THE
MUSIC
MAKER

THE MUSIC MAKER

HOW ONE **POW** PROVIDED HOPE FOR THOUSANDS

JACI BYRNE

Pen & Sword
MILITARY

First published in Australia in 2018 by Big Sky Publishing Pty Ltd

First published in Great Britain in 2019 by
Pen & Sword Military
An imprint of
Pen & Sword Books Ltd
Yorkshire - Philadelphia

ISBN 978 1 52675 486 8

The right of Jaci Byrne to be identified as Author of this work has been asserted by her in accordance with the Copyright, Designs and Patents Act 1988.

A CIP catalogue record for this book is available from the British Library.

Printed and bound in England by TJ International

Pen & Sword Books Ltd incorporates the Imprints of Pen & Sword Books Archaeology, Atlas, Aviation, Battleground, Discovery, Family History, History, Maritime, Military, Naval, Politics, Railways, Select, Transport, True Crime, Fiction, Frontline Books, Leo Cooper, Praetorian Press, Seaforth Publishing, Wharncliffe and White Owl.

For a complete list of Pen & Sword titles please contact

PEN & SWORD BOOKS LIMITED
47 Church Street, Barnsley, South Yorkshire, S70 2AS, England
E-mail: enquiries@pen-and-sword.co.uk
Website: www.pen-and-sword.co.uk

or

PEN AND SWORD BOOKS
1950 Lawrence Rd, Havertown, PA 19083, USA
E-mail: Uspen-and-sword@casematepublishers.com
Website: www.penandswordbooks.com

A True Story
Based on the World War II Diary of
Drum Major Henry Barnes Jackson

Dedicated to my late grandfather
Drum Major Henry Barnes Jackson, 1898–1964
5th Battalion
The Border Regiment
Service No: 3591894
Prisoner of War 1940-45
POW No: 4726

CONTENTS

PROLOGUE

France, 29 May 1940

We are in retreat. I'm in the second of two lorries taking our wounded back to Dunkirk, heading in the same direction as all of our retreating forces, every man in a desperate bid to return to Blighty to regroup, rearm and return to this war against the Jerries with a vengeance. We come to a crossroad and we turn left. I feel we should have turned right, but I'm in the back with the wounded. I call out to our driver, but he says the lorry in front is travelling too fast to stop the driver and discuss it and we must follow.

It is a fateful move.

We continue along the road for a couple of miles and then bullets start to fly all around us. Before we know it, we are surrounded by Germans.

In shock and disbelief, I look at my wounded men, my eyes scanning them one by one, mentally assessing their condition, as if I can now be of further assistance to the poor chaps.

I'm ordered to dismount from the lorry. Looking in the direction of the guttural voice that has just barked out the order I stare at his rifle, which is aimed right at me, and do as I'm told, clambering down from the back of the lorry in a reluctant manner before standing to face my captor. The Jerry officer tells me to take off my gun belt and throw away my revolver, which I have no choice but to do. Then he smashes me in the face with the butt of his rifle and, with a snap of my neck, my head ricochets in response to the loud crack, blood oozing from my nose and pouring down the front of my uniform. He takes two steps towards me and slaps my cheek. Then in broken English, he jeers, 'A long way from Tipperary, a long way now, hey?'

The Jerry's eyes flash in anger at my lack of response, and I look away. My insolence incenses him even further, and he orders me to look at him, but as soon as I raise my eyes to meet his, he screams at me, his face twisted with hate and loathing, spittle flying from his ugly mouth. I don't understand the language, but I do understand the meaning behind it. He's seen the insubordination in my eyes. He repeatedly punches me in my stomach until, finally, I buckle over in pain. He chuckles, raising one arm to get the attention of his men. They respond with laughter, and this is the very moment, the precise second in time, that I know I shall remember forever. Remember him stealing my dignity. Remember my shame.

But it is not over. Not yet. He orders me to stand against a wall and I fear my time is up. Such a short time has passed since I left Britain—a matter of weeks—my heart full of hope, the lads alongside me singing their patriotic songs of valour.

The Jerry officer bends down, picks up my revolver and hands his rifle to a grinning bastard behind him. Numb with fear, I watch as he raises my own gun to my head. His right arm straightens, his knuckles whitening as he grips the gun tightly, his finger closing in on the trigger. His left eye closes and he takes aim as my life becomes a rapid flicker of memories in my mind.

CHAPTER 1

OFF TO WAR AGAIN

1939

Whitehaven, England

There are times in a man's life when he must search deep inside himself. When he must strip away all that he thinks he is—or isn't— and rely on his very essence in order to survive. War is one of those times, perhaps the most fundamental of times. I know this, having served my country before.

I was but a mere boy when I ran away from home and my job at a colliery to fight Jerry in World War I—foolish lad that I was back then. The recruitment officer knew I was too young; I could see it in his smirk when I turned up to enlist. God, one look at my scrawny body, scraggly neck and sunken chest and he would have known—of course he would have. But the two bob and sixpence I waved under his nose for taking underage chaps the likes of me did the trick. Britain was getting desperate for men and, with a wink and a wave of his hand, the recruitment officer pointed me to the long line of new recruits. He said the food would do me some good—fatten me up a bit.

By the time I returned at the end of 1918 from what was named The Great War, I had just turned 20 years of age, but I felt like an old man, I can tell you. There had been nothing 'great' about it. The wind had been knocked out of me and I was no longer as puffed up as a toad by cockiness—more like a subdued pet frog. Working down the Haig Pit here in Whitehaven alongside my dad had been a haven compared to the muddy trenches I'd come to call my home. At least at the colliery I'd been able to return to a comfortable home to eat and sleep after work. At war, we'd bunkered down like scared rabbits in a warren, huddled together in dark, damp tunnels deep underground, tons upon tons of dirt above us as we attempted to

3

sleep in airless quarters far underneath the trenches where we fought by day. As for the food, well, I certainly didn't 'fatten up'.

My poor dad and mam were so pleased to see me return in one piece that they forgave me everything, and my skipping off to fight was never mentioned again. Still, I was pleased that we'd defeated the Germans, not that the bastards were admitting anything of the sort. They said it was simply an armistice—or something just as stupid. Said they could've won had they continued on fighting—said they'd been forced into agreeing to the terms of the armistice. But our country stood firm in the belief that Germany would never again be a threat to Britain.

How wrong we were.

Ever since that Hitler fellow in Germany became Fuhrer in August 1934, the pompous little man had continued to stir the pot; ranting and raving about the fact that we hadn't actually defeated Germany in The Great War and blaming the Jews for undermining him. Then in late 1938, after Germany had reoccupied the Rhineland and annexed Austria, Hitler turned his attention to Sudetenland in Czechoslovakia. We Brits were getting increasingly anxious. Where would Hitler set his sights on next?

In order to prevent another war, our prime minister, Neville Chamberlain, tried to appease Hitler by meeting him in Munich to sign an agreement, in effect giving Hitler Sudetenland on the promise that he would not invade the whole of Czechoslovakia. The prime minister arrived back in Blighty satisfied that he had achieved his goal of lasting peace. It was to be one of his greatest misjudgements.

Hitler had lied. Germany took Czechoslovakia in March 1939, and invaded Poland on 1 September the same year.

On 3 September 1939, Chamberlain gave a long speech from the cabinet room of Number 10, Downing Street in London which was broadcast on the wireless all over Britain. He told us that we were again at war with Germany. I shall never forget his closing words, which I have memorised: 'Now may God bless you all. May He defend the right. It is the evil things that we shall be fighting against—brute force, bad faith, injustice, oppression, and persecution—and against them, I am certain that the right will prevail.'

Being a drum major in the Territorial Army, I knew it was only a matter of time before I was called upon to serve my country. That time came in mid-September, and my first thought was: *Two wars in one lifetime, so much for never having to face the Jerries again,* and I prayed, along with the rest of my countrymen and women, that Chamberlain would be proven correct. That God would be on our side. I was no churchgoing man, but I knew I would certainly need His assistance if I was to make it through another war.

I was ordered to join my battalion, 5th Border Regiment, in the Wooler region in Northumberland, North-East England, and was advised that I would likely be in regimental aid, helping the poor chaps who were injured. I was not so stupid as to think there wouldn't be plenty of them. No, experience had taught me that much. I was no longer a naïve young lad; in fact, my fellow comrades considered me an old soldier, being that I was the ripe old age of 40.

I looked on the brighter side, which for me always meant the musical side. I was to lead the drum and bugle corps during drills, and I could take along my music sheets and some instruments to accompany me, which I hoped would offer my fellow men some entertainment during whatever leisure time we had.

The wife and our youngest girl were on holidays, visiting relatives in the south of England when I received my orders. Young Joan had been sick, the wife Mabel also sick before her, both of them hospitalised, and they needed the break to help them recuperate. When I contacted Mabel to tell her the news, I told her to stay where she was; that the eldest girl, Nelly, could continue to watch over her sisters and my dad. But the wife wouldn't hear of it and insisted on returning home. She is a good one, my wife—she was a strong woman in those days, and I needed her to stay strong, because she had to take full control as caretaker of the Whitehaven Town Hall, a position we shared.

I left Whitehaven on 29 September, a day shy of my 41st birthday. My Mabel led the farewell party, her beautiful liquid-centred toffee-brown eyes as sad as a lost dog's, my four daughters and my dear old dad all lined up on Bransty Railway Station beside her. Nine-year-old Joan jumped from one foot to the other on gangly legs, her red hair flashing in the sunlight, and I noted that she was already head and shoulders above her poor older sister Mona, 16, who was born with a 'growth defect'. My eyes swept over our third eldest daughter, Betty, who, although only 14, was a true beauty. She bore all of her mother's attractive features apart from one difference—her striking blonde hair. Rather a headstrong young woman was Betty but, no doubt about it, she was me all over in temperament. Not so the eldest daughter, 18-year-old Nelly, who was more like her mam in nature; sensible and far more compliant than her sister Betty. But there we have it. They were all there to bid me farewell. And, for that, I felt very honoured.

I choked up when I saw the boys from my local band arrive and when they broke into a tune to farewell me, their old bandleader, I had to swallow rapidly in order to keep my welling emotions in check. I didn't want the memory of me sobbing like a sissy remaining with them throughout the war. My band! How I'd loved every moment of being a part of it: the street parades, the conducting, the concert halls, balls and dances. Well, it was no longer to be and it saddened me that my Golden Age of Music, as it was then named, was over.

The drummer, my dearest mate and Mabel's younger brother, 26-year-old Ernie, had a tear in his eye. He was like a son to me, the son I'd never had. He hadn't been called up as yet, but I suspected it would only be a matter of time. Not so for some of the lads in the band who were staying behind for various reasons: age, reserved occupations, medical conditions and the like. They all assured me they would keep an eye on my family, and in them I had complete confidence. We were a close-knit lot in Whitehaven.

My emotional old dad was the last to hug me goodbye. He pressed a small gold clock into my hand, his consumptive cough masking his last words. I turned quickly to leave before I completely broke down.

And I was off. With a final wave as the train shunted out, I tried to take in everyone's features. I wanted—needed—an image firmly imprinted in my mind, although I couldn't help but wonder how much this picture would change by the time I returned. And, make no mistake, I was determined to return.

The train stations I passed through on my way to Wooler were filled with similar scenes to Bransty, and my spirits were buoyed by the crowds waving flags and calling out in patriotic cheers as I made my way to join my battalion. I finally settled back into my seat, my mind still focused on who I had left behind; foremost my darling wife.

Ah, my wife…

It was in the main street of Whitehaven, in April 1919, when I first saw her—my Mabel. I still love saying that—my Mabel. I'd taken a lunchbreak from work to get a bite to eat and perhaps down a quick pint of stout, and there she stood, patiently waiting her turn at the counter of Penney's Fish and Chip Shop. Oh, my Lord, was she ever a good-looking lass. She took the very breath out of me and I could hardly manage to voice my order for a tuppence worth of chips. Mabel Cranston was, and remains to this day, the finest woman ever to be put on this earth—and I'll not be disputed on that fact.

The first thing I noticed were her large brown eyes; they were ever so expressive, so much so they shone with every smile. Yes, her features were angelic, only to be matched by her soul, and I swear you could not have met a real angel to rival her, not even if you'd visited Heaven. And Mabel's skin, oh, it was so soft. Like rich, creamy milk. Her pert little nose was perfectly positioned on that wonderful face, and her naturally blushed cheeks looked as if they'd been smeared with ripe strawberries. As you can see, I fell hard, and it took me going to the local chippy many times in the hope of seeing her before I did once more. I was eating that many chips it was a wonder I wasn't the size of a barrel when I finally bumped into Mabel again, and by that time I was in such an anxious state I just blurted out a request for a date. Well, when Mabel nodded her head in the affirmative, I was dancing in clover.

But that was all in the past. The train began to slow, releasing hisses and sighs, smoke whirling through the air, and my thoughts returned to the present and to the task ahead. I was no longer a family man; I was now a soldier of war. My heart would not get me through the weeks, months, and perhaps years that lay ahead. From that moment forth I knew I had to start thinking with my head.

Wooler to Felton

By early December, after two months of basic training and lectures, which we found relatively undemanding, we moved from Wooler to the Felton area to undergo more intense training; Felton being a town approximately 30 miles south of Wooler. Our training schedule was certainly ramped up during our six-week stay at Felton, and the weather also made it hard going as winter came early and it was the coldest in living memory with many heavy snowfalls and ice making for challenging conditions.

1940

Felton to Swindon

In mid-January the battalion left Felton and headed for Camp Chiseldon in Swindon, Wiltshire, in the south-west of England, to make our final preparations for war. We moved by road and, despite the weather still being atrocious and our lorries sliding every which way, we arrived safely.

We were housed in timber huts, which were very cold—frigidly so—as the big freeze across Britain was still on, chilling us all to the bone. Having only one small heater per hut and the showers being icy cold, the pipes often completely frozen, it was rough going, but the food wasn't too bad, and we couldn't complain due to there being rationing on throughout Blighty at the time. So, we were mindful of that, of what our families were enduring, and camp spirits remained high.

Our company commander at Chiseldon was named Captain Sewell, and he proved to be a fine chap and quickly gained the respect of all. Camp Chiseldon indeed brought back memories to me, and I was familiar with the drill from the last war: practice on the firing range, using live hand grenades on the bombing range, and combat training in the nearby woods and local countryside. There was only one major change from the training schedule for The Great War and that was motor training—driving motorcycles, lorries and Bren gun carriers—our troops' general mode of getting around in the last war being on foot or on horseback. To add to all this, I found I was to study first aid and the basics of medicine in order to be in regimental aid, and so my days and nights were full with not too much time spare to pine for my family.

Speaking of families, the locals in Swindon were wonderful people, very tolerant of the thousands of troops amassed in their locale, and they kindly offered accommodation to the wives and girlfriends of soldiers when they visited. I'm sad to say my Mabel wasn't among those visitors, seeing as she had so much on her hands, what with her having to look after our girls, my dad, and tending to her demanding duties at the town hall. Still, as I said previously, I also had much on my plate with the intensity of training and my medical studies, and if there was any shard of time left to me, I played my music. I managed to put on a few musical shows which, as I'd hoped, were much appreciated by all the troops. As had long been the case, none of the lads called me by my proper name, Henry Jackson (Harry to my family and friends at home) when off duty, rather by my nickname 'Drummie', and there was many a night when that name was called out in good cheer. It was very humbling indeed.

I'm delighted to report that on completion of training for overseas service we were given final embarkation leave of 48 hours. At the end of March, the lads and I gleefully jumped aboard trains and headed home, the atmosphere jubilant as we sang and laughed all the way and, oh, what a joy it was to see my family once more before I headed off to war.

CHAPTER 2

BLOODY BATTLES AND GRAND PIANOS

1940

England

18 April—We are as ready for war as we will ever be and our battalion leaves Swindon early this morning. Now that Germany has invaded neutral Denmark and Norway, the call for arms becomes more desperate than ever. We arrive at Southampton docks this same day and board a troopship. After getting instructions on the use of lifeboats, we find our bunks and drop our kits before getting some grub.

The ship sails at night and anchors in the dark Solent and Southampton Water. I'm restless, so I go up on deck to clear the old head. The weather is cloudy and rain drizzles, but every now and again I can see glimpses of the half-moon through the clouds. I like to think I can see the face of the man in the moon smiling down on us. My gaze shifts to the deep, swollen black waters below, and I breathe in the salty air, and then watch on in awe as more and more ships anchor close by. I'm comforted by the sheer might of our force. As the last ship arrives, I retire for the night, for I shall need to be well rested for the days, weeks and months ahead—as I am now a man at war.

France

20 April—It's a mighty show of strength as our convoy of troopships, including the HMS *Ben-my-Chree*, the pride of the Isle of Man Steam Packet Company, arrive at Le Havre, France at first light today. This is the same port I landed at during the last war, and once again, as with Camp Chiseldon, memories flood back to me. I have to admit to my nerves jumping with a right mix of excitement and trepidation. Excitement at the thought of serving my country, as one can't help but be swept along with the fervour now infiltrating the ship, but trepidation for the imminent war I am about to enter.

This same night we board lorries and travel for three days to a small village called Bouessay in the north-west of France. This place gives no impression of war.

23 April—We set up our regimental aid post in a small two-room house that appears to have been occupied up until very recently. The larger room leads out to the main street via glass doors and has two sizeable beds in it, which will be perfect to accommodate our wounded. The smaller room has a huge barrel in it, and later in the day, when Lieutenant Sergeant Crosby and I arrive back at the house, we learn that the barrel contains undiluted whisky—our medical officer is in a proper dilemma because he cannot get any sense out of an orderly, who has sampled the whisky, and he finds him wandering around in a complete stupor. More men arrive to witness the scene, and it's an amusing distraction. After we have tired of the orderly's antics, and he falls into deep slumber on the floor, we are all allowed a small tot of whisky, which is enough to blow our bloody heads off. We have ourselves a merry old time for a short while, but the rest of the night is a bit of a blur! Somehow, we find our way to a shed to sleep, the larger room of the house being occupied by the medical officer and another officer.

The following day we are told that we are to stay here in Bouessay for six weeks of training on the tactics of war on foreign soil. Many of the boys feel this is not necessary, that they are well and truly ready to take on the Germans, some muttering their disappointment, and others not so quietly espousing their fervour to do battle with Jerry—their eagerness to kill. They complain at being further from the firing line than they would like to be. I keep my mouth shut. While I don't wish to douse the lads' zeal for action, experience has taught me that being on the front line is anything but fun. Indeed, some men are acting as if they're simply about to take a thrill ride at Butlins Holiday Camp.

On the third day the officers find themselves a better billet and an orderly, a driver, the medical officer's batman and I grab their beds. We just start to get down to it when we're called out. A Royal Army Medical Corps dispatch rider has run into four men, two having to be transported to hospital. Then, as soon as we get back to our beds, we are called out again as one of our lorries has run into another party of men. Six men are injured, including an officer who has to be sent back to Blighty. All this carrying on makes us wonder when we are going to be seeing some real action. It's rather humiliating that the only wounded we've dealt with so far are as a result of our own drivers' carelessness. Thank God no Jerries are around to witness the debacle. They would be laughing their heads off.

End April—After spending barely a week in Bouessay we are on the move again, our training aborted because they now need us closer to the front line in Belgium. It appears that the boys who are eager to get to the action are going to get their wishes granted.

Early May—We have travelled once more for three days and today we arrive at a place in northern France called Lille. We dismount, search for supplies, load up the lorries with our newfound booty, including a piano that I find in an abandoned building, and after the transport leaves us, we march north for two hours in heavy rain to Bondues, closer to the Franco-Belgian border.

Soaked to the skin, we arrive and I'm immediately sent off to find a building that will serve as a regimental aid post. I come across a hut which will suit our needs, but it's very dirty. With the willing help of local children, who find me a brush and some rags, some of the lads and I get the place cleaned up. The children then offer us some sticks and briquettes, which are compressed blocks of coal dust or other combustible materials such as charcoal, sawdust, woodchips, peat or paper and they are wonderful to get a fire going. Bless them. I soon get a raging fire going and lay my wet clothes out to dry before getting down to it on a stretcher for some much-needed sleep.

I wake to find a dining hall has been set up in a nearby disused cinema and the piano that I scrounged from Lille has been installed.

We have it pretty quiet here in Bondues, apart from the air raids which average around 10 a day. I witness a good many air battles and am pleased to report that oftentimes our air force is coming off best. Let's hope the pilots can keep it up seeing as our anti-aircraft can't do too much because Jerry is keeping its planes at a distance. So, for the time being, there's nothing for us on the ground to do but keep busy, and for me that means keeping up the entertainment. Along with my trumpets, sax, piano accordion and drums, I am able to get a band going and we get some concerts underway with great success. We also have a few church parades and I lead the drummers.

Lieutenant Johnston and I write letters to the local papers asking for sheet music, which we never receive because, unfortunately, the merriment is short-lived and events begin to move rapidly.

Belgium

11 May— We receive word that Jerry has invaded the Netherlands, Luxembourg and Belgium and we are ordered to take up defensive positions near the Escaut River in Tournai, Belgium. I suppose this is what we've been waiting for. Here we go!

We set off towards Belgium and, after a long 15-mile march in a south-easterly direction, we arrive at night at a small village called Froyennes, about 2 miles north-west of Tournai, which is a large town that saw many battles in the last war. We are ordered to set up our regimental aid post here in Froyennes. We're pleased to see that our air force is very active.

12 May—Refugees are streaming into our regimental aid post, all of them desperate to leave Belgium, and it is a pitiful sight indeed. We are told that mixed among them—the refugees—are the fifth columnists, one of Jerry's strongest forces, and they do great damage. We have no way of identifying them, but they are spies, the lot of them, and cowards at that, marching alongside the very people they are out to destroy. The bastards! We open our regimental aid post only to women and children for foot dressings. I wonder how some have managed to walk as their injuries are so atrocious, but we have to do the best we can before sending them off again to hobble on to who knows where.

13 May—Our air force has now become eerily quiet—no sight of them—and Jerry is bombing us almost every hour. We're surrounded by flames and, with the deluge of wounded troops now arriving, we desperately need medical supplies. My medical officer asks me to take a lorry into Tournai, which I'm told is also being bombed hourly and is partly in flames, to secure more supplies. I do so, with the aid of one man, and Jerry gives us hell from above as I drive along. I'm swerving and swaying, starting and stopping the lorry in order to avoid a direct hit. As we enter the outskirts of Tournai, I decide to take the vehicle near the canal away from buildings, which are in a state of near collapse. On the way, I pass a doorway of a large building and I see two nuns lying flat shielding terrified children who are crammed under their bodies, their poor faces telling a tale no book could ever depict in the same way, the memory of which will remain with me long after these brave women and their charges are dead—and that will be very soon, I regret to say.

The lorry crawls along as female refugees walking alongside plead with us to let them in the back of the vehicle, each desperately trying to get their children on board to safety, their frenzied screams for assistance stabbing relentlessly at my guilt-filled ears as they lift up their sobbing youngsters to us. But we can't take them. For whom would we take and whom would we leave behind, and what on earth would we do with the little ones? Take them to the front line? We are on a mission to procure medical supplies for our wounded troops and if we assist these poor women now begging for their children's lives, we are risking the lives of fighting men. This, my friends, is the true face of war.

Then Jerry stops bombing and we manage to direct some women and their children into cellars of a large nearby factory. We assure them that we will tell our transport officers about their plight, but their pitiful eyes express their cynicism before their resignation to their impending fate is depicted in their deflated, slumped bodies as we leave them.

We find the main street of Tournai in ruins. Jerry starts up again, but somehow, we manage to avoid a direct hit ourselves, and we reach our destination, load our supplies, and prepare to get the hell out of the place. We just start up the lorry, when a woman runs towards us, imploring us to help her get her invalid mother out of her house which has been bombed. She points to the building in question and, to my horror, I see it's in complete ruins. There's little chance that her mother has survived. Once again, I tell the distraught woman that I can only report the incident to the Royal Army Medical Corps, and I drive away feeling utterly hopeless.

As we make the slow journey out of Tournai Jerry planes come down low and machine-gun the masses of refugees. I pull up close to a building, and my companion and I crouch down and hold our breath until the planes pass over. When we look up again, my horror at witnessing the carnage is indescribable. The streets are littered with bodies, some in the throes of imminent death. It's an abominable sight. An unbearable sound. But then I hear a more shocking sound: the eerie sound of silence as death enshrouds its victims.

My head pounding, my guts churning with nausea, I start up the lorry, rev the engine and, dodging bodies, make a beeline back to base.

14 May—Our battalion receives orders to move forward and take up positions closer to Tournai, the very hellhole we got the medical supplies from yesterday. My medical officer asks me to go ahead of the battalion with his batman and find a house suitable for our needs. I'm not sure I'm up to the task as my mind is still reeling from the shock of the massacre I witnessed yesterday. But, naturally, I do as I'm ordered.

Thankfully, this time around I find Tournai to be a very different experience. No enemy planes pass over and luckily the area is almost deserted of life as we approach; only the dead are still strewn around, and some elderly people who refuse to leave. I understand their reasoning, for where would they go at their age?

After breaking into many houses and villas which have been vacated we come across a mansion in the Tournai suburb of Orcq and pull up and dismount to investigate further. I'm delighted; it has excellent cellars, a concrete roof and many exits. It's more than perfect for our needs. The medical officer is indeed pleased when he arrives with the rest of our battalion, and he and I go on a long tour of discovery. When the medical officer finds that the cellars are stocked with bottles of wine and also McEwan's Scotch, he's in clover. The kitchen is also well stocked with food and has a great cooking range which our runner promptly gets going. The runner then assigns himself to being the cook, a job which he holds easily and proves to be very good at. Within no time at all, many officers around Tournai get to know of our new cook's capabilities and often call around for a meal.

There is a grand piano in this mansion, one of the finest instruments on which I've ever played, and we spend a few short but merry days here, temporarily shielded from the ongoing war. This is how one has to live through wartime: enjoying the simple pleasures as they come, before facing what we all know we must. Living hour by hour, minute by minute. I'm glad to have been blessed with this God-given talent for music; to be able to entertain the lads and see the joy and hope in their eyes; eyes that may well soon be filled with nothing but terror before they become filled with nothing but lifelessness.

The mansion has magnificent surrounds and I enjoy taking brisk walks. I come across some wonderful sights of nature, and I make friends with a fine horse I find in an enclosed area, along with some deer. The poor animals are shivering with fright from the noise of gunfire. I return with some food. The deer are nervy and won't allow me to approach and so I leave some bits and pieces of food for them to get at their own pace, but the horse comes straight up to me when I hold out my hand with a few lumps of sugar, which he loves. When the army general eventually learns of my new friend, he takes the horse for himself. I will miss the animal, but at least I'm happy that the poor thing will now be fed well.

We hear that Winston Churchill has taken over as prime minister. He was always critical of Chamberlain's failure to fully comprehend the Nazi threat. Churchill is a military man; he trained at the Royal Military Academy and fought in The Great War and so the chaps here are excited about this news. We have great hopes for our new leader and his ability to get us through this war.

Once again, our mirage of peace doesn't last long. Things are starting to get hot and wounded are coming steadily into the regimental aid post. So far, our battalion is lucky and we've had very few casualties. Our boys appear to be taking their baptism by fire well.

The stretcher-bearers are proving to be very reliable. Two stretcher-bearers from A Company bring in a seriously wounded man. Jerry has been shelling them pretty heavily but, despite this, as soon as they deposit him, the stretcher-bearers bravely prepare to head back out to get others. I stop them, explaining that Jerry is still giving its all and I point out that they are not armed. But these men are made of bloody steel and they are determined to return for their injured, so I arm up and volunteer to accompany them back to headquarters, about a mile north of here.

We leave the grounds and run like the wind. We come across a large ploughed field, and we're about 200 yards from headquarters when Jerry starts with six-inch mortars right in the field we're in. Shells are flying all around us. We three drop into a partially made trench, where to our great surprise we find the company sergeant, Sergeant Major Mulholland. He raises his hirsute eyebrows, an expression that speaks volumes, and when he later nods, we all bolt out of the trench and run for our lives, finally making it back to the house where A Company is based, and we go down into the cellars.

I'm just taking a breather, when I'm told by a signaller on duty on the phones that Jerry has hit their ammunition wagon and it's exploding like hell. I remember that Company Commander Captain Dudding is at our regimental aid post having one of our cook's specials, so I decide to head back on foot to tell him. Again, I have many narrow escapes but arrive safely. I'm gasping for breath when I tell Captain Dudding about the ammunition wagon and he can hardly believe my words, but when he looks out of the window, it is plainly visible. Flames resulting from the direct hit are now shooting into the sky. The captain abandons his meal and makes off as fast as he can. I'm later told that some chaps at headquarters had to unload pits that were also filled with explosives in order to avoid a similar situation. I shudder at the thought of having to do such a perilous job.

17 May—Things are getting worse. Whenever one of us so much as shows our head, Jerry snipes. By late afternoon some of our boys are hit and the medical officer decides it's getting too dangerous and asks me to try and get to headquarters again to ask the commanding officer if we should retire from our position. I creep out of the entrance of our regimental aid post and get on a motorbike, but Jerry soon puts paid to that, and I'm catapulted off the wrecked vehicle and have to carry on by foot, dodging from cover to cover until I'm within sight of headquarters. I then have to make a dash for the gateway in between rifle bursts, following directions from our lads who are defending the outer walls.

The commanding officer is busy attending to refugees but after I explain our company's situation to the adjutant, he goes to see the commanding officer who decides we are to stay put for the time being. The adjutant also tells me that our 1st Battalion has got a good cutting up after making a bayonet charge. This is devastating news.

Again, I head off on foot, feeling like a small bird trapped in a wire cage during a hailstorm, as the whistle of Jerry bullets and mortar shells scream past my ears. I hear one shell falling directly overhead and I drop flat on the ground, praying this is not it for me. The shell lands nearby, barely 20 feet away, but it feels so near that I wriggle my feet to ensure they are still attached to my body. They are, I'm glad to report, and when I look up again, a deer is in pieces next to me and my discarded tin helmet is covered in its entrails. I think about my mate the horse for a slight second, thankful that it's been taken away, before I take off once again and finally make it back in one piece.

Barely half an hour later a dispatch rider arrives with orders that we are now to retire to headquarters and I feel my innards shrink after what I've just gone through. Tragically, the dispatch rider is killed on his way back and I think to myself what a waste of life. All the commanding officer had to do was give me the okay when I was there and the rider would still be alive. Still, orders are orders, and there's no time for retrospection.

18 May—Our company loads our lorries in preparation for our departure, and after a difficult journey, dodging bullets all the way, we finally arrive at headquarters. We make our regimental aid post in a small dugout which has a concrete roof and our anti-aircraft position themselves upon the roof. The dugout is sheltered by a long, high concrete wall. Our artillery boys put up a wonderful barrage for about eight hours, so much so that Jerry asks for an armistice to bury its dead. It is granted, although I wonder about the dead civilians now rotting in the streets: the stench of their corpses pervading the very air we breathe. Who provides them with the courtesy of a burial?

It is eerily quiet while Jerry buries its dead—unfamiliar calm blankets us as we are able to look outside to the daylight and walk about without fear of being under fire. Then, the next day, in the late afternoon, Jerry starts another barrage, and the place is again alive with shells and tracer bullets. One can only assume Jerry's fervour is an outpouring of grief and rage in retaliation for the losses just buried. In response, our boys hit back with a vengeance, and it's a bloody battle once more all through the long night until dawn.

Our wounded are now flocking into our regimental aid post and, although all is quiet again throughout the day, in terms of Jerry fire, we are kept busy attending to our brave soldiers as the field ambulance dashes backwards and forwards collecting wounded and bringing them in. A lieutenant corporal is brought in and we can see he's in a very bad way. He pleads with us to put him out of his pain and we give him morphia and prepare to operate, but soon we can see that there's no hope for the poor chap and, sadly, he dies about 10 minutes later.

Darkness falls—and then Jerry blasts us. Our guns respond and on it goes until dawn when it becomes quiet again. Then, a few hours later, Jerry gives us its absolute all, so much so that at 10:00 pm we get orders to load up our lorries and make off by convoy back to transport lines. It is no easy feat under the torrent of gunfire still raining down, us men running and scrambling, desperately loading what we can onto lorries. Finally, the last ambulance gets away with the remainder of the wounded, and the convoy begins to follow. My lorry is about 300 yards away under trees, and we scramble for it. We are doing all right for the first 100 yards as we are under cover of the five-foot-high wall but, after that, we have to run out in the open.

We jump aboard, all men intact, and we're the last to leave. It's been about an hour since the first lorry left and our vehicle is packed so tightly there's hardly any room for the orderly, batman and myself, let alone the four stretcher-bearers who are desperately trying to squash in. But we can't leave the stretcher-bearers behind—these brave men who risk life and limb to save our wounded. Never.

As the lorry pulls away the last stretcher-bearer leaps aboard the side of it and grabs onto my neck, his legs dangling in the air while I grasp onto the crossbar for grim death. We move very cautiously, as it's a clear moonlit night and we are easy targets for Jerry. While travelling through the woods, we are advised to wear gas masks, gas being suspected. We're painfully aware that there are very few worse ways to die than by gas—it is horrifically slow and excruciatingly agonising—and it's not a theory any of us fancy testing, so we do as we're told. The orderly assists the stretcher-bearer, who is still clinging to my neck, on with his gas mask and we travel until we come across a field ambulance and the four stretcher-bearers leave us. I'm not sad to see them go because my neck by this time feels as if it's about to break. However, on discovering that I have a little shrapnel in my hand, which must have happened while we were on the move, I decide that it's probably a good thing that the pain in my neck overrode that of my hand throughout the journey.

Franco-Belgian Border

We arrive at dawn at a place called Cysoing, just inside France, 9 miles south-east of Lille. After scraping the shrapnel out of my hand and dealing with some cases of shell shock (one being Company Sergeant Major Smith), another terrible consequence of war, we join our boys who have taken up positions in well-made pillboxes, these being remnants from the last war.

The medical officer and I head off in a lorry with a driver in order to find a place suitable for our regimental aid post, and we soon come across an enormous brick kiln which we feel will suit the purpose. We find some single beds in an old house nearby, load them onto our lorry and take them back to the kiln. There are some sheds not too far away from the kiln in which to park the lorry under cover. I hop out to direct the driver, who begins to drive through, but then three Jerry planes fly overhead, dive down, and machine gun us. The driver and the medical officer frantically jump out of the lorry and crouch in a corner of one shed, but I'm still outside, watching bullets pinging around me like hailstones in a Cumbrian storm. I think my time is up, but I make an instant decision to risk life and limb and run like the bloody wind. Thankfully, I also make it to safety inside the shed.

We find that in sheds next to ours are the Cheshires [the Cheshire Regiment] and its transport. Then our Bren Carriers arrive and take up the remaining sheds and we all sigh with relief because we feel safer now that the tanks are here.

Once again, on finding a piano in one of the nearby houses, and by request of the medical officer who is a bit of a jazz fiend, I keep the lads going with music. Despite still being under attack, the atmosphere brightens somewhat.

Our runner proves that he is not only a grand cook, he's also a plucky young lad, because he goes out heedless of shellfire to milk cows and I'm delighted to report that he returns safely with enough supplies to keep us all well-fed: milk, some laying hens for eggs, and other fowl he plucks for roasting. Along with a supply of food we found previously in a deserted house, he serves us up a delightful feast. What a wonderful young chap he is.

We soon realise that there has been no sight whatsoever of our planes for days. Jerry must know this too as it is doing what it likes to us now, and this is unnerving to say the least. But when we are told that French–Moroccan troops are close by to our right, and an elite French division to our left, the news cheers us.

24 May—We all gather in one of the Cheshires' sheds to tune in to the King's Empire Day speech on a wireless set they have, but Jerry guns soon upset the party and smash the set to smithereens. It's not good for our morale.

A few wounded are brought in and one man is a sergeant from our company from Workington, but we find that the poor fellow is dead. Then, not long after, we hear that the French troops have cracked up under the pressure of heavy fire and are in full retreat, and we're advised that we are now in serious danger of being cut off. At 10:00 pm orders arrive for the stretcher-bearers to get back to their ambulance, which they do. At 11:00 pm we get word that our battalion is to retire to Lesquin, about 6 miles north-west of here, between midnight and 3:00 am, with the exception of our company which has to wait for another two companies to arrive in the morning, and then we are to move on with them.

By eight in the morning there's no sign of the two expected companies, so our medical officer tells me to go to our last base headquarters to see if they are there. On the way a French plane, which we have got to know has fallen into Jerry hands, flies over and does a bit of bombing, but I manage to avoid danger. The expected companies are not there, so I report this back to the medical officer who then asks me to go back once more and wait until 9:00 am to see if they arrive. But by the given time there's still no sign of them and, on my return, the medical officer decides we are to make off without them.

25 May—We arrive at midday at the small village of Lesquin and meet up with our battalion. At 4:00 pm I'm asked to lead an advance party to a place called Le Bizet, just over the Belgian border. It's roughly 15 miles north of here, just past Armentieres.

On the way my advance party pass what is left of a battery of French artillery; guns all over the place, horses and men cut to pieces. It's a sickening sight and I wonder when one becomes immune to witnessing such atrocities? Never, I hope, for to become so blasé one may as well opt out of the human race, although truth be told, after seeing these poor devils and creatures lying around in twisted and discombobulated shapes, their torsos, limbs, and even faces missing, I question being a member of such a race. Human, but not humane. Still, I cannot allow myself to think this way, for the mind must stay strong if it is to carry the physical form safely through this war.

CHAPTER 3

CAPTURED BY THE JERRIES

1940

Franco-Belgian Border

25 May—My advance party arrive late at night at our destination of Le Bizet in heavy rain and bunk down in a deserted shop to try and get some sleep, but it's impossible as large, bulky tanks pass us throughout the night. I'm told they're in retreat, all making for Dunkirk.

26 May—Our battalion arrive at around 7:00 am and I find a barn for us but, at midday, we hear heavy gunfire and there are many air raids. It's here that we learn just how dire the situation now is, and we're advised that we will also soon be making for Dunkirk, and then we'll head back to Blighty for fitting out before returning to fight. So, it seems our forces are in full retreat, but we swear that we will return stronger and more prepared. It is now patently obvious that we will need all experienced hands on deck if we are to have any chance of winning this war.

At 6:00 pm we pack our lorries and head off north to regroup and receive further orders regarding our retreat, but at 10:00 pm our lorry gets bogged and we have to abandon it. Another lorry alongside is on fire, the flames are fierce and we are aware that it may soon explode. We try to rescue our belongings from the back of our lorry while we have time, but the only box we can get open is the medical comforts box. I manage to get my music case, but my trumpet is in a box right at the front and I can't get near it and we're ordered to walk away. To me, this feels like the last straw. Our driver then tries to set fire to our vehicle, rather than allow the enemy to retrieve our supplies, but he fails in his attempt and we leave it when another lorry comes along, and we stop it to hitch a ride. This lorry is packed with equipment and about 12 men and, in order for us to fit, we have to throw away all our packs, and those on board also have to offload some supplies. I absolutely refuse to discard my music case and I hand it to an orderly to take care of. I'm still very sore at losing my trumpet, but at least I have my music case containing some smaller instruments.

By now we have lost our convoy and we get to a crossroad and the driver turns left. About half a mile down the road, we meet a Frenchman who tells us that Jerries are on the road ahead and marching towards us, so we turn sharply and finally re-join our convoy. I see a car behind us and recognise the driver; he's the headquarters company commander's driver. He beckons me to join him and I dismount and do so. Although the car is crammed with men, I'm in clover in this vehicle and we travel faster than the convoy, dodging in and out of the three rows of vehicles and Bren Gun Carriers all moving at a very slow pace.

27 May—At daybreak the skies open and it teems down. Then Jerry planes start bombing the convoy and it's hard to keep moving. Men are riding on anything they can or walking on each side of the road alongside the slow-moving and overcrowded lorries and tanks. Regiments are now mixed up and confusion reigns supreme... a sorry sight indeed as confused, disorientated and war-shocked men stagger on through the mud.

The car I'm in is now doing nicely. A voice calls out and directs us up a road where our battalion is to head. We proceed along the road and eventually reach our destination—a farm at a place called Roesbrugge-Haringe, approximately 20 miles south-east of Dunkirk, which is to now be our base headquarters. I'm absolutely exhausted and collapse on a stretcher in a barn for a couple of hours' sleep.

I awaken with a start, realising I have lost my music case and doubting I will ever see it again, being that the orderly I handed it to was not from my battalion. I curse my stupidity for accepting the ride in the car and leaving my music case behind, and I reluctantly rise and wander outside to find our battalion has arrived. I don't have much time to fret over lost instruments because the medical officer orders me to set up our regimental aid post as soon as possible as there are incoming wounded expected very soon. I find a small shed and quickly sweep and scrub it clean before kitting it out. As soon as I'm finished we are back in action as casualties start arriving.

28 May—The wounded are now streaming and screaming in, but it seems hopeless as we only have our medical comforts box containing the most basic of medical supplies. The worst cases are put in a barn to await the field ambulance to be transferred to hospital. I'm returning from attending to these men at the barn when our medical officer tells me there is a man out of the mortar platoon lying out in the open suffering from shell shock.

Dodging Jerry crossfire, I go out to him and find it's one of my drummers, Edward Orr. The poor man is in a terrible state: convulsing, ranting and raving and calling out my nickname *Drummie! Drummie!* over and over again. He's a big fellow, and I have a hell of a time dragging him back. I can only manage to get him so far and then a sergeant and a private from the Bren Carriers come to my aid. Poor old Edward, I wonder if he'll live to regret my actions, dragging him out of the line of fire rather than letting him take a bullet, because he'll never be the same man again. Shell shock is like a deadly dance with an octopus; the creature's tentacles wrap around one's nervous system and squeeze the sense out of one forever. I know this only too well after seeing the results of shell shock in the last war.

On my return Lance Corporal Gill is brought in, his foot shattered to pieces. The medical officer decides to remove the foot and gives the poor lad the last of our chloroform. Our patient goes out to it but, having lost almost all of our supplies, we have only one lance and a pair of scissors to do the job. The medical officer works hard with the lance, sweat pouring from him until, finally, he asks me to have a go. I do so and try to finish the job with the scissors, all the time blanking out what I'm doing and trying hard to convince myself that I'm carving up a Sunday roast at home. Finally, I finish and poor Gill's foot is discarded in a corner of the room. I turn around just in time to see an orderly collapsing on the ground. He's fainted, but there's no time to worry about him as things are now certainly ramping up, and we are in dire need of help. We have few supplies, no decent surgical equipment and too many wounded by far.

It's now late at night and we haven't seen the field ambulance in two days, so our medical officer sends a runner out to see where they've got to, but the runner returns with a major from the Royal Army Medical Corps who says that they can't get the ambulances through from where they are situated. The major turns to me, stares at my face and points to my hand. I look down and see that I've cut my thumb and blood is pouring out. After the medical officer sews up my thumb he invites me to join the major and him for a quick coffee over at the officers' mess as we're all fagged out.

It's here at the mess that our medical officer says someone will have to rush the wounded to Dunkirk and get them aboard a boat or they will not survive as they are all too badly injured. I volunteer to have a go. Two officers' mess cooks named Tom Penrice and Walter Hardy overhear the conversation and ask me if they can join me, and I say it is up to them. The medical officer at first does not like the idea of me going and wants an orderly to take my place, but I put up a good case, and he finally relents and includes Penrice and Hardy in the deal.

29 May—It's the early hours of the morning and we carry all the infirm 300 yards and place them in two lorries and, while we do so, the major shows the first driver a map leading to Dunkirk. Penrice gets into the first lorry while Hardy and I get into the second with the most seriously wounded and we start out shortly before dawn.

France
In Retreat

Arriving at our transport lines, a sergeant named Weston tells me that he has just received orders brought by a motor cyclist sent from headquarters that a full withdrawal to Dunkirk will be activated shortly. Just before we head off, Weston gives me a bottle of wine and says, 'Well, I hope to see you soon, Drummie. But for now, it's goodbye and good luck, and you'll need every bit of it.'

I am soon to discover that truer words have never been spoken.

In Capture

We're travelling well when we come to a crossroad and we turn left. I feel we should have turned right, and I call out to the driver, but he says that the lorry in front is travelling too fast to stop the driver and discuss it and we must follow. It is a fateful move.

We continue along the road for a couple of miles and then bullets start to rain down on us in a deluge to rival an Asian monsoon. I have to fling myself over one of the wounded and, when I look up again, I see that Hardy has a bullet hole right through the rim of his tin helmet, but, wonderful to relate, none of our men are hit. Next, Germans surround us like a swarm of bees.

We are ordered to dismount and the lorry drivers and Penrice and Hardy are taken away, but a Jerry officer points to me and beckons me to him. He tells me to take off my gun belt and throw away my revolver. He smashes me in the face with the butt of his rifle, and my head ricochets in response to the loud crack, blood oozing from my nose. He takes two steps towards me and slaps my cheek and then, in broken English, he jeers, 'A long way from Tipperary, a long way now, hey?'

His eyes flash at my lack of response and he continues to hit me, his face twisted with hate and loathing, spittle flying from his ugly mouth. Then he orders me to stand against a wall. This is it. I feel my time is up.

The Jerry officer bends down and picks up my revolver. He hands his rifle to a grinning bastard behind him. I watch on as he raises my own gun to my head. His right arm straightens, his knuckles whitening as he grips the gun tightly, his finger closing in on the trigger, and then his left eye closes and he takes aim as my life becomes a rapid flicker of memories in my mind.

I've been in critical situations many times in my life, but I never felt that I was about to face my Maker. I don't feel that way now. My life rushes past me like I'm watching a film—a very short film. This is how the beginning of the end has been explained to me by men who have come so near to it. Short. Sharp. Swift. I realise that this is the very truth of the matter; life is short. Bloody short. My dear wife

Mabel's angelic face appears in my mind's eye, her own sparkling eyes and peaches-and-cream skin glowing with innocence and calm. The image fills me with love. I didn't often tell her how much she meant to me. My eyes well up with tears of deep regret as I pray that I will live to tell her how deeply I love her but, as I stare down the barrel of my own gun, I doubt my prayers are going to be answered.

Then something miraculous happens. The officer lowers the gun, walks towards me and rustles through my pockets and, when he finds a small but treasured gold clock my father gave me, his eyes light up. Appearing satisfied with his booty he strides away, and I think I might be safe—for now. I stand there, watching him fondling the clock, seemingly disinterested in me, and so, stomach churning, I make a decision and walk away to turn my attention to my wounded.

I begin to gather bales of straw from nearby fields, ripping them apart, scattering the straw around like a man possessed, and then I proceed to carry the wounded from the two lorries. The German officer with my clock laughs at me and flicks a limp, disinterested hand in my direction, so I continue on.

It's hard going. The wounded are heavyweights, some of them barely alive. Regardless, even the near-dead manage to offer their thanks, and I can feel my heart swelling to twice its size throughout this exceedingly humbling experience.

The night that follows is one of the worst I have ever spent in my life, and I've spent many shocking ones in the last war. I help my boys, moving them about, getting water to their parched lips and adjusting bandages. Blood is everywhere. I believe I will never get the smell off me, the metallic, earthy, horror-filled odour assaulting my nostrils.

30 May—I'm pleased when daylight comes and the wounded are moved inside an empty bunker by Jerry. I follow and continue to assist my men to the best of my ability until, at about 4:00 pm, a Jerry doctor arrives. After a couple of hours, I watch on as the wounded are loaded into Jerry ambulances. I smile as I farewell each man, my words of encouragement sounding hollow to my ears. I doubt I will ever see them again and my heart is bleeding with sorrow for what they will have to go through. They will not see their homeland for a long time, if ever. However, I must now face my own fate. After all, I'm a prisoner of war, at least I hope that is my fate; I dare not allow myself to think of the alternative.

When my injured men are driven off to who knows where I'm ordered by the clock-thieving German officer to march by gunpoint to a nearby field where I find other prisoners assembled. Penrice and Hardy and the two lorry drivers are here and I rush to greet them, thankful for their safety, and comforted by their familiar faces.

We are soon crammed like cattle to slaughter into lorries and driven in the dark of night to a large mansion, housing thousands of other prisoners. My heart sinks at the terrible sight, and the ugly truth now hits me—Jerry is surely winning this war.

I am not here long before another batch of prisoners arrive and I see six more of our lads; one is a fellow named Adair who is a signaller, and another is one of my drummers. They tell me they had been asleep in a barn and were awakened about 3:00 am yesterday to find the battalion had moved on and the enemy were all around them. It's a bittersweet reunion as we swap stories of the fates of others, whilst debating what may lay ahead for us now that we are captured men. The 11 of us make a pact to do whatever it takes to stick together.

We can't find an inch of ground to sleep on, except for a cellar with a foot of putrid water slopping around in it, and it absolutely stinks. One of the lads spots some boards wedged amongst the filth, and we scramble to help him dislodge them and place them over the fetid water in an attempt to get some sleep. Sleep is hardly the word for it for, as soon as my weary eyes start to close, all I can hear are the mournful groans of fellow prisoners, the odd scream piercing through the blackness and landing like a spear through my heart. But they are only expressing aloud what I am keeping tightly contained within, for I fear that once I start to scream, I won't be able to stop.

CHAPTER 4

THE NIGHTMARE MARCH AND THE LABOUR CAMPS

1940

France

31 May—Whatever sleep we do manage to get is short-lived, because an hour or so later, very early this morning, we are ordered to fall in, and we start what is called by us prisoners, for obvious reasons, as The Nightmare March. There are many horrific incidents that happen on this march that I will leave out of these memoirs but, on my life, I swear they will never be forgotten—and never *ever* forgiven.

We march all day and into the evening. There are many French prisoners with us, all appearing to have been well prepared for capture as they have suitcases, extra bags and clothes and food provisions in their large haversacks. At around 9:00 pm, we arrive at a sizeable church and the French are marched inside to sleep, while we Brits are kept outside and have to sleep amongst the tombstones in the graveyard. It is a terrible experience; bitterly cold and frigidly frightening, sharing the damp soil with long-ago extinguished souls and, being the second day without food, we are all starving.

Before dawn the German guards come around hitting us with the butts of their rifles, and we're on the road again, marching without any food or water. I hear that a few poor chaps tried to capture some of the multitude of rats that scuttled by us overnight for food and, while the thought disturbs me, my achingly hungry stomach considers the future possibility of having to do just that, as I am in no doubt that this journey will be a case of either thinking on one's feet, or certain death.

When the sun comes out it gets hot and we're all parched. The French townsfolk, bless them, place buckets of water on the side of the road, and it's a scramble to get a drink before the merciless guards come along and kick the buckets over out of sheer spite. They wish us dead. It makes it easier on them.

Every now and then we make a dash for tins of food, also left by compassionate villagers, and Penrice, Hardy and I finally manage to grab one each. I get a tin of condensed milk, and I thank God for the small mercy. The Jerry guards are absolute bastards. They find it amusing to stop us British prisoners while they allow the French to get far ahead before making us run to catch up to the Frogs. Naturally, many poor chaps are hardly able to walk, never mind run, and they have to drop out. On hearing shots, we know only too well what has become of them, each gunshot reverberating through our bodies as we trudge onwards, thoughts of our fallen comrades a terrible burden to bear.

Having marched for approximately 20 miles in the glaring sun, sweat pouring out of us after being stopped many times while the sadistic Jerry guards play their game of slow down and catch up, we approach a large field where we are to stay the night. But by the time we get there, the French are lined up for something to eat. Then, by the time we get to the servery, we find that the French have eaten all the soup, and so we are once again hungry and exhausted as we get down to it and attempt to sleep. I'm grateful for the warmth of my two companions, Penrice and Hardy, who are huddled next to me, as the only covering we have between us is my overcoat.

It's the same routine today, off again with nothing in our stomachs. My left leg begins to trouble me and I can hardly drag it along. I'm far older than my fellow compatriots, and I fear I will not make it, but my mates encourage me onwards, and after 5 miles or so my leg miraculously comes right again. Another blessing bestowed upon these aching bones.

It's been another 20-mile march today, but at the end of it we do manage to get a cup of the so-called soup on offer: hot water and a few pieces of macaroni. Still, it's something.

Each day is a repetition of the last, and many, many boys do not make it. Is there ever a more sickening form of torture than hearing one's comrades falling to the ground before screaming and begging for mercy? Perhaps there is, perhaps it's the silence that follows. Hauntingly quiet. Not even the birds sing following the loud crack of gunfire, which pierces the air and echoes throughout the countryside, shattering nerves and playing with minds. But on I toil, marvelling at my ability to remain alive when so many younger and fitter men than I have perished, while simultaneously wondering whether I will be next to take a bullet.

8 June—We finally stop at a prison in Doullens, France, having marched for nine days at an average of 20 miles a day. Some of the places we have been on this march are Froyenncs, Arras, Saint-Pol, Cambrai, and Bapaume, but there has been no sequence to the march. We have been zigzagging everywhere, and we soon discover the reason for this; it has simply been a propaganda exercise for Jerry to show the people of France the defeated remnants of the British Army and what a sorry lot we are.

The three of us, Penrice, Hardy and I, are ordered to join a working party in a large warehouse that Jerry is turning into a hospital supplies store. We have to carry huge bags of grain and the Jerry officers don't think twice about using their fists or even feet to hurry us along. There are 12 of us in this party and when we are finished for the day we are marched back to the French prison only to find that the men we were with have left without us, their destination unknown to us. More prisoners roll in and tell us that a large proportion of their men were shot on the march along the way. I wonder where this farce is leading, as I'm certain do all the men. Needless to say, spirits are at an all-time low.

We are marched to the train station in Doullens this same evening, only to find the French already occupying every single one of the train carriages, or rather animal cages because they are open wagons. What is this blasted favouritism all about? We're forced to climb onto these already overcrowded carriages with the aid of the guards' bayonets, and we are crammed so tightly that if one lifts up a foot to relieve cramps one cannot get it down again. During the night the train stops and we have to just stand there. No other choice. No sleep. No food or water.

A few chaps manage to climb up the sides of our carriage. I watch on longingly as they settle into sleep perched precariously on the thin rims, parts of their bodies crushing the heads of others. But just as day breaks another train slams into us and some of the blokes who I had previously thought so lucky to be getting some horizontal shut-eye during the night are knocked off the carriage and injured. One chap falls between our carriage and the next, and I shall never forget his screams for help. When he is eventually recovered, both of his legs have been completely severed from his body, and he dies within five minutes. A Frenchman is also killed in a similar fashion, his death also pitifully horrific.

We travel by train until midday and then we have to march until nightfall where we sleep in a field. It is here that I want to make my escape but one of my two pals will not do so. I will not say which one. As we have agreed to stick together, I succumb to his wishes. We do get a little soup, though.

Stalag XXI-D, Trier, Germany

10 June—We travel all day on foot without a crumb to eat and by nightfall we're herded aboard another cramped cattle train and travel through Luxembourg to Trier, Germany's oldest city. We march to Stalag XXI-D which we're told is a prisoner-of-war holding camp. There are thousands upon thousands of captured soldiers here and my heart sinks at the sight. We finally get a fifth of a loaf of bread and a piece of cheese per man. This is a luxury, and I have to be careful not to eat too fast only to lose it all again. My stomach is delicate, and I can feel my old ulcers playing up.

At 7:00 am we stand in long queues, as ordered, and here we stay all day long. By 8:00 pm we are still standing, having had no food or water. At least, most of us are standing. Those poor chaps among us who could not manage to do so any longer have been taken away. There's no need for me to elaborate on their fate.

We are then marched to the train station and, once again, we're loaded onto rail carriages. At least we get a little bread and cheese here, and this time, famished, I gobble it down.

Camp Schubin, Poland

12 June—We arrive in Poland at 11:00 pm at a place called Schubin; all of us are weak and hungry, many barely alive. We stagger from the train trucks and march to camp. I cannot describe the horror. The stench of wasting bodies. I feel as if I'm one of the walking dead, but I manage to make it to the camp, which I'm told is to be my home for a good while. We get a drop of so-called coffee—burnt barley without sugar or milk—and then we must get down to it out in the open where we are to sleep each night for the next fortnight as we're informed there are no barracks available to us. No tents, no blankets.

This place is full of Poles—soldiers captured during the invasion of their country in 1939. We are formed into companies and sections and I am made a section leader, perhaps due to my age. The conditions here are shocking and the food indescribably awful and meagre at that. It is hard to keep going, and many don't, succumbing to dysentery, which is a horribly painful and degrading condition to suffer. We are all in a filthy condition. The heat is unbearable, made more so by the reek of human wastage.

3rd week of June—The German guards come around and hand out cards this morning, one for every man, so we can write home and I, along with everyone, am delighted to be able to send news to my loved ones advising them that I am alive. We are given strict instructions that we must not mention our whereabouts or the censor will destroy the letters. I pray that my news brings some comfort to my darling Mabel and our girls, not to mention allowing her to continue to get my pay packets.

I hear on the grapevine that Britain is doing it tough. Germany has been heavily bombing, mainly in the south, and while it is worrisome news, I'm grateful that the wife and family are in the north and hopefully safe in the town hall residence in Whitehaven. I think of my daughters cleaning the grounds and I recall their grumbling voices and doleful faces when they had to come home from school or work to face their daily chores before sitting down to tea, my memory vivid of them scrubbing the town hall steps. Ah, it brings a fond smile to my lips. If only the girls knew what a relatively easy existence they have, certainly in comparison to this hellhole, but then, of course, no father would ever wish these conditions upon his offspring. They shall never hear it from me. On my word, if I survive, I shall never speak of this damned war again!

Late June—Thank God! We are billeted in barracks today, even though we have to sleep on straw and there are hundreds of us to one barracks.

1 July—Our photos and fingerprints are taken today, giving us further hope that our country will be advised of our whereabouts; that, at the very least, they will know that we are alive.

3 July—Once again today, we are given a card to send home. I hope I hear from Mabel soon as to think of her worrying about me is torturous, especially as I have far too much time on my hands nowadays. The camp routine is monotonous; we all feel utterly useless, and I can understand why some of the lads are starting to lose their minds a bit.

9 July—I still haven't had any news from home, but we are given another card today and I try to write in tiny print in order to cram in as much as I can, although there's not much to write about when one knows the censor is scrutinising every word.

12 July—Today we discover that all of the cards we previously wrote were a Jerry hoax. The bastards brag that they have destroyed them all, burnt every card we've ever written! They strut around, taunting us, as they laugh and gesticulate with their hands to simulate a fire burning. Needless to say, this sends our spirits plummeting. But not only are our spirits flagging, men are beginning to die like flies all around me. I imagine this is not only due to physical exhaustion as a result of the arduous journey here and starvation and disease, but from the sheer mental anguish caused by Jerry's cruelty, which is beginning to increase daily.

18 July—Penrice leaves the camp today, his destination unknown, and I wonder if I shall ever see him again. It feels as if I am losing mates on a daily basis, whether by death or by German decree. None of us know when they leave this camp for the next whether the conditions will be for better or worse. I wish Pen well; he's stuck by me and Hardy just as he said he would do, and if it were not for the warmth of his body next to me at night, and his constant words of encouragement, during the interminable journey here, I'm sure I would not have made it this far. At least I still have Hardy.

I find myself attending more and more funerals, often as a coffin bearer. Today it is of a chap who was brought in dead from a working party. The Jerry guards say he died from pneumonia but, as I march alongside the makeshift coffin, blood is running from it and dripping in gory, gelatinous globules onto my boots. I feel my chest rapidly rising and deflating with anger, and I strangle a scream of injustice, knowing that if I start to protest, I will be shot.

28 July—Sadly, Hardy leaves Schubin today. As with Penrice, Hardy and I have been through so much together. After two long hellish months fighting to stay alive at the hands of the Germans, my good-natured and high-spirited mate is leaving me. And, once again, I pray for him, as I still pray for Penrice.

29 July—I am made company commander of Number 11 Company, a hollow privilege indeed, given the circumstances.

Exin, Poland

13 August—It's now my turn to leave Camp Schubin. I go to a place called Exin, about 10 miles west of Schubin, and I'm pleasantly surprised by the conditions. I'm housed in a former school building along with only 140 prisoners. Although we are under guard I'm told this is not an official stalag. The working hours are long. We're up at 5:00 am for a 6:00 am start, and we return at 7:00 pm, but we're treated okay and the food is better than I've been used to, in as far as quantity is concerned.

After being put on various jobs, such as digging large trenches alongside roads for drainage, I get a job helping a Polish electrician fit out a building which is to be a cinema. I formerly told Jerry that I was a tradesman, which is probably why I was sent here, and I am a tradesman of sorts, but a fitter knows next to nothing about electrical stuff. Still, I'm happy to report that my boss is a patient chap and, although they are rather a rough lot, I find the Poles to be good people and very kind-natured. My boss has a wireless set hidden in the rafters of his home, and he brings me regular news of Blighty. This is surely one of the most wonderful gifts anyone could give to me—news of my glorious homeland, although it is disheartening to hear that Jerry is still bombing Blighty.

I start to earn the equivalent of 70 pfennigs a day. There are 100 pfennigs to a mark. This money is special camp paper money and is of no value on the outside, but a few of us chaps soon find we can trade things with the Poles for German money, for which we can get them to procure things for us outside camp. Prisoners are forbidden to have German money, so it's quite a challenge to do so behind the Jerries' backs.

Camp Schubin, Poland

9 September—I am just settling down in my new place when I'm sent back to hell—Camp Schubin—with 11 others, because being tradesmen we are told we are now wanted at Schubin. I'm devastated at this as, for me, it's now back to the drudge, the tedium, back to the overcrowded barracks, lousy food, stench and dysentery.

Camp Wollstein, Polish–German Border

11 September—It has been only two days since my last diary entry and I'm on the move again. I thought I would be glad to get out of Camp Schubin, but today, when we arrive at a place called Wollstein, about 125 miles south-west of Schubin and close to the German border, my heart sinks. The conditions are woeful. We are crammed in flimsy tents and sleep like hogs in a sty on beds of putrid straw. It's also mind-numbingly freezing and we have no blankets at all.

12 September—I awaken to a thunderous explosion this night before pandemonium breaks out and bodies dash out of tents in every direction. We are under attack from above. Another bomb drops, and another. When it's all over, we are ordered back to our tents and try to sleep but it's a futile exercise as our nerves are shattered.

13 September—This morning the Jerries taunt us, telling us that it was three of our own planes that dropped the bombs on the camp last night. We know this. Who else would it be? We ignore them, but it's spine-chilling to know that we were bombed by our own comrades. Thankfully there are not too many casualties.

Stalag XXI-B, Warthelager, Poland

2 October—We are all pleased when 200 of us are moved to a place called Warthelager, a few miles north of Posen. When we arrive today, we find the camp houses 1200 prisoners. We are billeted in very basic huts holding 200 men apiece. It's not so bad—anywhere is better than the last hellhole—and here at least we have a roof over our heads, although the huts are very dark and have cold concrete floors. Apparently, they were once stables. Each hut is then issued with a small stove, but the acrid smoke they produce is unbearable, and one can hardly see through the billowing haze.

When we are told that we can start on foundations for new huts we get on to it straight away. It keeps our minds off our desperation for news from home. Having heard not a thing since being taken prisoner four months ago, we are fretting that our loved ones may be getting one of 'those' telegrams. But gradually the mail from home starts trickling in, although I'm not one of the lucky recipients.

It is now the end of the month. We get a postcard each to write home, and we are told that from now on in we will get a postcard one week, a letter card the next. We pray that this time it's not a Jerry hoax.

Early November—We have learnt that this place is a Jerry training area. Oh, how I wish I could get news to Blighty regarding this.

It is now getting very cold and it starts to snow, but work goes on, and our new huts are well in progress. Our boots long ago well and truly wore out, and we are all walking around in wooden clogs, similar to Dutch ones, and they are exceedingly difficult to work in. We still receive only one meal a day, which has never varied from the time I entered the first camp—thin soup. And if we are very, very lucky we get a fifth of a loaf of bread. It's certainly not enough food to sustain us, let alone provide us with the energy to work, and we are all suffering from malnutrition.

When we hear that a number of Poles have managed to obtain a wireless set we pile into their barracks to listen to the news, but sadly we learn that Jerry are bombing London heavily. The Poles sympathise with us. They're decent blokes who are eager to befriend us and are very poorly treated by the German guards. One day, after listening to the English news, the Poles type it out on leaflets and distribute it around camp. Unfortunately, one leaflet falls into Jerry hands, and the Gestapo are called in to investigate. When they cannot find the culprits, for not one of us is going to tell them, one night we hear them marching hundreds of Poles away. Only 40 men return. To think they were doing this for us, the poor devils.

It's now early December. The weather is appalling, with snow mounting up so high we can only leave the huts every second day after clearing it. The thermometer is showing that it's 18 degrees below freezing and it's all we can do to keep warm.

Mid December—We move into our new billets, which provide us with better conditions than the former stables. In desperate need of hearing from the wife, I have to satisfy myself with writing poetry. I hope to read it aloud to my wife one day and, hopefully, that will be soon. I name this poem 'Thinking of You…'

THINKING OF YOU WITH AN ACHE IN MY HEART
WONDERING WHERE YOU ARE NOW
STRIVING TO SMILE, AND TO PLAY MY SMALL PART
LIVING THE DAYS OUT SOMEHOW

THINKING OF YOU AND THE THINGS THAT WE PLANNED
THE CASTLES WE BUILT IN THE BLUE!
THE SCHEMES THAT WE MADE

WHEN THE FUTURE LOOKED GRAND
THE DREAMS THAT JUST DIDN'T COME TRUE
TRYING MY BEST NOT TO SIGH OR COMPLAIN
BUT WHEN THE NIGHT COMES AT LAST
I GO TO MEET YOU DOWN MEMORY LANE
SO SWEET ARE THE THOUGHTS OF THE PAST

THINKING OF YOU OVER THERE FAR AWAY
WONDERING WHY THIS MUST BE
LOOKING AHEAD TO THE JOY OF THAT DAY
WHEN YOU WILL BE BACK WITH ME.

Drum Major HB Jackson
POW, Warthelager
Poland 15/12/40

Christmas Day—We get Christmas presents of two loaves of bread, a cigarette holder, two packets of tobacco, and two bottles of beer per man. And then, in the afternoon, the guards come around handing out one Red Cross parcel to be shared between four men. They distribute them smugly, as if they are bleedin' Santa Claus and his elves—as if they'd paid for the parcels themselves. Oh well, small mercies I suppose. I would dearly love to give the chaps a musical show, but I've not an instrument with which to do so. It feels like I've lost both my arms.

The mail is coming in about every fortnight, but I am still unlucky and receive nothing. I've been seven long months in capture without one letter. It's very dispiriting.

CHAPTER 5

SAD NEWS FROM HOME

1941

Stalag XXI-B, Warthelager, Poland

It's now January, my eighth month in capture, and I cannot believe how much time has passed since I last made an entry in my diary, but one day simply rolls into the next here at Warthelager, and one's mind is primarily on sleep, food and the endless wait for mail. To consider anything else signals the end of one's chances of making it through this war. Of course, there is lots of talk of escape, but it's mostly fantasy. Stuck here in Jerry-occupied Poland, not to mention the flat, lifeless terrain, we are advised by the Polish prisoners that we are bringing on an early death sentence if we attempt an escape. With Germany flying their flag at an all-time high, and the news trickling in of our forces' further retreat, for the time being the general consensus is to stay put. But once our troops swell and advance, hopefully with the aid of other countries, we will be making our run for freedom from here and joining up with our troops again. I swear on my life we will!

1 February—It is still bitterly cold and I am the only one taking a working party out today. It's 30 degrees below zero, an unimaginable temperature, even for us Brits. The ground is piled high with snow, as it has been since November, and God only knows how we'll keep on managing. One chap is punished for insubordination and is ordered to get down on his hands and knees and put his face in the snow. He has no gloves and, when he hesitates, two Jerry guards push him down to the ground before repeatedly kicking him. This goes on for an hour, and our chap is a total mess when he returns to the barracks.

About 50 parcels arrive from home with warm clothing in them, but I am once again unlucky.

9 February—Today I return to the camp from a working party to find four letters waiting for me! I have three from the wife and one from her mother, Elizabeth. A red-letter day indeed. Oh, what a relief it is to know that the wife realises that I am alive. Along with every other bloke who has received mail, I rush to my barracks, hop on my bunk, and get down to reading.

But on reading the third letter from Mabel, I am sent into shock. The wife asks me if I received her letter dated 18 August last year telling me of my father's death, but of course I didn't. These letters are like reading a book from the end.

Oh, I'm truly heartbroken, now both my parents are gone, but they are still so clear in my mind…

I was the only child born to John Henry and Eleanor Jackson, at Rosemary Lane, Whitehaven, England, on 30 September 1898. My parents had been married the year previously and mine was a loving family. My dad was a coal hewer, and he worked long hours deep underground loosening rock and minerals with a pick. Even now I can see him in my mind's eye; his weary face, caked in black muck, lighting up when he returned home to find me and my mam waiting for him. Dad would hold out his permanently stained hands and filthy fingernails in greeting, hands that no amount of scrubbing could get clean.

When Mam wasn't cleaning the house, or washing Dad's sooty clothes, a thankless job, she could be found in the kitchen, elbow deep in cooking. And although my dad's wage was poor, Mam always managed to cover our table with delicious food, and I don't ever recall her complaining about lack of funds. Worrying, yes, but more for my dad's safety than about his meagre wage. But despite her ever-present worries of imminent danger and our lack of spare money, or perhaps it was because of it, my mother wanted more for me, and it was she who instilled in me the love of music. For Eleanor Jackson was a woman of refinement, if only in her own mind. I remember my dad saying he couldn't believe his luck when my mam took him on as husband. In fact, he said it so often I sometimes felt like an intruder in their lives.

From a very young age, my mam took me to each and every concert that came to town. My earliest memories are of the brass bands that would play in the streets. Seeing my enthusiasm for music, she begged for and borrowed musical instruments, and I banged around on them like other lads did toys. When I was six years old, Mam took me to visit a bloke in Whitehaven town who locals called The Music Man, and he agreed that in exchange for meals from my mother, he would teach me how to play music.

The Music Man introduced me to the ins and outs of music—reading, timing, rhythm, melody, keys and expressions. It was like learning a foreign language at first, stepping into a whole new world; but I soon took to music like a monkey to bananas, I was that hungry for it. Within no time it seemed, I was so enthralled it was a wonder I didn't change shape into a tuba or saxophone or some form of musical instrument.

Well, my dad took it all in his stride—my obsession with music—but that's not to say he ever saw a future in it. Not at all. I was only seven years of age when he sat me down and said, 'Son, a man's passion for the arts, whatever that may be, is fine and dandy, but more than anything a man needs to be a good and decent human being. I have faith that you will achieve such ends.'

No doubt he was preparing me for my future, because unbeknownst to me and my dear mother at that time, my father had plans for me to follow him down the mines. I cannot imagine why. As I got older, Dad started spruiking his job and trivialising music; mining was a good, honest job, he repeated on a regular basis. Earning a living through music was for sissies. Family tradition was everything (his father was also a miner), and perhaps I was getting all ahead of myself.

I said nothing in response, but the mere thought of spending my life down a suffocating pit, covered in muck and sweltering in the dark and airless underground, horrified me. For my father's job was a perilous one indeed, and every person in the district knew how common it was for a man not to return home from a shift at the pits one day. The Wellington Pit disaster in May 1910 in Whitehaven reinforced that. One hundred and thirty-six men and boys were killed in an explosion and ensuing fire. They were all buried alive after the mine was ordered to be sealed to starve the fire of oxygen. It took several months of agonising wait until they reopened the mine and then began the gruesome task of recovering the badly decomposed bodies to hand them back to their distraught loved ones for burial. I remember hearing sad tales of some of the dead men being found with their arms around the charred remains of terrified boys, some as young as me, their final messages of love desperately scrawled on walls. Our town was full of coffins. Haunted me for months, it did. I was nearing 12 years of age and I feared my turn was coming to work at the pits.

Finally, having had enough, in 1912, miners throughout England, including my dad, downed tools and took place in the National Coal Strike. They hung on for 37 days until the government finally ended it by passing the Minimum Wage Act, and conditions, in so far as money went, improved somewhat. God knows, this win only served to encourage my dad because when I was nearly 14, a short time after he resumed work following the strike, Dad made the big announcement over tea one night that he'd got me an apprenticeship as a fitter—in the mines. I was to leave school on the spot.

I felt the very blood inside me freeze—could almost see it crystallise into snow. I looked up at my mam's face and saw that it was also as ashen as mine. She let out a gasp, her voice so quiet as she said the words, 'No, John… no.'

But my dad was having none of it. He laughed. He actually laughed! 'A fitter, a bleedin' fitter, Eleanor!' he sang out happily as he heartily scooped up a spoonful of stew. 'No bleedin' hewer for our lad Harry here! A fitter no less! Now, I ask you, how many lads get such an opportunity, eh, my lass?'

So, as my dad's word was law, my fate was sealed. I started my apprenticeship the following week—and I hated it. The work was interesting, I suppose, learning all about the ins and outs of machinery, but the mines, oh, they were everything I'd imagined they'd be and worse. Much worse. The darkness. The cloying atmosphere. The feeling of being like a rat clawing its way through underground sewers. The dust causing gagging and coughing. Oh, it was all too indescribable.

Then, in June 1914, war broke out and I was desperate to enlist, but my dad said no. Besides the fact that I was too young, Dad said it was a perk of our job—mining—that we didn't have to go and fight, seeing as miners were exempt from fighting in war, as our work was vital to the nation. He straightened his normally stooped body, a result of spending half a lifetime down the pits and gave a conspiratorial wink in my direction—and that was the end of the matter as far as he was concerned.

Not for me. I stood the job for as long as I could, and then, in March 1915, I made a snap decision. I was sick and tired of hearing how poorly our chaps were doing in the war. Many of my mates were over there fighting for their country, and I was damn well going to do the same! I was a tad over 16, and I was a working man after all. An adult. I left my job after my shift had finished one afternoon, and I skipped all the way to the enlistment office. I never returned to the colliery.

It's all water under the bridge now, I suppose, but I never thought I'd be in this position when my father died. Locked up and useless to do a thing about it. Mabel says in her letter that Dad was very weak towards the end, but he'd insisted that no one was to write and tell me how bad he really was. He said I had enough on my plate. Ah, that was my dad, always thinking of others. This has knocked the very stuffing out of me. Every son should be there to comfort his father in his dying hours. To tell him all the things we men keep hidden deep inside—until it's too late, as it is to be for me and my great dad now. And to think I was his only son. His only child. I have nothing left of him here; the Jerry officer who captured me put paid to that when he took my last memento—Dad's gold clock.

Jerry has taken everything.

Everything.

CHAPTER 6

KEEPING OUR SPIRITS UP

1941

Stalag XXI-B, Warthelager, Poland

11 February—I answer my letters today. It is hard to express in writing my grief at my father's death, especially knowing that it is now months after the fact and his funeral is well and truly past. I feel so bereft, but I do my best, thanking my dear wife for all her help with Dad and, of course, I send my love to all.

The weather is starting to fine up and the snow is gradually clearing away, which is good as it's been bitterly cold. One simply cannot come to terms with the degree to which the temperatures drop here in Poland.

12 February—There's a big thaw on and a large bridge near here is badly damaged.

18 February—We have just had another three days of snow. This Polish weather is strange indeed.

22 February—Today I, along with all the boys, receive a Red Cross parcel, which is very welcome.

Our company has started a small library, but many of the books have been provided by Jerry and are full of propaganda, such as titles like *The Atrocities of the Poles*, which show horrible photos of decomposed bodies of minority Germans supposedly killed by the Poles. Documents on the *Origin of the War* and *Why Britain Cannot Win the Trade War* are others. Needless to say, we all scoff at such rubbish.

27 February—We are ordered to move back into our old huts, which we begrudgingly do today. This is because Jerry needs our new ones for themselves, and we now realise why we built them in the first place. For incoming Jerry troops. Of course, we're not happy about this, but what can one do?

Jerry troops start to arrive and within no time they step up training. It's not pleasant to watch their fanaticism, what with their swastikas, Nazi salutes and goosesteps. We boys have a laugh once we're in our barracks, attempting to copy their silly style of marching, swinging one leg up while keeping the other rigidly straight on the ground.

I'm comforted when I receive my second lot of mail this afternoon: two from our youngest girl, Joan, telling me that her class has pitched in to send me a present but she can't decide what it will be, which makes me chuckle; one from Mabel's mother; and four from Mabel starting from 5 November 1940 to 25 January this year. Life is beginning to feel like an endless wait for mail, an endless search for food, and an endless yearning for freedom. At night, I dream of our chaps coming to free us, and me joining them once again in the fight against Jerry. But then I awake to reality and watch the Germans swaggering around the place like stud bulls on show, bragging and shouting in their guttural accents about how bloody wonderfully well they are doing in this war.

6 March—Today I receive 11 letters. There's no sequence to the mail, as the dates are all over the place, and one has to wonder about the Jerry mail system. Still, in whatever order news from home comes, I'll take it!

I'm not overly surprised to read from Mabel that she has moved the family out of the Whitehaven Town Hall, it having been too much work for her. I understand, but I do feel useless knowing how hard the wife's been having it. She says she's moved back to Bransty, to The Green, only a few doors from her parents' place, and she's back to selling insurance. What a woman.

In one letter I find a photo of Mabel and our daughters—a really good one it is, too. I boastfully show it around. No one believes the wife's age, and many lads comment that she looks just like one of our girls. Even the German censor, who once again came down to our camp to remind us of what we're not to write in our return mail, remarked on what a grand family I have. It makes me very proud.

Four girls, all as pretty as their mam…

Soon after our marriage, Mabel told me the news we'd been expecting—she was indeed pregnant—and she immediately left her job as a domestic servant. I was all for this because the old crow she worked for was very demanding. It seemed as if my kind-hearted wife was to be everyone's prey. But I have to say that I was indebted to her employer, if only for the fact that when I first met Mabel the old woman had taken a liking to the special on offering at Penney's Fish and Chip Shop—a ladle of mushy peas topped with a spoonful of chips smothered in salt and vinegar. She sent Mabel out, bowl in hand, on a regular basis to fetch her some. So, if it weren't for that, I wouldn't have met my girl, and therefore I wouldn't have been as proud as a peacock to see the wife blooming in pregnancy with our first child.

Our Nelly, Eleanor to be precise, she being named after my mam, was born 26 February 1921, only six months after our wedding date—much to the shock of the local town gossips. Mabel's mother, Elizabeth, was also not impressed, to say the least, and I squirmed on seeing the mother-in-law counting the months on her fingers, her glare of indignation directed firmly at me. Then, she clapped her hands and demanded that we explain away Nelly's untimely arrival as being a premature birth. Premature, my foot. Anyone who knew anything about babies could have seen when our chubby and happy little girl was born that she was well and truly cooked. Anyway, I wasn't overly interested in people who had so much time on their hands as to be wasting it nattering about others. No, I had formed my own band, and between band practice and dances, work and our new baby, I was extremely busy.

I'm delighted to say that every two years after Nelly came into the world, we had another daughter. Our Mona was born in July 1923, and in March 1925 along came our Betty (or Elizabeth, who was named after Mabel's mam after several tantrums were thrown by the mother-in-law due to our Mona not taking her name and Nelly being named after my mam). Women! I can tell you, I was surrounded by them.

And then our lovely little family was struck by sadness. Mabel first picked up that all was not right with young Mona. She just didn't seem to be growing like Nelly had. Mona struggled, and her little arms and legs appeared stunted. Dwarfism, the doctors called it, and the light in our world dimmed somewhat. I had seen dwarfs before but only in the circus, and they were a form of entertainment—a spectacle to be laughed at. I hated that; even as a young lad I can remember thinking it was unfair to mock them, the circus freaks as they were called. Well, it seemed I had spawned such a creature. Our Mona's condition took me aback when Mabel first told me the diagnosis, I can tell you, and I worried that her mind was also affected, such was my ignorance on the subject. But in time, our daughter certainly taught me a thing or two. For there was nothing wrong with *her* brain! I'm proud to report that her mother's loving care ensured that Mona was not treated in any way differently to her sisters and, although we knew it was unlikely that she'd ever go on to meet a chap and have a family of her own, Mona became the best asset we ever had. For she fussed over her siblings and parents as if she were born to be a mother.

Of course, after going through the situation with Mona, I decided enough was enough, and I told Mabel as much. No more children, I said. As it turned out, it seemed someone higher in authority than me—He who lived in the heavens, if you get my drift—decided otherwise. Five years after Betty came into our world we were surprised by the news that we were having another one. We held our breath, and we prayed that this child would be healthy like Nelly and Betty and would not have to suffer the afflictions that Mona did. And while I was praying for that, I thought it couldn't hurt to put one in for another blessing to be bestowed: that it would be a boy. But it was not to be and, in April 1930, our Joan popped into the world. She was a tiny little thing was Joan, thin and bony, pale skin and flaming red hair. I took one look at her and chuckled, as she reminded me of a plucked chicken. But Joan had a grand set of lungs on her and, even though she was perhaps the wrong sex for the likes of me at the time, I was happy because with that hair colouring she was her proud dad all over. And our Joan was 'normal'.

Still, after Joan's birth, I really put my foot down and told Mabel that four girls were enough for any man to contend with in that day and age. Joan was to be the last. And she was.

I show the photo of my family to two young fellows from the 4th Battalion Border Regiment named Fred J Kirkbride and Walter H Ferguson. Walter often comes to my bunk for a good old crack [chat] and exchange of news. He's a good bloke. In fact, when he received 200 cigs from the *West Cumberland Times* two days ago, Walter rushed straight down to my bunk to give me a packet. Very welcome they were too. We have to hide them from the guards—the cigs—because the Jerries are on rations and they will confiscate them for the slightest reason and keep them for themselves.

There's a lot more activity around camp of late. Jerry troops are coming in for a few days' training, and then they are off again. They are all very confident that they'll wrap this war up by the end of this year. Many of them brag that they will invade England in April.

We are desperate for some information on what's happening on the warfront at home but, although they are a boastful lot, Jerries are very cautious regarding specifics. It's very demoralising for our boys and hard to keep our silence, which of course we don't when the Krauts are not around, and at least this helps to boost each other's morale again. We continue to have a good laugh some nights back in our barracks when a few of the chaps walk around mimicking the Jerries. One of the lads put on a hilarious show for us last night, imitating their goosestepping, him squawking and flapping his arms around, his eyes rolling around in his head as he stuck his neck out at a near impossible angle. Despite everything, we have decided that it is imperative we keep our sense of humour. Without it, we are truly doomed.

19 March—Today I receive 26 letters, which keep me going for days. We Brits are rather lucky in respect to mail and parcels from our loved ones, which we've also started to receive, especially when compared to the poor Poles. The Poles are mere emaciated frames and are naturally intensely anxious as to when this war will be over, because they are getting further rationing. We try and toss them food scraps over the fence, but if we're caught even fraternising with them these days we are in serious peril. Desperate as anything they are, the poor chaps. The Jerries loathe the Poles.

1 April—It is a year at the end of this month since I left Britain, me standing aboard the troopship, my mind focused on future battle and full of hope for success, but now I fear it will be another year until this war is over. Pray to God that I, that all the chaps, make it through.

2 April—Many more German troops have arrived and have been grandstanding around the camp lately, wearing full battle dress, and today there is a great exodus from here. Word is out that Yugoslavia is now in the war, and we think that's the place they are heading for.

6 April—Jerry troops continue to pour in and three days of manoeuvres are carried out with many generals present, including General Goering, head of the Nazi Party and commander-in-chief of the Luftwaffe, the Jerry air force. Goering is Hitler's supposed successor should anything happen to Hitler. These new troops are a fierce-looking lot: their caps with gold bullion and golden eagles, their black jackets emblazoned with swastikas, shoulder boards and collar patches, their breeches tucked into high, immaculately polished leather boots. Goering, of course, is wearing a flamboyant uniform of his own design, his fat fingers squashed into a multitude of rings. We watch on in disgust as the camp becomes emblazoned with red, black and white banners bearing the swastika. There must be a reason for all this, but we are certainly not told what it is.

8 April—Today we learn that the word out was correct and Jerry troops have marched into Yugoslavia, but so did our troops. Pray to God we are the victors. The Germans here are in high glee and say that the war will be over in a matter of weeks because they have three-quarters of a million troops in Yugoslavia, and we only have 200,000. But I continue to have faith in our boys. I only wish I could be alongside them to fight these bastards. I know they speak rubbish, the Germans, spouting propaganda in the hope of demoralising us, but one would be a liar if one didn't admit to feeling down sometimes. It's the sheer inertia of our situation that brings about this melancholy. We came here to fight, not to sit around dependent upon our enemy for our next bite to eat and dreaming of revenge.

9 April—We are told by the Germans this morning that the whole of Greece has fallen, but later this afternoon we discover that it was only the Greek city of Salonika that fell. Jerry's constant bragging and confidence is starting to tell on some of our chaps, and they are showing signs of despair, but it's not wise to speak up as the punishment is shocking. Today one of our boys who does so—voices his anger—has to stand at the camp gates for four hours with his hands in the air while the Germans taunt him and prod him with their bayonets. Understandably, he comes back a complete mess and, though we try to buoy him with encouraging words, I doubt his mind will hold up. A strong mind is everything in this place, and without it one may as well be dead. I keep reminding myself that if I can survive this, I can survive anything, and I want to take that attitude back to England with me and hand it on to my girls. Music is my saving grace and, although I can't play due to having no musical instruments, I do spend a lot of time thinking about, singing and composing music. For me, where there is music, there is hope.

29 April—Rumours are buzzing around camp, but one hardly knows what to believe as most of them are started by Jerry who are increasingly tightening conditions. For the last two months, we have been made to pay for our cards and letters to write home, and we only get one a week now. But we will not be dispirited, and we while away our time bartering with the Poles outside to get Jerry money to buy bread for us. Of course, this is forbidden, but to date I have managed to get a lot of bread into camp for the boys. One day I actually got 30 loaves, and my working party brought them into camp right under the Jerries' noses. Today I was carrying 15 loaves in my haversack and I hid them in the Jerry camp until we were ready to go back to our camp. I suppose I will be caught one day and will have to take the punishment, but it will be worth it. My mate, Sergeant Rimington Davies, is also doing the same thing, and many times our beds are covered with loaves after we get in from a working party at night. The lads all come in for their bread, and it's a grand sight to see their gleeful faces when they discover the size of our booty. Rimington is also managing to get one or two eggs on occasion, but no one knows from where—and he's not telling.

The camp is still alive with rumours of the Germans winning the war. Jerry have even published and distributed a supplement to their newspaper, *The Camp*, which is filled with the 'supposed' news of the progress of the war. If one believed the rubbish they publish, which none of us do, the war should have been over long ago. Every week they report the sinking of thousands of tons of shipping and tell of conducting air raids galore all over England wherever and whenever they like, with not the least resistance from our chaps at home. This extra supplement claims they have chased and defeated our troops in the Balkans. Still, it's hard to maintain morale when all we're fed is propaganda, and some of the blokes are taking it to heart, and their mental state is suffering as a result.

It's very wet and still keeps cold here at the end of April. We walk out of our camp this morning and we, the sergeants of our companies, are told that we cannot go out with our respective parties. Jerry say this is a punishment on account of our men not being ready by 7:00 am. It is a ridiculous claim because our men *were* all ready to go before the guards came. Anyway, it is pouring down with rain, and we sergeants are pleased to stay indoors and have a good old crack amongst ourselves. But the Germans remain determined to mete out their punishment and this evening, while on parade, we are informed that our overdue Red Cross parcels will once again not be handed out until we get our men out promptly at 7:00 am. There's also to be no smoking or eating in ranks from this point on. The answer from all our boys is: 'Stick it up your arses!'

We are all fed up to the eyeteeth with this carry on. We know that there are now 600 Red Cross parcels in store for the 200 men in our hut. It's been over a month since we've had one. Jerry are so confident that the war will be over soon that I think they are trying to show us who is boss by controlling the parcel supply.

30 April—I speak to a Jerry corporal this morning who is here with his battalion for a rest, having served in France. They are staying in our former huts that we worked so hard to make comfy. He says that the war is nearly won and that Germany will have it all wrapped up by the end of June. I attempt to hide my cynicism and ask him why he says such a thing, and he replies that Jerry troops are now making for Spain to meet ours and, when they have 'shooed' our troops out of Spain, England will soon discover that they have no friends and are on their own. His confidence amazes me, and he continues on, telling me that they will then proceed to England and 'wipe us all out' and then the war will be over.

Of course, this is how Jerry troops are staying strong. The poor bastards are terribly brainwashed. Later this afternoon, while I'm in one of the huts doing my usual daily job of sneaking the lads' bread over to them, I see the latest *Camp* paper claiming that the English people are so fed up and getting so restless they are almost ready to surrender. It goes on to report that our prime minister, Winston Churchill, is no longer war minister and that if the Americans should decide to provide us with help it will be too late.

I feel like spitting on the paper, but I think I might just take it to the latrine block; it may come in handy for toilet paper, which a few of the lads are enjoying doing—wiping their arses on Jerry propaganda.

CHAPTER 7

RUSSIA CHANGES SIDES

1941

Stalag XXI-B, Warthelager, Poland

1 May—We are given a day off work today, it being a general holiday for the Germans in celebration of the birth of so-called 'National Socialism' [Nazism]. It means absolutely nothing to us. We loathe the idea of celebrating any such thing, nor do we consider it a 'holiday', not here in this horrible place called Warthelager, but if it means no work in such terrible weather then we'll take it. Yesterday and today it's been snowing hard, and it's very cold. In fact, it has been a terrible week for rain, snow and sleet. On the job I'm in charge of, there's about two feet of mud we have to walk about in, making it miserable going, particularly in our pathetic shoddy footwear.

8 May—Posen, a very large town about 8 miles north of here, is bombed today. Ten aerial torpedoes are dropped resulting in considerable damage. I hear from a Pole that 60 people were killed and 200 wounded.

The Camp paper this week is awful to read; we don't seem to have a dog's chance in hell of winning this war. In it are the chief points of Churchill's speech explaining about the defeat of our troops in Yugoslavia and Greece and, by the tone of his speech (according to *The Camp*), Churchill is talking about defeat. Many of our lads are really taking it to heart and it takes all of one's efforts to keep their spirits up.

9 May—I receive my second parcel from home today, which was sent in January. I also get a letter from Mabel (which was posted on 14 April), and she says she thinks the war will be over by the summer. I hope she is right, but from where I'm standing it seems impossible to believe that it will be over this year.

14 May—We hear through the 'grapevine' today that Herr Hess (now *he* is supposedly Hitler's proposed successor should anything happen to Hitler) flew from Germany to Scotland for a meeting with officials from the British Government, confident that he could get them to persuade England to surrender. Apparently, his plane was shot down and he bailed out and was promptly arrested. What a pompous idiot! Naturally the Germans here are very quiet about it, and we can get to know very little, but I think this rumour has a lot of truth in it and believe that Jerry's silence is testimony to this and they are embarrassed, as they well should be! Some successor Hess is now. We lads cannot contain our amusement, and we show it.

16 May—The Jerries retaliate against our attitude towards Hess, and they start to conduct intense searches of our barracks, giving us further proof of Hess's failed madcap scheme! As a result, many of the boys are getting caught with bread but, up to the present time, my mate Sergeant Davies and I have managed to evade detection. Thank God, as the punishment is not pleasant at all. But I have no doubt my turn is coming.

One of the things we British are disgusted with is the sight of Polish women working around here, including the old and very young. All through the bitterly cold weather, they continue to toil carrying heavy pieces of wood for carpenters' building works or shifting heavy falls of snow. Now they are digging up the land and working on manure heaps. It's hard to stomach and raises the boys' ire when around Jerry, and some of the lads make snide comments to them regarding the Germans' inability to treat women with respect. But of course, the ignorant guards simply laugh and make lewd gestures pertaining to women, further displaying their hatred of this poor race of people.

19 May—We get word today that British forces are advancing on Iraqi-held Fallujah and the Russians are heading towards them. We have all fingers and toes crossed for a good outcome.

Two chaps out of our company make their escape tonight. They are two medical orderlies named Kingsbury and Bain. It was well planned, for they had tomorrow off duty and hoped that their escape would not be noticed until the end of shift tomorrow.

20 May—Our two chaps' escape is discovered. They were shot at by Jerry Tank Corps soldiers, but still they have not been brought in and, although Jerry won't say, we believe they have managed to get away. I hope and pray that the lads succeed, but they will have to have tons of luck on their side.

21 May—We wake this morning to hear terrible news, and all spirits plummet. Lance Corporal Kingsbury has given himself up. He had waited at the appointed place for his mate, but Bain didn't turn up, so he came to the conclusion that Bain had been shot. We all pray that this is not the case and that Bain is still on the run. Kingsbury's punishment is unmentionable.

23 May—The weather has turned very warm, which helps to cheer us somewhat, and then spirits soar when our company receives some musical instruments and music sheets from the Red Cross. How I have longed for this day to arrive! I get an accordion and soon have the boys going with two songs called 'All Pals Together' and 'Memory Lives Longer Than Dreams'. In the afternoon we get our 'band' going. It consists of two accordions, two trumpets, one clarinet, one violin, eight mouth organs and a set of drums. The Jerries flock around the wires and can't understand how we project such wonderful spirit but, damn it, we will show them.

I receive two very welcome letters from Mabel, and I am chuffed to hear that I have been 'adopted' by the local Cubs led by Miss Tweddle. Like her name suggests, spinster Tweddle is a funny old bird, but she takes her role very seriously, for which I'm very grateful!

24 May—Poor Bain is also captured today, about 20 miles away. It is a crushing blow to our boys' morale as he joins his mate Kingsbury for punishment.

25 May—The Jerries boast that they have sunk one of our biggest naval vessels, HMS *Hood*. A severe crush to our naval force indeed.

28 May—The status of this war swings like a pendulum, for we are elated to hear today that the German battleship the *Bismarck* has been sunk.

29 May—I have been one year in capture. It feels like 10, and sadly one cannot see an end in sight.

Two more chaps from another company make good their escape today. They have been on a working party at the train station for a few weeks and have been preparing for a long time. This morning they got dressed in civilian clothes behind some stacks of bricks, and when a goods train arrived at about 8:00 am they climbed aboard carriages at the rear of the train. It is not until the time of writing (1:00 pm) that they are missed. Jerries soon arrive on the scene to question us, but naturally receive no information. We wait until the guards are out of sight, and then offer up our collective prayers that this time our men will be successful.

3 June—Two hundred of our men arrive at our camp from one of the main camps today. They are all dressed in new battle dress and well and truly show us up. They tell us that they have been getting Red Cross supplies regularly. We don't let on that they are in for a bitter disappointment here; it is no use dousing their spirits when they'll find out soon enough.

Once again, there is great activity here at Warthelager with German troops and tanks moving out. From the rumours we are getting from the working Poles, there seems to be a chance of Russia breaking ties with Germany. Both countries invaded Poland in September 1939, Russia only two weeks after Germany, after agreeing to divide it between themselves and signing a pact of nonaggression. However, it now appears Hitler wants all of Poland. I hope these rumours have some substance to them as we could do with a hand from the Ruskies, although they are an unknown force and it is well known that, like the Japs, they do not uphold the terms of the Geneva Convention which they did not fully sign. Apparently, they can be brutal towards their enemy and prisoners, and we are mindful of the fact that at this stage we're still their enemy and, should that change, it may well be a case of swapping bad for worse. One simply doesn't know.

5 June—Another one of our chaps makes his escape today. He also leaves a work party at the train station after they are all counted. I cannot say too much about this case for obvious reasons, but I know all the details. Tonight, at roll call, it is arranged for a chap out of another company to fall in with ours to cover for the escapee and this is done successfully, so we have given the chap a good start. We have heard nothing in regard to the two who escaped last week, and our thoughts remain with them.

6 June—We are all inoculated today for tuberculosis.

Our chap who escaped yesterday has been caught after only a few hours at liberty. This news plunges us into despondency; our hearts continue to ebb and flow like the ocean we crave to see again, one minute swelling with waves of hope, the next crashing with despair.

But on a more positive note; since receiving the instruments and sheet music from the Red Cross we now have social activities in the camp in the form of concerts, and they're very heartening. There are two concert parties run by proper committees with a producer, stage manager, prop men and electricians—just like a Blighty show. No one could believe what is done in regard to props and talent unless the concerts were to be seen. Each party (one belonging to our company) has an orchestra. Some of the lads dress up as 'girls' for chorus work and I have never seen better female impersonators anywhere.

All sorts of rorts are now underway. There's a chap in camp who runs a pawnbroker and auctioneer business and he seems to do very well for himself and, so far, he hasn't raised the suspicion of Jerry.

16 June—I'm in a work party near the Jerry huts today when I see it is deserted of fighting troops. I would love to know what's going on.

17 June—This morning I see that there are some new Jerries on guard duty drill (to relieve the former guards who have been sequestered to fight, I believe.) What a poor sample of humanity they are; many of them are almost cripples, and it's an indication of the Jerries' desperation if you ask me.

18 June—We have just heard that Turkey has made an agreement of nonaggression with Germany. One's head spins with the constant turnaround of allegiances.

22 June—Jerry guards boast today that Germany declared war on Russia a week ago. Of course, we now know that Russia was the one to break the alliance but, with its usual arrogance, Jerry is very confident of beating the Russians in only six weeks. I think this is the reason its troops are deserting this place, to head to Russia.

27 June—And it's on—Russia and Germany are now sworn enemies. Hitler has sent some three million Nazi soldiers pouring into the Soviet Union, but we have very little news of the fighting between them. All that is said by Jerry is that everything is going according to plan, but I've come to believe nothing of their propaganda.

It's becoming very noticeable now that the Jerries are getting very severe. For the least offence, such as a slight movement while on parade, the offender is put in the clink for five days. The Gestapo are coming down very hard on the Poles. Outside the camp, two Polish girls, while passing, respond to some of the boys by saying 'good day' in their own language and they're put in the clink by the Gestapo. Yesterday my mate Sergeant Davies told me, that while taking a working party to the train station he was saluted by a Pole, and the poor Pole was wrenched from his bike by a Gestapo, his bike pump smashed and the air let out of his tyres, before being beaten senseless. In defiance, another Pole also saluted Davies and he was also struck down, and the two were taken away by the same Gestapo. Savage bunch of bastards are the Gestapo.

We continue to hear nothing about the fate of the two men who escaped over three weeks ago, but rumours are rife that Jerry are now shooting escapees on sight rather than bringing them back to camp and having to feed them. Pray to God that is not the case.

28 June—Although the war between Germany and Russia has been on for a week now, nothing has been done for our protection, such as trenches dug, but it is noticed that everywhere Jerry has converted cellars into air raid shelters for themselves, and all of them are carrying gas masks. Later today Hitler issues a statement on the Jerry position with Russia. He announces they have destroyed 4000 planes, and 1330 tanks have advanced over 200 miles, and they have taken 80,000 prisoners. This news has put Jerry in high glee, and they are once again talking of the war with Russia being over in six weeks.

29 June—The Jerries are coming down harder and harder on the

Poles. Today, Sunday, according to the word of a Pole, all Polish men were examined coming out of church, and those found to be without an 'Arbeit' [forced to work] card were put into a cart and driven away. He tells me that many batches of children have been herded into Posen to be put to work in factories. Also, if a Polish woman is living by herself and not working, she is sent away to work, and a German woman is given her house.

The bread has been rationed from this week, so it is now impossible to get any from the Poles. Last week, an order was issued for all foreigners to hand in their overcoats. I, along with one or two others, refused and, so far, so good.

20 July—We have heard many reports from Jerry about them driving the Russians back. By their reports, they are about 125 miles from Moscow but, according to our 'bird', there have been many Germans killed. We also hear that the Russians have officially joined the Allies, and this is confirmed when we see definite signs of food blockades by the Russians. The Poles can hardly get a crumb to eat, and even Jerry can get very little, but at least we now have the Ruskies on our side.

5 August—Things are now getting desperate in regard to food. We have not had any potatoes for over a week, and the Poles are literally starving to death. They are mere skeletons. Bones walking. It is hard to witness.

13 August—We are staying inside today, having come in from work due to very heavy downpours of rain. We notice the Jerries are very quiet in regard to the situation between them and Russia, which immediately raises our suspicions that all is not going well for Jerry. Let's hope this is the case. One doesn't know quite what to believe, but there have been a few air-raid warnings around here these last few nights, so we assume we are correct and the Russians are gaining ground.

I have a long conversation with a Jerry guard tonight who, up until recently, had the job of getting work parties out and looking after the cleanliness of our huts, so he is often hanging around with the boys. He is well-liked and can speak English but, when it was discovered that he used to work in America, he was demoted to a guard. He tells me that Jerry 'Big Men' have also been looking into his family history and have discovered that his father was a 'Red'. The poor man is frustrated with his current status because the underprivileged people in his home town used to turn to him for advice, and he used to write letters for them, but all that has been stopped after him coming under Hitler's ever-increasingly paranoid radar. It appears that Hitler is now turning against even his own men.

The Jews here at Warthelager are treated abominably, even worse than the Poles, and they are a desperate lot indeed. A Pole told me, and other men on different work parties also heard the same, that on Sunday last two Jews who had tried to escape from Posen were hanged in public. They also tell us that the Jerries have organised special killing squads assigned to particular areas in Russia; their target—Jews. Once again, this is by order of Himmler. One simply can't imagine any such thing, although we know this persecution of the Jews is going on in the camps.

16 August—At about 4:00 am today we were woken by the noise of bombs being dropped in the distance, and at 5:00 am one bomb was dropped pretty near to us, but at the time of writing, this evening, we still know very little about the raids. It's terribly trying on the nerves.

30 August—I'm told today by two German guards that we are to be moved from here. One guard says this will happen in three weeks' time, while the other says it will be very soon. One wonders if even they know what's going on. When the second guard moves on I press the first one for further information on the upcoming move, and he confirms that all British prisoners are to leave Poland, but he doesn't know where we are to be sent. Then he suggests we may head to Russia because Jerry troops there have taken so many Russian prisoners that they don't know what to do with them all. They have nowhere to put them, and they have very few supplies and little food to feed them. He says there is talk that we Brits are to move up to Russia to build more barracks to house ourselves, while the Russian prisoners will come to camps here in Poland. This is to make escape harder than if interned in their own country. If that's the case and we swap places with the

Russian prisoners, I wonder where they think they are going to get food for us? It's not a thought I fancy sharing with the lads so I decide not to until I can get some more information on the subject.

31 August—Today I'm out on the job in a working party, making a new range cooker, when I'm stopped and told that all machinery now has to be cleaned in readiness for our departure. Sure enough, later in the day our large concrete mixer is ordered to be stopped, cleaned, oiled all over, and made ready for transportation, but we are still not told where we're to go or when we're to depart. Rumours are flying around all over the place, most of them based on the theory that Jerry is under threat from Russian advancement. We also hear that our troops have walked into Iran, but on questioning a guard about it he laughs at me and walks away.

We begin to notice that the Jerries are getting very indignant, and then things start getting much worse in regard to their food and cig supplies. Indeed, just about everything is on severe rationing. The poor Poles can hardly get anything, and without doubt the best-fed chap is the likes of us, the British prisoner with his Red Cross parcel, which we are receiving every week now, along with cigs. In fact, the Jerry guards are now asking our boys for cigs; we try to hide our supplies, but they still manage to find some. The Poles are allowed only five cigs per week, but I'm pleased to report that we are able to pay back a little to the Poles who were so good to us previously.

Our mail is now becoming very unreliable under what Jerry calls a new system for our company; the censor only delivers mail to a certain number of lads, the next week some more lads, and so on. It means that one is without mail for two or three weeks and then gets a large number of letters. Unfortunately, I am an exception and am getting no mail whatsoever, and neither is my mate Davies, because we have been telling a few home truths about the conditions here in our letters home and the censor doesn't like it. He tells me that I am now not even allowed to write to Mabel.

CHAPTER 8

DEFIANCE WITHIN THE CAMP

1941

Stalag XXI-B, Warthelager, Poland

2 September—We have another air raid tonight, but once again we cannot get to know the extent of damage done.

The Poles continue to be persecuted. On our job last week, a small engine broke down, and it was suspected that the Poles had been doing a bit of sabotage by putting sand in the engine. The Gestapo were on the job every day but couldn't find anything out. On Sunday, the Poles had to work for no pay at all and, on Friday, they were told they would now have 10 marks deducted from their usual pay. The average wage for their working week is now only 24 marks.

The weather is now very wet indeed.

15 September—We still haven't heard anything further about being moved from here, and machinery still sits clean and packed up. Today I am put in charge of a working party on a new firing range. It's raining slightly when we leave camp, but it gets worse. I instruct the men, 60 of them, after getting wet through, to come into a shelter. The guards try to get them out to work again but are unsuccessful. The Jerry boss of the job arrives, but we men decide to stick together and head back to camp. The boss decides to let us go but, just as we are marching away, a Jerry corporal fronts up and tells us to stop and stand where we are until he brings his commandant to 'sort us all out'. He walks away, and I tell the men to take shelter again and wait.

The corporal returns, not at all happy to find my men under cover, and he tells us that the commandant is on his way, and the men are ordered to form up again, shivering with cold. I appeal to the corporal, explaining that the men are wet through and that they have to use their coats for covering at night on account of only having one blanket and also because there are no fires now. But he just scoffs at me, and we wait in the teeming rain until a motor car arrives on the scene and the commandant alights.

I have not mentioned this man before nor will I name him now, for obvious reasons, but we have had many a bad experience with him in the past, and what follows will be enough to show what type of person he is.

The commandant starts shouting, and we're marched to another part of the rifle range whereby he picks the youngest and smallest person out (Sergeant M Fraser) to go before a jury for inciting mutiny. Fraser's entire body slumps in fear and all our chaps' eyes are filled with pity when he's wrenched out of rank. Then the commandant places two armed guards at each end and front and back of us and says we will have to stand there until we go back to work. He shouts in his gravelly voice, advising that if anyone moves he will be treated as trying to escape and will be shot on the spot. I speak up and say that Fraser did not incite mutiny, and the commandant steps in front of me, his icy-cold eyes narrowing, and it's all I can do to keep myself standing upright. He smiles sadistically and tells Fraser to step back into rank before turning back to me, making his intention perfectly clear. Perhaps it is me who will have to face a Jerry jury, and we all know what that outcome would be. Guilty as charged. The commandant spits in my face and I remain there, his dirty spittle dripping off my face, my eyes averted from his. He finally walks away, and I release a small sigh of relief, though my military-trained body remains as erect as a steel pole. The commandant continues strutting up and down the line, shouting words of abuse and striking men in the face as he makes his demands for those who want to work to step out of line. One or two men finally step out, and I'm sorry to say that the rest of us gradually break away also. What other choice do we have? Our lives are worth nothing to these bastards.

16 September—My pal, Sergeant Davies, has been made 'the confidence man' for our company, meaning he will represent prisoners to Nazi German authorities. When he reports in sick today, I'm ordered to go out in his place supervising a new bridge construction job.

This night the sergeants of all companies are called into the office and told that the Jerry commandant has decided that any sergeant, whether sick or not, will have to work just the same as their men.

19 September—While I'm out with my party of men today, the commandant tells the rest of the sergeants that they will not be paid for going out on supervisory work. He is determined to get his pound of flesh for what he sees as our insubordination the other day at the rifle range. This means that we will have to take charge of jobs and men but will get no pay, yet sergeants looking after the cleaning of billets in camp will get payment.

20 September—We, the sergeants of our respective companies, hold a meeting this evening and decide that in the Geneva Convention there is nothing to state that supervisory work is not to be paid. A letter is drawn up stating what our views are and is signed by all sergeants present and handed by Davies to the Jerry sergeant major to be sent to the American Embassy for ruling. Of course, we suspect the sergeant major will take it straight to his commandant.

21 September—As expected, the commandant arrives at our barracks tonight and calls for all sergeants to turn up. When we do so, he asks for one of us to explain to him where in our pay books it mentions about being protected under the Geneva Convention. I, being medical sergeant of our battalion, step forward and give my name. The commandant stares coldly at me for the longest time, and I fight to keep upright as my stomach is churning. He knows damn well who I am. He holds his face close to mine and shouts something in German before stepping away. I've no doubt as to his meaning. Then he orders another sergeant to step forward, and he tells us both to hand in our pay books to the sergeant major, and he leaves, none too happy. The Jerry sergeant major waits until we hand him our pay books and tells us that they will be handed to the commandant and then sent to Posen. We wonder if this is the last we'll see of our pay books.

22 September—I ought to have been in charge of a working party today, but I refuse to do so and I stay in. I know I'm risking things, but someone has to stand up to these bastards. We have another meeting later on this day, and the other sergeants decide to go out on supervisory work without pay until the answer comes back from the American Embassy. I am very much against this, and so I report in sick the next morning and take my chances with the commandant, who previously ordered sick men to work. However, I find that my medical officer, Lieutenant Colonel Hankey, agrees that I am not to go out and instead he gives me a job in camp for the day and so, for today, I'm safe.

29 September—More and more sergeants are now refusing to go out to work without pay, of which I am still one. It's the eve of my birthday, and tonight my mate Sergeant Davies and I manage to get 50 bottles of beer costing 22 marks. Never mind how. I get the band going in our barracks, and we have ourselves one right royal night with no interruptions whatsoever from Jerry, which is indeed surprising.

1 October—All of us sergeants are called together this morning and asked by the German sergeant major which of us are willing to go out to work. Only five out of 30 are now willing to do so. He rants and raves and threatens, but no one moves and he storms out and doesn't return all day. Of course, I, along with the other rebels, am waiting for the commandant to dole out punishment.

3 October—I'm surprised but delighted when I receive 11 letters and two cigarette parcels today as I haven't had anything in so long due to my mail being stopped because of the censor not liking what I wrote. I certainly don't question it. One letter is from Mabel's cousin, R Cranston from Kendal, with an enquiry about a man named Pearson, who was wounded and is said to have been in one of the two lorries of wounded men I was in charge of when captured while making for Dunkirk at the end of May 1940. Pearson's people have had no word of him since June 1940, when it was reported that he was severely wounded in his arms and legs. I cannot help them much because the last I saw of my wounded was when they were put into

German ambulances, supposedly to head to hospital. I can remember my capture like it was yesterday; I can remember the hellish night I spent assisting the wounded—the memory will never leave me. But I regret to say that my memory regarding names and faces is rather bad these days, and also many of my fellow prisoners' minds are almost a blank regarding specific details of their capture and the march afterwards, so I can't get any information out of them. Mind you, it's no bloody wonder we would want to forget the horror of our capture and ensuing journey to Poland. I also receive an enquiry from the Red Cross with regard to the same person. I write back to both correspondents and tell them the little I do know and pray that my letters will get past the censor.

We are moved into huts that are a slight improvement on our old ones.

6 October—Today, Monday, we have a visit from an American Red Cross representative, but he doesn't see much of the bad conditions as we have just been moved into better billets, probably because Jerry knew this visit was coming following our letter and pay books being sent to the American Embassy, which this visit would indicate have been received.

Early November—Our medical officer, Lieutenant Colonel Hankey, and I go to Posen with two Jerry guards to purchase some new musical instruments. I have no idea how the colonel managed it, but it's a great experience after being caged up for so long, although we are a centre of interest, looked upon with scorn by the German populace, but with sympathy by the Poles. It's a grand city, and to our eyes it is very busy indeed.

Working parties of men from other companies leave here heading to various places which they are told are small working camps.

We still have had no word of when we will be on the move.

11 November—With the instruments we secured in Posen, and others we scrounged from around camp, I have started a light orchestra, drawing players from all the companies in the camp. At present, we have the following instruments: a piano, two violins, two clarinets, one alto sax, two tenor saxophones, three trumpets, two trombones, three accordions, one bass and drums. We hold our first concert for tonight, with many Jerries in attendance, and I'm happy to report that it's a huge success. Some of the pieces we play are the 'Old Comrades' march, 'Rose Marie' selection and 'Waltz' and I have a grand time conducting.

I am still stopping in and not going to work, but I'm now the only sergeant doing so. I'm determined to stick it out until my interpretation of the Geneva Convention comes through. I'm hoping I will hear something soon as things are getting pretty rough on me, although I've still not been sent to the clink. If one can't fight these bastards on the battlefields, one can do so on principle.

The weather is getting very cold again, and we have had a great deal of snow already.

Things seem very quiet around camp, and it looks, to our eyes, that the war can go on for years yet. The Germans are very confident they will soon be victorious, but they always are.

18 November—Today we learn that our aircraft carrier HMS *Ark Royal* has been sunk and a battleship badly damaged. This news is terribly disheartening for us, which only spurs the Jerries on to high glee and they increase their cruel taunts.

19 November—The censor comes into our barracks today to once again harp on about what we are not allowed to say in our letters home. I ask him when we are to expect the return of our pay books, which another sergeant and myself handed in to the commandant to send off to the American Embassy weeks ago. The censor laughs and tells us that all other sergeants, with the exception of the two of us who handed in our pay books, are going to be recognised under the terms of the Geneva Convention. I challenge him and ask why that would be the case, and he blurts out that I am to be investigated for not providing information to the families of men who were wounded when we were captured. He says it is well known that I was the driver of the ambulance heading to Dunkirk when captured. Of course I was not the bloody ambulance driver. I'm well aware that the censor read my letters responding to Mabel's cousin and the Red Cross in regard to Pearson, which placed the blame on the Germans, and he obviously went straight to the commandant, who seized his opportunity to get a trumped-up charge made against me in retaliation for me stirring up trouble and forcing his hand under the Geneva Convention. I'm furious, and I let the censor know in very few words what I was and what I wasn't. I also ask him why the other sergeant who also handed in his pay book should be punished. I ask what bloody false charge they have concocted for him, but the censor is not in the least bit interested. He shakes his head, says something about my mail being stopped again and walks away.

20 November—An order comes in from high command for our wages to be lowered from the equivalent of 70 pfennigs a day to 50. The lads are very sore about this, but it does not affect me as I still refuse to go out. Surprisingly, the next morning, I get an offer of a job on the administrative staff of the camp to be in charge of cleanliness in return for pay. This, I accept.

22 November—Our sister company, BAB 2 [Bau and Arbeits Battalion. *Bau* is the German word for construction, and *arbeit* for job, meaning a prisoner-of-war construction and labour battalion], leaves here today for another camp about 60 miles away. While they were here, many of the lads who had been on cemetery work told me of the sad state of Russian prisoners whom they were forced at gunpoint by Jerry to bury at Posen. Most of the poor men had died from starvation, but some were not quite dead when they were buried. Our chaps were understandably traumatised by the memory of conducting such a shocking task under threat of being shot themselves. They told of their horror on witnessing the still-alive Russian prisoners' eyes, of their pleas for mercy as they covered them in dirt and left them to suffocate to death. One wonders how we are ever again supposed to sleep at night after all we have seen in this damned war.

I hear today that a Polish church near here has been destroyed by the Germans for no apparent reason.

I receive no letters, but surprisingly I do get a parcel from home. As usual, not long after, the guards arrive to confiscate things and they take my boot polish, saying prisoners of war are no longer allowed this. I laugh at them and ask what the hell they think we'll do with the stuff? Eat it? Make ammunition? However, the guards have little sense of humour and I soon shut my trap before they take me away for being insubordinate.

I have heard nothing further regarding the false charges against me, so I can only assume they can't make them stick.

7 December—We hold our second orchestral concert tonight, which is a bigger success than the last one in November. Some of the pieces we play are: 'Light Cavalry', 'Florentiner March', 'Ave Maria' and 'Wine, Women and Song'. The Jerries, seated in the front rows, beam with delight at being entertained, but it's the faces of our boys that we concentrate on and we bow to *them* on *their* applause.

11 December—We learn that Japan bombed the American naval base at Pearl Harbor in Hawaii and, as a result, the Yanks have announced war on the Nips. It gives us all hope. But later today, when we get the news, to the Germans' delight, that both of our ships HMS *Repulse* and HMS *Prince of Wales* were sunk yesterday, we are devastated, and whatever joy I have managed to lift through my music sinks faster than did the bodies of our sailors now entombed on the ocean bed. I think to myself that the ocean floor must be littered with twisted metal and human remains.

13 December—The Yanks have now officially declared war on Germany and Italy after the Krauts and Eyeties had declared war on America. This is great news—the Yanks joining us in our fight against the enemy.

14 December—It is Sunday today and two parties of men from our company, numbering about 60, are ordered out to work. They refuse, because they worked the previous Sunday and were told they would get a day off in lieu, which they didn't. They argue that, according to the Geneva Convention, they are entitled to this. The Jerries are incensed at their refusal to work and they mock the lads, singing out the words 'Geneva Convention' in childish voices, like schoolyard bully boys. Then, everyone in our company is ordered out on parade, and two companies of Jerry guards turn out in a show of force. The aforementioned-despised commandant arrives in his chauffeur-driven car and a repetition of the rifle range job occurs. He orders machine guns to be brought out. His henchmen line up and take aim at us and we are horrified.

Men from other companies are looking on in shock from various places, and the commandant shouts out directives for them to either return inside their huts or be shot. The commandant's heavily armed men run towards many chaps who are still looking on, some of whom are out at the cookhouse getting water and, along with the rest of the men, they rush back inside their barracks, aided by rifle butts and stern verbal abuse.

The commandant asks us who wants to be the first to be shot by machine gun and, when he obviously gets no response, he orders those who are prepared to go to work to take a step forward, but no one does, I'm proud to report. Then, in typical fashion, the commandant picks out six of the smallest chaps and tells each man that he will be taken away to prison where life will be 'very hard'. They are marched away, but this still does not move our boys. Finally, the commandant tells us he promises on his honour that we will get a day off in lieu in the near future; he will release the six men from threat of prison; and will guarantee that the company will not suffer in any way for their initial refusal to go to work. In order to protect our men from having to endure prison, and intimidated by the machine guns surrounding us, we sergeants say our men will go to work. I have no choice but to join them.

After about an hour on the job the Jerry interpreter Kauffman arrives and gives orders that our company's entertainment is to cease. There are to be no rehearsals for any Christmas concerts. I have a rehearsal of the camp orchestra scheduled in the afternoon, and I damn well intend to carry on. I discuss this with all of my players, and most of them agree to also defy orders, so we do so and have ourselves a merry old time. But when I'm coming out of the hall, Kauffman races over to me and throws a fit, after which he storms off to see the commandant, and I have to wonder what my punishment will be. Whatever it is, I am prepared for it, so sick of this torturous treatment am I.

18 December—One of our sergeants refuses to go out to the job this morning and he gets sentenced to 21 days in the clink. I have not been punished for my recent defiance in holding rehearsals and I believe this is due to the fact that, as much as the commandant hates me, he loves music, and that's why he is holding back, although rehearsals have been halted. However, to err on the side of caution we players agree that we had better not attend rehearsals for a while.

Christmas Eve—We were to have had an extension of lights until midnight, but at 9:30 pm the lights go out, although small celebrations continue under improvised lighting.

30 December—We have got Christmas over with, and it was far quieter than we had all hoped. On Christmas morning a short church service was held for which I was allowed to play the piano. In the evening, we were permitted to sing carols at another church service, that being the extent of the Christmas celebrations.

Naturally, given our music ban, there was not one concert. Christmas is normally one of the rare times our boys are allowed to be entertained exclusively, with only a handful of Jerry guards in attendance. This is because Jerry doesn't celebrate Christmas in the same way we do. On questioning a guard about this, he tells me that as much as the Germans *do* enjoy Christmas—it has always been celebrated throughout Germany, and a large percentage of the population are Christians—Hitler has ordered a ban on it.

'How can the Fuhrer possibly encourage celebrations for the birth of a Jew?' the guard asks me and goes on to explain that Hitler has now renamed Christmas 'Rough Night', or something just as bleedin' daft. Made it all about Nazism. He even changed some lyrics in carols in order to remove all reference to Christ and replaced the word Saviour with Fuhrer!

I have to say that as much as the guard tried to justify his leader's actions, he seemed none too happy about it.

CHAPTER 9

STOMACH AND HEART ACHES

1942

Stalag XXI-B, Warthelager, Poland

It is now 1 January. Although it's a new year, there's been no change to our miserable situation. The weather is bitingly cold, and snow is very thick on the ground. The temperatures are so far below zero that even the mercury in the thermometer cannot tell us how cold it is. I have heard recently that the Gestapo are so freezing they are searching the Polish homes for woollens and thick clothing which they take for themselves.

We have had news (from where I can't disclose) that our troops are doing well in Africa, but out in the Pacific things are not going so well and the Japs seem to be making ground.

My stomach has been bad for quite a while now, and this afternoon I was told that I'm to go into the camp hospital tomorrow morning. The old ulcers are playing up and the pathetic amount of food we are getting is not helping, but I must not complain. Compared to the wretched Poles, who are so hungry they're barely able to move let alone toil in these freezing conditions, I'm doing okay.

22 January—I have been in hospital for three weeks now, but I cannot say I have improved much, although it is rather cushy and comfortable here, certainly compared to camp conditions. The hospital is heated which brings some comfort, as the weather outside is still awfully cold.

There is a strong rumour that our company is leaving here very shortly for a place called Katowice, 250 miles south of here, near the Czechoslovakian border. I wonder if I will go with my company when that happens, or remain here in hospital? I would much prefer to be with my mates.

News trickles into the hospital, and I'm told that one of the boys at Posen was shot for threatening a guard.

23 January—We get the English news on a wireless set (again, from where we get it I cannot say) but it's pretty bad. The Japs have invaded Borneo and the Philippines and are advancing towards New Guinea and Burma. Our troops in Africa, after driving the Italians and Jerry almost to Tripoli, have started retiring again, and the enemy has taken an important town back once more. The only part of the news that is any good at all is regarding the Russians, who are in advance.

25 January—*The Camp* paper today claims that the Japs are now in full control of the Pacific. Although we know this is an exaggeration, I cannot describe the effect this kind of news has on us prisoners of war. One can hear small groups discussing the situation from all angles and imaginary views. Many men get depressed. It's only natural, but one must strive to remain positive.

Last week a few Polish Jews were hanged in one of the forts at Posen. The Jews are still being persecuted very harshly, and there are some shocking rumours flying around regarding the poor beggars.

27 January—The latest news today, in regard to our company moving, is that we are now going to be sent into Germany to a place called Heidelberg, about 600 miles south-west of here. God only knows why.

Once again, we manage to listen to some British news, and our troops are still retiring everywhere. We later hear an unconfirmed report that the Australian prime minister has appealed to the British to 'do something' about the Japanese advancement. What does he expect of us? Our boys must be exhausted. They're fighting in Europe, the Mediterranean, the Middle East, Africa and Pacific-Asia.

13 February—I'm still in hospital. I should have been going to Posen for an X-ray, but I have been told that the ambulance cannot go due to having no petrol.

The Japs have forced a landing at Singapore. Nothing seems to be boding well for us.

The weather is extremely cold and snow is blanketing the grounds outside the hospital. Some of our heaters are now broken, the remainder being next to useless. The boys here don't mind that too much though, because the longer the bad weather lasts, the worse it is for Jerry in Russia, and we desperately need the Ruskies to overcome Jerry. Freezing ourselves is about the only sacrifice we can make for the war effort.

We have had only one Red Cross parcel each since Christmas. This is explained by Jerry as being due to poor transportation, but they are probably keeping the parcels for themselves.

I have not been completely idle during my stay in hospital, and I'm delighted to report that today I have just finished putting together an arrangement to a song which was written by Corporal McBride. It's called 'Absence Makes the Heart Grow Fonder', and McBride should be very proud when he hears my rendition. Truer words as his lyrics have never been written. I pray that it will pluck at the lads' heartstrings when I play it for them on my return to barracks and give them hope that their women back in Blighty are waiting with open arms for them to return home. Some of the lads are getting rather despondent about that, their women remaining faithful I mean. Having heard no word from their women back home in quite a while, it is starting to mess with their minds.

Fort Rauch, Posen, Poland

20 February—This morning two of us patients get a speedy dispatch in an ambulance to the main hospital at Fort Rauch, Posen. The nineteenth-century fortress that greets us on our arrival is a formidable sight.

I have to hand a letter from Colonel Hankey to Captain Lansdell saying he thinks I have a duodenal ulcer and to put me under treatment following an X-ray, and also to try and get me sent back to my company after treatment on account of my music. Colonel Hankey finishes the letter with complimentary remarks on my musical capabilities, which makes me feel exceedingly honoured. But Captain Lansdell tells me that once a chap gets sent to this place it is a hard job to get him back to his company. This concerns me and I'm not happy about it. Not at all. After being with my mates for so long back at Warthelager, I would not like to leave them for an indefinite period of time. I also want to get back to my music, so I remain hopeful that I am an exception to the rule.

21 February—I am on nothing but sweetened water with tablets, but I am feeling okay. The news coming through is only sporadic, but we do know that in South-East Asia things seem to be getting desperate for our chaps. The Japs are all over the place and seem to be meeting with little resistance. We hear that after they invaded Singapore earlier this month there were many deaths and hundreds of our troops were taken prisoner, the remainder of our forces withdrawing so that now the Japs are in full control. They have even bombed Australia.

As for Jerry, we hear that they decided last month that they need to completely eradicate the Jews. I cannot conceive of how they can have such hatred for the Jews, nor how they ever imagine they can simply erase an entire race of people. I say this to the patient in the bed next to me, who tells me that he saw three Jews hanged here last summer with all the other Jews made to watch. The three were hanged in the morning and were left hanging until 10 o'clock at night, and only then were their horrified spectators allowed to leave. Rumours are still rife regarding the treatment of the Jews, some of them truly disturbing, and I also hear more and more horrors regarding shocking experiments being done on the poor beggars in the name of science.

26 February—I've been here in Fort Rauch Hospital a week and my 'diet' today is changed from sweetened water to milk and custard, thank God. My stomach seems to take to it okay. I'm rather cosy, actually. This hospital is well supplied, and we're all being tended to. The only snag is the strict no-smoking rule; however, this only makes life more interesting, and gives us a challenge to overcome boredom when the lads and I manage to get around this rule by sneaking a few puffs whenever we can.

Our latest discussion is regarding Churchill's most recent speech, which we all agree was very tame indeed. If only our prime minister could experience the conditions here in these prison camps, not to mention some of the terrible things we hear about our boys in South-East Asia at the hands of the Japs. Of course, Churchill would know what is going on, and his stance makes us all exceedingly angry. We need such a figurehead as he to stand up and serve it to the enemy, for this is certainly not the time to be timid about anything.

13 March—I am allowed out of 'bed' today. I have been put on ordinary rations but unfortunately the hospital is now on half rations so my intake is rather meagre. Just my luck.

The news from the Far East is now drastic. The Japs seem to be doing whatever they like. But, on the home front, it is heartening to hear that Jerry is not so successful. Pray to God the Allied forces can overcome them soon.

I receive a note from one of the lads from my old camp at Warthelager saying that two of our boys called Teasdale and Bowden were bayoneted for being insubordinate. Teasdale is in hospital and Bowden is up for court martial for taking a rifle off a guard. Things are getting grim indeed.

Stalag XXI-B, Warthelager, Poland

31 March—I am moved back to my old camp, Warthelager, today after the hospital at Fort Rauch receives a phone call asking if I am fit enough to travel back due to my company being on the move shortly. Thinking it is the camp's colonel calling, the hospital answers 'yes' but when I arrive back at Warthelager the colonel is furious and says he did not make any call to the hospital and neither is my company moving just yet.

4 April—I am now writing on Easter Saturday. I am not feeling at all well, my stomach being practically as bad as ever. Still, it's good to see my pals again and when they give me all the latest crack and report that our air force attacked Lubeck in northern Germany, one of Jerry's major ports, and destroyed over a third of the city, I'm buoyed by the news. We have a laugh at the fact that Hitler is outraged at this latest hit. The little man is getting a bit of his own medicine, at long last.

BAB 21, Blechhammer, Upper Silesia

5 April—Even though I'm still not feeling well, I feel lucky to have been brought back to Camp Warthelager after all, as we start our move via train today, this being Easter Sunday, and I am pleased to be doing so alongside my mates. Somehow, I manage to perk up and, after a very fast journey, we arrive at a train station called Ehrenforst in Upper Silesia. We then march for about two miles to a labour camp in an area called Blechhammer, which is a sub-camp of a place called Auschwitz. This is a very large camp, and there seems to be many other camps in the vicinity. We pass a civilian concentration camp, and all the prisoners are terribly emaciated and have their heads shaved. It is a pitiful sight indeed.

The weather is pretty good, and we are accommodated in barracks, but there's no running water or proper sanitary facilities. We find we're caged in, completely segregated, and we miss having the Poles for friends. We soon discover that the Jerry guards here are real brutes and very on edge. We are formed into a battalion named BAB 21.

Mid April—We read in the latest edition of *The Camp* that two Polish railwaymen were executed for taking sugar from Posen to Warsaw and selling it at a higher price. Also, two nurses were executed for stealing patients' rations. Despite people starving, it appears Jerry don't give a damn. They are only on the hunt for blood for the slightest misdemeanour, and we have quickly learnt that one has to tread very warily indeed here at Blechhammer.

27 April—My stomach has come good again, and I have been put in charge of the hospital, under the supervision of Captain Davidson, Royal Army Medical Corps, of Aberdeen. We have been kept very busy for the last couple of weeks. The hours of working at this camp are very long—at least 14 hours a day—and the work gruelling, and it's telling on many of the boys' health. Conditions are appalling and the Red Cross parcel issue seems almost extinct. The food is getting less and less.

The Jews here are in a terrible condition but, despite that, they are made to carry huge sacks of produce out of barges and then, after depositing it, they have to run back down into the barge again with the aid of a whip. It is gut-wrenching to witness, and sometimes I just sit on my bunk in silence and reflect on mankind's cruelty to their fellow men.

The only good news to come in is that our chaps are still doing some heavy bombing of Germany.

9 May—Our padre, who has been visiting other camps today, brings us the news back from BAB 20 that a lad has been shot on the spot for smoking. The padre says this was the second case recently. A commission that was visiting came on the scene about half an hour after the incident, but he doubts anything will come from it. We have all learnt not to expect much as a result of such visits.

12 May—Five of our sergeants and two corporals leave our company today, to go where we do not know.

Red Cross parcels are now starting to arrive.

It's now the end of May 1942. I have been two years in capture. It's hard to comprehend and simply too depressing to dwell upon. I wish I had some musical instruments to take my mind off things. Of course, we were not permitted to bring them with us from Warthelager and we are told that we must first 'earn' the right in order to be permitted to play music here—whatever that means.

The news from South-East Asia is not good at all, and we hear that the Japs are now in full control of Burma, which our military leaders are calling a catastrophe. And then we hear that Rommel is attacking at the Gazala Line.

5 June—I'm delighted that we were issued with some musical instruments this morning after Jerry learnt of my musical abilities from Captain Davidson. I thank my captain profusely and get down to organising a band straight away.

I have discovered that two lads from my battalion are at the next camp to ours. They come from Frizington in Cumbria. One is named Ashbridge, and the other Clements, and they tell me they have been two years in this camp. I now often have a crack with them through the wires, and I even had young Ashbridge across at our camp last Sunday on a scheduled visit, which was permitted because I lied and said that I was his uncle. No one questioned this and his visit was very welcome indeed. After Ashbridge left here, I was filled with melancholy for home, particularly for the wife, so I wrote her this poem:

DAYBREAK
IT'S DAYBREAK, WHAT DIFFERENCE WILL TODAY MAKE
I ACHE EACH MORNING, EACH DAWNING, FOR YOU
EACH DAY WITHOUT YOU IS A BLUE DAY
ALONE I'M SCHEMING AND DREAMING OF YOU
DARLING, MY LONELY HEART IS LONGING TO HEAR
YOU SINGING LOVE'S OLD REFRAIN
IT'S DAYBREAK, WHAT DIFFERENCE WILL TODAY MAKE
TILL FATE WILL GIVE US EACH OTHER AGAIN

Drum Major HB Jackson
POW BAB 21
Blechhammer
Upper Silesia
Sunday, 31 May 1942

CHAPTER 10

INHUMANITY AND TRAGEDY

1942

BAB 21, Blechhammer, Upper Silesia

8 June—I'm inoculated for typhoid fever today, the water here being disease-ridden and the worst I have ever experienced, even when I was in the last war.

There are all nationalities working at Blechhammer, including many Italians who volunteered and are now trying to escape back to Italy.

The news that dribbles in regarding our progress in the war in Europe is quite good, and it appears that our air force is working hard and bombing many industrial sites in Germany.

10 June—A young girl is found murdered in woods near here today after she had been violently raped. This is the third such victim in five weeks—such terrible and cruel acts. One cannot but think of one's own girls back home and imagine the rage and grief within if it were to be one of them that was so brutally violated. Thank God my four daughters are all safe in the north of Britain.

Mail starts to arrive and I receive letters from the wife and all our girls. The wife's letters are very optimistic on the whole, and Mabel seems to be doing okay and going strong at her work selling insurance. She tells me that she's piling the notes away for when the war is over, which she thinks will be very soon. I'm very proud of her. What a good one I have in my Mabel. Practically all the letters the boys are receiving are about the war being over shortly. Let's hope that this time it is correct as this life just about gets one down, what with all the cruelty from the Jerries, who continue to be a savage pack of beasts here.

Thirty-six Poles were hanged here last week and hearing such things can drive one to despair. Sitting around listening to such horrors puts years on one. It can only be experienced to be imagined. The nearest to a description I can think of is locking up many sparrows in a very small cage. We are all simply animals to Jerry, a source of amusement, objects to wield power over. I remember, after the last war, hearing of German agents conducting experiments by infecting sheep bound for Russia with anthrax and inoculating mules and horses of the French cavalry with equine disease. This is what we are to Jerry—a bunch of experimental animals. Roll on Duration [war end], I say.

23 June—We hear today that Tobruk in Africa has fallen once more to the Germans. This news is drastic. The Jerries are in high glee and are once again talking about victory being theirs in a very short time. We are devastated to learn that in the battle the enemy captured 28,000 men, amongst whom were eight generals. A few days before this news, in a reprint of the English papers, we read that the Jerry general, Rommel, was trapped by our General Ritchie at Tobruk. Jerry denied it and had a good laugh at us, saying that Rommel, who they name the Desert Fox, has always outsmarted Ritchie and did so again.

End June—As it turns out, the Jerries were correct about Rommel. To say that this latest news is very discouraging to us is to put it lightly.

4 July—We are permitted to hold our first concert in our new camp tonight but, after what we deem a very successful first night, a few of the Jerries who attend find fault with some of the remarks our boys make on stage and demand that these scenes be cut out in the next concert due to be held tomorrow night. We refuse to do so, because it is so childish of Jerry, and we protest that they misconstrued our actors' remarks, but our arguments fall on deaf ears.

5 July—Tonight's concert is cancelled.

7 July—I go with Captain Davidson, Sergeant Davies and two Jerry guards to Gliwice, about 30 miles away, to purchase more instruments. The captain says we can start rehearsals again but he won't tell us how he wrangled this. No matter, Davies and I are simply amazed at this turn of events! Captain Davidson has 4000 marks to spend and we have a rare old time in a big music store. We get a piano, one alto sax, one tenor sax, one bass, two trumpets, and many other instruments. I take along some chocolate we scraped together from Red Cross parcels, which I give to the two assistants in the music store, and after they taste it, they are very accommodating.

Mid July—Concert rehearsals are underway again.

End July—We are now getting very little news, but it seems that Jerry has been stopped advancing in Egypt. Also, we hear that the Yanks have started air missions over Germany. All this news is heartening.

9 August—We have received no mail for a fortnight now as it's all being held in the German office due to the fact that an order came through from Jerry's head office last week saying that we could only receive the same amount of mail that German prisoners of war receive. They say that they have complained about the manner in which the English distribute mail to German prisoners of war—very few letters are getting through to their men—but nothing has been done about it. So, each month we can now only receive, and are only allowed to send home, the same amount of mail as the German prisoners of war until something is done by the British to rectify the situation.

10 August—We are all devastated when this morning a boy named Preston of the Gloucester Regiment is found hanged. He took his own life, and he was only 22 years of age. It hits us all very hard; young Preston was well liked and no one saw it coming at all, the poor young lad. I will now post a poem written in honour of him:

In Memoriam
Private Preston—Gloucester Field Post 19401 A
An obituary for a comrade who died by his own hand in
Blechhammer Prisoner- of-War Labour Camp
10/8/1942
THRO' TWO AND TWENTY YEARS OF LIFE
HE CAME! WE KNOW NOT HOW
THIS LAD, SO BRAVE THROUGHOUT THE STRIFE,
SHOULD LEAVE THE STRUGGLE NOW.
WE DARE NOT JUDGE! WE CANNOT TELL
WHAT ANGUISH FILLED HIS HEART

BUT THIS WE KNOW, WHO KNEW HIM WELL
HE'D ALWAYS PLAYED HIS PART!

WHILE FACING HOSTILE HORDES IN FRANCE
HE WAS UPSTANDING—BRAVE;
PREPARED FOR EVERY WHIM, OR CHANCE,
THE BLOODY CONFLICT GAVE;
WHEN WOUNDED, CAPTURED, SUFF'RING SORE,
RIGHT GALLANTLY HE MARCHED
FOR SEVEN WEARY MILES AND MORE,
THO' HUNGRY, ACHING, PARCHED!

WHAT IF THE PAIN WHICH SEARED EACH LEG
DID MAKE HIM BITE HIS LIP?
NO PLEA FOR MERCY WOULD HE BEG—
HE GRINNED AND KEPT HIS GRIP!
ALL THRO' THESE DREARY CAPTIVE YEARS
HIS COURAGE NEVER FAILED;
AND YET WE WONDER BY WHAT FEARS
THIS BRAVE HEART WAS ASSAILED.

AS FAR AS WE CAN TELL, OR KNOW,
NO DARK CLOUDS MARRED HIS SKY—
THERE WAS NO ONE SMALL THING TO SHOW
WHY HE SHOULD CHOOSE TO DIE.
HE SEEMED TO HAVE ALL HE COULD NEED
TO BRING HIM FUTURE JOY;
A MOTHER'S LOVE, A HOME INDEED
TO COMFORT ANY BOY.

HE EVEN HAD A WIFE TO TAKE
(HE'D EVEN BOUGHT THE RING!);
AND EVERYTHING CONSPIRED TO MAKE
HIM HAPPY AS A KING.
PERHAPS IT WAS THE WEARY WAIT

THAT HE COULD NOT CONTEND;
BUT, OH! WHAT IRONY OF FATE
GAVE HIM THIS AWFUL END?

WE LAID HIM IN A SOLDIER'S GRAVE,
PERFORMED THE SOLEMN RITE,
FOR WE REMEMBER HE WAS BRAVE
WHEN CALLED UPON TO FIGHT;
THIS TRAGEDY, SO DEEP,
WE HOPE THAT IN A BETTER LAND
HE'S FINDING REST, IN SLEEP!

AND WHAT OF THOSE HE LEFT BEHIND
TO MOURN? GREAT GOD, LOOK DOWN!
OH! THOU, WHO DOS'T DELIGHT TO BIND
THE BROKEN HEART AND CROWN
WITH COMFORT TO ALL WHO MOURN AND GRIEVE,
MAY THESE SAD SOULS NOW SEE
THEY'LL FIND, IF THEY WILL BUT BELIEVE,
SOLICITUDE IN THEE!

Private J Bush, Royal Army Service Corps

13 August—We bury Preston today. The Jerries allow only a party of 30 men to attend as mourners, but they will not allow us to give Preston a military funeral due to him taking his own life. We are incensed at this and, in defiance, we make a Union Jack for the lad's coffin. Also, we're told that there is to be no bugle played, but I am asked by the boys to take mine and again, in defiance of Jerry, I damn well do so and play 'The Last Post and Reveille'. I decide that whatever the consequences, I will show Jerry that we will not be prevented from paying our respects. We *will* give the young lad his due send-off after him enduring such suffering. We will not be like them, they with their hearts of stone.

After the funeral we agree that we must strive to prevent more suicides. We must buoy each other up and support our fellow soldier. Our collective sanity depends on it.

CHAPTER 11

THE WAR SEEMS INTERMINABLE

1942

BAB 21, Blechhammer, Upper Silesia

I am now writing on 25 August. Last week 245 sailors arrived here to make up our new 3rd Company. They are a fine set of chaps and soon settle in, although they bring us sad news: the HMS *Eagle* was torpedoed by Jerry last week while on convoy duty to Malta and was sunk with heavy loss of life. They also report that a large landing by our troops at Dieppe, France, met with little success; all our men were either killed or captured. The Germans here are ecstatic about this, what they call 'their latest victory'. They jeer and say that our leaders had bragged about the landing being the start of England's 'Great Second Front'. According to the Jerries, their forces well and truly routed our boys. I got into a very bitter argument regarding this with an under-officer who completely lost his temper. He argued that we are a defeated nation, and this I could not, and *would not,* accept and I told him as much. To date, the under-officer has not retaliated with punishment, but I'm waiting for it.

We are getting news of home from a 'bird' in our camp about twice a week now. This has taken some time and labour to arrange and, if caught, the punishment will be severe, but we believe it is well worth the risk.

1 September—We are experiencing very hot weather at present. Today we receive mail which we are assured is now running as before. Unfortunately, some of the boys receive bad news concerning the behaviour of their wives, and some decide to file for divorce as a consequence. One feels very sorry for these lads as this life is bad enough without having that on their minds.

12 September—The mail has been held back again.

We hold a concert tonight and my lads are on fire. Our audience is ecstatic, and the Jerries also appear to enjoy it with no complaints this time of us insulting their delicate egos!

16 September—We learn that an attack was made on Tobruk by sea by our naval force, but it was a failure. While we are bitterly upset about this latest defeat, we are hopeful when we are told that our air force is still active and the highly-populated German city of Dusseldorf got a colossal bombing.

By the end of September, we hear that General Rommel left Africa to seek medical treatment in Germany. The Jerry guards don't want to hear about it, but now it's our turn to have a good laugh about their so-called Desert Fox, or Deserting Fox as we now name him behind their backs. Also, the Japs are being given a bit of their own medicine by the Allies after America sent forces in to support the Aussies who are said to have been engaged in fierce battles with the Nips.

1 October—I'm sent to hospital today because my stomach is playing up something shocking and I am practically eating nothing. What would I do without bicarbonate of soda? I honestly don't know. Many chaps are also now ailing with their stomachs due to inadequate diets.

The mail restriction is still on.

7 October—I've been in hospital for a week now, but my stomach problems are not much better, and I'm on nothing but sweetened water. The weather outside is very good and, when we pop outside for a cig, we see many Germans leaving the camp. We hear that Jerry is now even calling upon its older guards and under-officers to fight because they are needed in Russia. If it carries on like this, there will be no guards left and we'll be marching ourselves right out of here!

We have had one or two air raids near here in the past week. In the German papers many articles are written about the poor treatment of German prisoners of war by the British. I will not comment here, but one can only imagine my thoughts, especially when word comes in

Private Jackson, Royal Field Artillery, 1915.

Jackson proudly posing on horseback despite being underage at sixteen, 1915.

Bransty Railway Station, Whitehaven, where Jackson left to join his battalion in September 1939 and returned in May 1945.

Henry (Harry) Barnes Jackson and his beloved wife, Mabel.

The 5th Battalion Border Regiment's RAP at Orcq, near Tournai, Belgium, early May 1940, just before Jackson's capture.

The start of many POW funerals attended by Jackson during his time in concentration camps throughout Poland.

Another POW funeral. Jackson was often a coffin bearer and bugler for the Last Post and Reveille.

POW Camp Warthelager, Poland, in snow. Jackson was interned here from October 1940 – March 1942.

POW Camp Warthelager in spring. Warthelager was a training camp for the Nazis.

POW recreational activities in camp, in this case a boxing match.

Recreation: POWs playing cards inside cramped barracks.

When Jackson's wife Mabel finally heard news of his capture, she sent this photograph in January 1941. Clockwise from Mabel (centre): the youngest and the author's mother, Joan; next youngest, Betty, second eldest, Mona and eldest, Nellie.

Recreation: POWs dressed up as women to provide amusement during races.

Finally, to Jackson's delight, the first musical instruments arrived from The Red Cross. Camp Warthelager, May 1941.

POWs eagerly watching band practice led by Jackson, who often covered up escapes by replacing band members.

Jackson (front row, second from left) and his first band. Camp Warthelager, 1941.

Responsible for arranging stage performances, in his diary Jackson proudly referred to the female impersonators as his 'girls'.

With only one meal of soup a day, the POWs relied on Red Cross parcels to survive. Jackson (sitting highest) wrote in his diary: 'God bless the Red Cross!'

Jackson (facing the camera) expressing delight as he helps unload Red Cross parcels.

Jackson and his best friend, Sergeant Davies, were in charge of constructing this bridge in the snow near Warthelager, Poland, in September 1941. In his diary, he records temperatures of 32 below freezing!

Jackson conducting the band.

A ghostly photograph of Jackson and his band preparing to perform for the Nazis at Blechhammer, part of the Auschwitz concentration camp complex, March 1943.

A caricature of 'Drummie', Drum-Major Jackson's nickname. After the Nazis named him their kapellmeister (maker of music) in Blechhammer (1942- 1944), his pals also called him 'The Music Maker'.

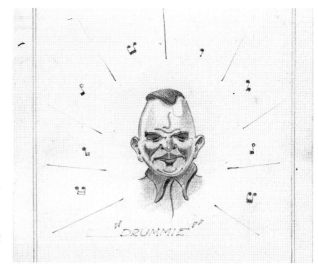

Private Preston's tombstone, Blechhammer, August 1942. Preston's comrades defied the Germans and gave him a full military burial, despite it being denied to suicide cases.

Jackson (seated centre) holding his battalion's (BAB 21) pet kitten outside the barracks, Blechammer 1943.

Jackson (seated right) and friends, Blechhammer 1943.

Jackson playing the Last Post at yet another POW funeral, Blechhammer.

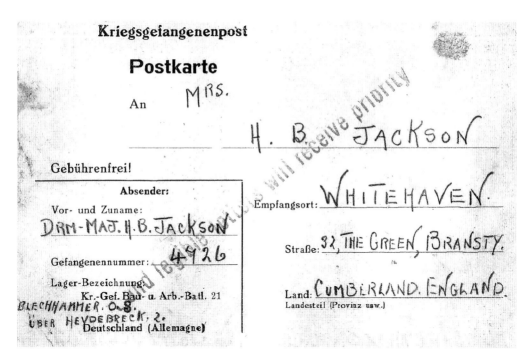

A postcard from Jackson in Blechhammer that eluded German censorship, reaching his wife Mabel in Britain.

POWs freezing outside their barracks, Blechhammer, winter 1943.

The Pirates of Penzance play, Blechammer, September 1943. Jackson wrote: 'I had over two hundred pages of manuscripts to write for the orchestra, having had only a piano score on hand.'

Circulated throughout Nazi concentration camps, The Camp, was a propaganda newspaper aimed at intimidation. It contained such tragic photographs as this one taken at Buchenwald.

Jackson's 'girls' showing their appreciation for their director onstage.

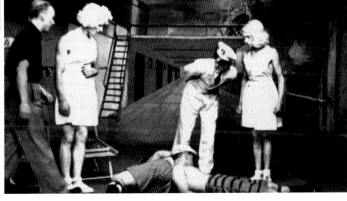

POWs performing the musical, Anything Goes.

GLAMOUR GIRLS" OF THE STALAGS

Repatriated prisoners of war have been full of praise for the efforts of amateur actors and musicians whose shows have done much to brighten the lives of British prisoners of war. Drum-Major Harry Jackson, The Border Regiment, has played a leading part in organising orchestral concerts, operatic shows, and dances, and, amongst the photographs he has sent to his wife at The Green, Bransty, Whitehaven, is the one above of a quartette of "girls" in the camp presentation of Gilbert and Sullivan's "Pirates of Penzance."

A clipping from the Whitehaven News, 18 November 1943, sent in by Jackson's proud wife, Mabel.

Jackson, the Nazis' kapellmeister sitting centre stage with his band in Blechhammer POW Camp (1942 – 1944).

Jackson's formidable mother-in-law, Elizabeth Cranston.

The Fox and Grapes Pub (circa 1950s), Queen Street, Whitehaven, where Jackson loved a stout (or three). He lived in a flat above the pub from 1952 until his death in 1964.

Jackson (third from left) in 1946 eating from a pie cart with friends after his homecoming from six years of war, five of which were spent in Nazi concentration camps throughout Poland.

Jackson (centre) relaxing with wife Mabel (left), and family and friends, 1947.

Jackson with his first band, The Exelda Dance Band (circa 1920s), the name he also gave to subsequent bands.

that at Camp Lamsdorf about 1700 of our chaps who were captured at Dieppe in France are being kept in handcuffs which are only removed for two hours a day. The poor chaps are said to be in a terrible state, and one almost can't hear it described. The word out is that Lamsdorf is a place of horrors. Our hatred of Jerry is at an all-time high.

12 October—I'm released as a patient from hospital today, but I will soon have to return to work there.

19 October—I've been working at the hospital for a few days now and I have been kept as busy as ever. Two of our boys named Wynn and Potts are brought into hospital today with severe wounds to their thighs, having been shot at close range by a Jerry guard. It seems that their working party was lined up ready for marching back to camp, and the guard asked either Wynn or Potts to carry another guard's case. There was a slight debate between the two as to who had to carry it, when two policemen arrived and advised the guard to shoot at them. He did so, right into the back of both men's legs. The bullet went right through Wynn's thigh and then also pierced Potts's thigh, shattering both men's legs. Neither of these men knew what was going on. They came in here in a shocking state, and I only hope to God that we can save their wounded limbs.

The health of this camp, in general, is very poor, and I am expecting many cases to enter hospital this winter. It is always so damp, which contributes to failing health, and there is a constant cloying mist surrounding the place, adding to an already eerie and depressing atmosphere.

29 October—We bury Wynn at Cosel today. He took the brunt of the bullet and, as I feared he would, he died after an operation to remove his leg. Potts is still alive and has his leg still, but he's too sick to make it to his mate's funeral. Once again, I play 'The Last Post'. Poor Wynn was out of the Royal Engineers and came from Stoke.

I notice one of the graves at the burial site belonged to a young chap out of the Kensington Regiment who was shot recently for smoking on a job. The Jerries are now very trigger-happy, and the guards are gaining great pleasure from reducing the number of prisoners for the slightest thing. The atmosphere around camp is electric.

9 November—Jerry guards surprised us with a search for German money very early this morning. Then, in the afternoon an order comes through from the German High Command that all entertainment has to stop once again, and they come to take away all our musical instruments. I feel this is the last straw, removing the only joy I have in this godforsaken hellhole, making me want to scream with anger!

11 November—We are now getting pretty good news from our 'bird' that American troops have successfully landed at different points in North Africa. The Jerries are very skittish about this, so we assume the news is true. As a result, the guards take out their frustration on us for the slightest thing, and we are being subjected to very severe searches. In the last five days, we have had our rooms and belongings searched numerous times, but as yet they haven't found our wine supplies. For quite a while now we have managed to make some excellent wine. It is very intoxicating! Some of the boys have even invented secret distilling plants under lifted boards, and more wine cellars have also been constructed under the huts.

Mid November—Some of our distilling plants are discovered and taken away, but we lads still have some stash left. Jerry then starts taking all unopened Red Cross tins away, thinking this will stop us making our brews, but it doesn't, and they can't keep the spirit of us lads down. We just laugh at Jerry and carry on regardless, building more distilling plants.

Mid December—Christmas is drawing nigh. This will be my third Christmas behind barbed wire. I wonder if I shall be free for the next? Many of us are starting to feel prematurely old and, given my age and state of health, I am certainly feeling like a decrepit old man, but somehow I keep on going. I suppose it is due in no small part to my music. I have started a light orchestra here, having got some of our instruments back (I cannot say how), and I'm given permission to hold rehearsals and the musicians are making good progress. I'm hoping that this year we can hold a Christmas concert for all our chaps.

The mail is coming in only sporadically now. It's been over three weeks since I have had any. I am surrounded by men, but I feel so lonely. I yearn for my family; I even miss Mabel's family, the Cranstons, and that's saying something.

There was never a dull moment with that lot. I can clearly recall the first time I met the Cranston clan…

Unlike me, Mabel came from a large family. The first time she invited me to her home to introduce me to her folks, in late 1919, I was quaking all over like an underground explosion at the colliery. Mabel is the eldest in a family of 11 children—five girls and six lads— and, while I was fearful of her father's scrutiny, I can tell you it was no easy task to keep myself from wetting my pants on meeting her army of siblings. Being that I was an only child, the mere thought was terrifying.

I jangled the brass doorbell of Mabel's home at number 7 The Green, Bransty, Whitehaven and waited for quite some time before Mabel answered the door and shyly ushered me through. Chaos is the only way I can describe the scene that greeted me. My head was spinning as Mabel introduced me to all 10 siblings.

Her teenage sisters—Betty, 19, Elsie, 17, and Georgina, 15—were very interested in me, the strange chap whom Mabel had brought home. They twittered around the place in a gaggle of giggles, their hands held to mouths, whispering to each other, and I've no doubt it was in reference to me. Mary, eight, hid behind Betty, her eyes as round as plates. I later found out I was the first suitor to ever grace their parlour.

Then I met Mabel's male siblings, starting with her brother William, who at only 13 years of age scanned me with an air of fierce protector while his brothers Alfred, 10, Ernie, six, and Geoffrey, four, grinned at me from behind William's lanky frame. The youngest two, twin boys, called out for Mabel's attention and, with one swift movement, she scooped up her two-year-old brothers, Bert and Jack, one on each hip, as if they were one-pound bags of flour.

Finally, Mabel's father, William Snr, stood from his hidden position in a rocking chair, holding a pipe firmly between his teeth as he shook my hand vigorously. I could almost hear his mind thinking *Thank God, you're taking one of this brood off my hands*! William was a signalman for the railways. He was a well-dressed man and stood tall as he continued to pump my hand up and down as if he were directing a train to pull up. He asked me if I liked gardening, his face turning down at the edges a little when I answered in the negative and told him that music was my passion. William sighed, and pointed out of the window to his garden plot abundant with vegetables. Then he promptly took off in that direction, leaving me to wonder if I shouldn't have lied somewhat about my lack of green thumb in order to impress the man a bit more.

And then… I met the matriarch of the family. And make no mistake, Elizabeth Cranston was a true matriarch. For she was a force to be reckoned with, I can tell you! As small in stature as she was, Mabel's mother swept regally into the room and, with a clap of her hands, every single body in the parlour froze on the spot and a hush descended. Despite a fire raging in the fireplace, the room seemed to turn to ice as Elizabeth's eyes studied me from head to foot without so much as a how do you do.

Mabel plonked the twins on the floor and raced to my side. 'Mam, I would like you to meet Henry Barnes Jackson,' she said, and I noted my full name was on display. No one ever called me that; I was just plain old Harry from Rosemary Lane. It was only then that I noted Mabel had not formally introduced me to her father beforehand, and in that very moment I knew that this family was ruled by Elizabeth Cranston.

To this day I can't say the woman has ever warmed to me, nor I to her. It soon became as plain as the nose on my face that Elizabeth resented me removing her eldest from the family. My poor Mabel did most everything around the home, every evening when she returned from her job as a domestic servant, and even on her only day off on Sunday. Yes, Elizabeth could no doubt sense that Mabel's loyal servitude was coming to an end.

And end it certainly did. I made bloody sure of it. I married my beautiful girl on 18 August the following year (1920) at a grand service held at the Wesleyan Methodist Church, that religious denomination being the ultimate condition laid down by Elizabeth Cranston. My folks were none too impressed about the venue, they being staunch members of the Church of England faith, but if that was the only obstacle to me taking my prize, then I wasn't going to object. Betty, Mabel's next youngest sister, was a bridesmaid, and I felt for the poor girl because it was unlikely Betty would ever marry. Unlike Mabel, Betty was not graced with beauty, and there had never been, nor was there, a single man on her horizon. Now it was she who was to become the family slave. And Betty's mother made it patently clear that this arrangement was not up for debate, nor would it ever be; her daughter Betty would never 'desert' her as her Mabel had done.

Of course, Mabel was still called upon to attend to family duties, but it was never to the extent it had been before I came on the scene. I put paid to that. Only on the occasional Sunday and on family holidays was Mabel required to be in attendance to Lady Elizabeth and her tribe of children. Although I must concede there were a lot of holidays. Working on the railways, Mabel's old man had acquired a disused railway carriage and, being the handy bugger that he was, William had had it relocated to a plot on Braystones Beach, about 12 miles down the coast from Whitehaven. He'd converted it into a fine bungalow and at every opportunity the family travelled down there. Mabel and I occasionally joined them and I have to admit it was a right treat for the likes of me. Not so for poor Mabel who had a large gaggle of kids to tend to on top of cleaning and cooking chores so as to give her mam the break Elizabeth demanded.

But now, thinking of them all, as daft as those days were, I would give anything just to sit in the Cranstons' parlour and feel a part of a real family again.

CHAPTER 12

DESPERATION TAKES ITS TOLL

1943

BAB 21, Blechhammer, Upper Silesia

I am now writing on 11 January—we have got Christmas and New Year over with. We made the best of it and, since our 3rd Company is made up of sailors, we had the raisin wine, which they are still making. I will now tell you how.

Our method is to get a barrel (never mind from where) and almost fill it with boiling water. Then we put in raisins and any other dried fruit which comes in the Red Cross parcels. After two days, we add yeast, then after about a fortnight or three weeks, we strain it and we have ourselves a party!

Over Christmas we gave three concerts in the camp, and then we gave one in a large cinema for a few other camps. The orchestra performed well, and we are now preparing for another concert. There are some Jerries who are true bastards and try to intimidate us during performances in an attempt to assert their authority, one being the same under-officer I argued with last year when he said England was a defeated nation. He's a right pig and he has been giving me a hard time ever since. He attempted to stop band practice last week, and I told him what I thought he was in no uncertain terms. For this, I have been rewarded with six days in the clink. It would appear that at last he has taken his revenge. I knew it had to come, and I am now waiting to go in because at present the clink is at full capacity.

The weather is terribly cold and the snow very deep. I had a fall on ice last week and fractured a rib but, after a few days in bed, I am feeling okay again.

The mail has started arriving **once** more, and more of the boys say they are getting bad news from their wives and girlfriends regarding their relationship. I try to talk to some of these chaps about it, and from what they tell me I'm not altogether convinced that the situation is as bad as they interpret. They say that they just 'sense' something is wrong—that their girls are not as affectionate in their writing. Nerves are shattered, tensions are running high, and paranoia is rife, so it's my belief that some of the lads are overthinking things. I tell them this, but then a true 'Dear John' letter arrives and paranoia sets in once more. As soon as the emotional winds of insecurity blow in everyone gets tossed about. I thank God that my faith in my beloved Mabel remains strong.

1 February—I have done my sentence in the clink and came out this morning. It wasn't too bad at all, much to my surprise, although I was searched many times for cigs while in there, but I always managed to get them in without being caught after being supplied by one of the lads, along with my food, when I came out to the latrines. Bless them!

4 February—Lieutenant Reigerfeld, a British soldier, is found trading with a German girl whom he was courting. He gets clink, but his poor girl is brought up for court martial and, whilst on the stand, condemns the Nazi method of government. She is sentenced to death to be hanged in public this same day. Poor Reigerfeld is taking it badly, and one wonders what state he will be in when he's released from the clink.

18 February—The Jerries are getting pretty gloomy over the Russian and African affairs. It seems to be gradually sinking in that all is not boding well for them. We hear that German troops have surrendered to the Ruskies in Stalingrad, meaning that the Nazi Government has had to concede defeat for the first time ever. The Allies appear to have Libya under control, and Nuremberg has been heavily bombed. Of course, *The Camp* paper disguises the facts very cleverly via propaganda but we can tell by the long mournful faces of Jerry, and by the severity of the punishment they are handing out for the least thing, that they are not happy at all.

The weather here is very mild now to what we have come to expect.

We hear that at Cosel typhus has broken out. Also, one of our boys recently died of ptomaine poisoning from spoiled food. It is a shocking way to go, and I will not fill in the blanks here.

19 March—Our battalion (BAB 21) and the next one (BAB 48) have been joined, totalling 1200 men.

Things are very unsettled. I thought I was going to be sent to Lamsdorf with some others as that's what I had been told previously but, thank God, I am to remain here instead. This is due to the Jerries making me the camp '*Kapellmeister*'. *Kapellmeister* is a German word, which means designating a person to be in charge of music-making. The lads here now call me 'The Music Maker'. I love that title—*Music Maker*—it reminds me of my old music teacher when I was a lad in Whitehaven who was known to locals as the Music Man. He'd be quite delighted at my new title if he were still alive. I'm to conduct a large orchestra. The only snag is that we'll be playing music exclusively for Jerry, but our lads will be able to watch on during rehearsals. It's one of the few joys they get in this place, and it helps boost morale.

28 March—The orchestra is now playing wonderful music and during rehearsals the hall is crowded with our boys listening in. I have a straight orchestra of about 30 players. The instruments are now: two pianos, one organ, six violins, three clarinets, four saxophones, two horns, two bass, one baritone, three trombones, six trumpets and drums.

29 March—We have had wonderful weather up to now but today it starts to rain, much to the delight of the Jerries who are looking forward to a good crop of vegetables for themselves this year. Not so good for the likes of us prisoners, their 'slave labour', who have to work in such dreadful weather. This camp is also packed with foreign workers: Italians, French, Slovakians, Dutch, Romanians, and Ukrainians who volunteered to work in the hope of getting better fed. There are also hundreds of Ukrainian women working and they toil like men. Most work at a place we call 'the factory' which is now almost at full pressure. The factory is a synthetic oil refinery and produces benzene. Jerry needs the stuff to be pumped out in order to keep its fuel supplies up.

About the most unfortunate among us by far are the Jews, who are in abundance in this camp. The Jews wear blue-and-white striped thin cotton pyjamas bearing large yellow stars and numbers. All of their uniforms are in a filthy state and appear to be one-size-for-all, right down to women and children who are swamped by the clothing. Prison numbers are tattooed on their arms, and their heads are shaved. The poor beggars are made to work very hard, given little food, and are whipped mercilessly to keep them going. Many commit suicide, through sheer desperation. They have no connection with the outside world. Our boys try and give them cigs and scraps of food, but if one is caught, it is the end of the line for them.

Another group made to suffer indignities are the strafe Poles [*strafe* is the German word for punishment], men who have committed 'crimes' such as stealing bread and other such minor offences. Incredibly, there are strafe Germans in here too: soldiers who have fought for their country but have done things at the Russian front they should not have done. I hear that some are even being interned for having been late back from leave, with many sentenced to years of imprisonment. Their clothes are painted with broad yellow stripes. A demeaning situation for them indeed.

8 April—We witness a truly horrible scene today. A little Polish boy in the camp who is in charge of emptying refuse by means of a horse and cart is killed. The lad was slight of build and malnourished, and only had the use of a whip to get the lethargic horse to move. Our boys often helped him carry the foul bins out to the cart, but only when the guards were not looking. However, today we see he is under the scrutiny of a guard, and a mean bastard this one is too. Sadistic as Satan. The poor young lad, as thin and fragile as the wafers Jerry gives us, staggers and falls to the ground from fatigue. Suddenly, the Jerry guard strides over, takes the boy's own whip from him, and strikes him cruelly across the face with it, again and again, as we call out to the monster, pleading for the young one's life, but our objections fall on deaf ears. The poor little mite's eyes bulge out of his head in fear and pain as he lies dying on the ground. Then, too weak to even cry out, his eyes become lifeless.

The guard then turns on us. He orders us inside our barracks on threat of being shot and only walks away after we do so. We are shocked, but later agree that the poor lad has gone to a better place. For surely this place is hell on earth, and the Jerries are the very devil personified. Especially this bleeder. I hope to live long enough to name him one day, but for now I will hold my tongue, although the very mention of this Jerry guard's name makes my gut turn over.

29 May—I've been three years captured to the day, but it seems like an eternity, and I find it so hard to come to terms with. I don't write as frequently these days as things are pretty well the same day in, day out—simply trying to survive despite the starvation and deprivation. Only my music and news of a defeat against Jerry or the Japs keeps things interesting, along with news of an escape.

Speaking of escape, one of my violinists escaped along with two other men a fortnight ago today. The two other men were captured the next day, but my violinist is still at large. The evening he escaped my orchestra was to give a concert in the next camp, so, to cover his getaway, I had to take another chap along to the concert to play the escapee's violin. We had arranged all this previously and were very well organised, although my violinist's replacement was not a particularly good player, but the rest of the orchestra just drowned him out, and Jerry didn't seem to notice. It was wonderful to know that we were outsmarting Jerry, if only in a small way, and I think the orchestra played better than I have ever heard them play! Anyway, my violinist got a good head start, and our lads have spent hours talking of him and sending their prayers.

We're getting a few air-raid alarms but see no action. We hear the Allied forces are making progress against the Germans, but the Japanese are causing all sorts of trouble in South-East Asia. We are now hearing terrible things about the Japanese forces and their treatment of their captives. The Nips didn't sign the part of the Geneva Convention pertaining to prisoners of war, only the clause relating to the sick and wounded. In 1942, they promised to abide by the Convention's terms, but it seems that they aren't. They signed The Hague and Forced Labour Conventions in 1930, but they have continued to violate all international agreements. Our 'bird' says the Japs are savages and that earlier this month the Nips went on a three-day massacre of thousands of Chinese. They have done this before; a couple of years before this war broke out, we heard of Japan's invasion of China. In Nanking, thousands of Chinese soldiers were stranded and this was followed by a shocking killing frenzy after which the Nips turned on civilians—raping, mutilating, crucifying and provoking dogs to maul. Horrific stuff!

So, while things for us Brits can't be called easy, I suppose we must be thankful that we have some protection under the Convention, and I have to say that while we have some right brutes for guards, indeed they are in abundance here at Blechhammer, there are a couple who we have a crack to. They're not as brainwashed as some and we don't think they agree with the Nazis. Of course, they would be shot if caught discussing such things with us prisoners, but we are aware of their discomfort with the Nazi regime. One such guard was coming back from leave when he was killed last week. He had lost his son, wife and home when his place in Hamburg was heavily bombed whilst on leave. He was supposed to have stepped out of a train only to be run over by another, but we boys think he committed suicide.

1 June—The orchestra is playing exceedingly well, and some of the pieces they have managed are 'Euranthe', 'The Magic Flute' and 'The Bohemian Girl'. Not an easy task at all. I'm very delighted with the chaps and our troops are loving rehearsals. I must say it's hard playing for Jerry. We musicians feel like animals in a zoo, jumping through hoops for our captors. However, we manage to express our defiance in small ways, such as refusing to make eye contact with Jerry and bowing only slightly on their applause. It's the only way we can save face.

I'm sad to say that my violinist is captured near Berlin after being away for 16 days. He is near death when he arrives back in camp today, and the chaps are plunged into sadness at the sight of the poor bloke. We had such hopes for him. Perhaps the sad truth is that there is no exiting this place, except in a box dripping with old blood. My violinist is then taken away, and we don't know what will become of him. We fear they will shoot him as they previously threatened to do to all escapees.

6 June—Two more chaps make their escape today. For this, the Jerries put us through the mill and make us stand outside our huts from 6:00 pm until 9:00 pm whilst they search our rooms, some of which are turned completely upside down. They are raging and shouting, shoving chaps in the back and chest with their rifle butts, and sending some to the clink for the slightest thing. I am glad to report that my journal is safe. I have a special method of hiding it, which of course I will not divulge here, but I realise that to date I have been fortunate, because if it ever falls into Jerry hands, I will be lucky to escape with my life.

8 June—One of the two escapees is captured today and we assume he will face the same fate as his predecessors, which is still unknown to us, but as far as we know the other one is still at liberty.

12 June—Eighteen chaps are sent to the big camp at Lamsdorf today—Lamsdorf being a place of terror.

13 June—Jerry officials arrive here this morning to further investigate the escapes, and when they get no answers they come into the hospital and threaten to send everyone who is sick to join our 18 men at Lamsdorf. Our hospital is full, but fortunately for many of the sick they are not singled out, although sadly some men still are, and they're beyond terrified to be taken away, but we are all so proud of them for not revealing anything. I'm lucky that I was on duty at the hospital rather than a patient in it, or I could also now be on my way to Lamsdorf.

The other escapee is still at large—or dead.

July—One of the chaps who was sent to the lunatic compound at Camp Lamsdorf is shot dead for climbing the wire in an attempt to escape. It must be a true hellhole.

We discover that a building, heavily surrounded by barbed wire and Jerry guards to the left of our compound over the other side of the canal, which has been in construction for many months, is a brothel. It opened about 10 days ago. I believe many of the women are prisoners and were forced into prostitution on offer of better conditions and more food—some French, some Poles. The rest are Germans: either strafe Germans or German women who were previously prostitutes. No Jewish girls are allowed to work on account of the Jerry policy of 'racial hygiene' and certainly no male Jews can enter the grounds of the brothel—not that the poor chaps would have the strength or money to do so. German soldiers are allowed with any of the women, but naturally prefer German women. Prisoners (those who have earned merits or who grease the guards' palms well enough) are only allowed with the French and Polish women. Every night we can see streams of men coming and going in all directions, and outside the building there is a tremendous queue. On Saturdays and Sundays, all day long, the queue remains with hundreds of men going backwards and forwards. It is a sight to behold, and one hears terrible tales of the poor girls who service so many desperate men. They are forced to undergo crude sterilisation procedures. Some do not even survive the operation, and those that do face contracting horrible diseases. Where the men get the money from to pay for the service is anyone's guess, although we later hear that there is quite a wrangle going on and some blokes are even sending home for money to be sent so they can visit the brothel. I am certain they don't tell their loved ones what the money is for! We have even heard that some Jerries send requests home to some prisoners' loved ones asking for money for chaps to go to the brothel. In the unlikely event that funds do come through, the Jerries pocket it for themselves. They think it's amusing and do it as a form of punishment, but I can tell you that the responses from wives and girlfriends cause a hell of a stink and, unfortunately, some poor chaps take their own lives as a result.

15 August—Some men are taken away from our camp on account of them going insane. We believe they are going to be taken to Lamsdorf, a place filling up so fast that the Jerries are killing the more serious cases. This thought makes one ill. There is no doubt that the length of time served as prisoners is having its effect on some. Thank God, I have my music to keep me sane. Speaking of which, I have been very busy lately doing the orchestral score for

The Pirates of Penzance. The rehearsals are going well and the boys' singing is wonderful.

16 August—The weather is still bad and rain every day seems to be the usual thing.

News is coming through about fighting in Sicily. The Allies are in control and the Germans in retreat. Now on to Italy!

Lord 'Haw-Haw', whom we hear on the wireless set some mornings, is very severe about our terror raids on German towns, but of course he would be. The traitor fled Britain to Germany before the war and the Hitler-loving fascist broadcasts Nazi propaganda daily to Britain in order to rile us. Shame on him.

The Russians seem to be doing well but, according to the Jerries, they are losing an enormous amount of men and equipment. But we know the Jerries are nervous. They appear to be very preoccupied with Germany's flagging war efforts and we often overhear them muttering amongst themselves. Then, when we learn a few days later that the Allies are in full control of Sicily, we know Jerry is running scared. However, the guards' preoccupation with their sorry state of affairs works in our favour as they appear to be overlooking minor misdemeanours.

17 August—Some of the chaps are taking advantage of the Jerry guards slackening off and there is every kind of racketeering going on nowadays. Many of our boys are paying Frenchmen to exchange with them for a night off. The Frogs put on our boys' uniforms and come into our camp with the working party, while the soldier or sailor puts on Froggy civvies and spends the night out. I will not say where they go or what they do, but you can imagine, as there are few forms of release in this place.

21 August—When the Jerries discover the rort with the Frogs this morning, while we are on parade, there's a search for two Frenchmen among our company. A Frenchman is discovered dressed in our uniform and he's taken away after being kicked and knocked about. He gets two years' clink. Then the Jerries set out to find our boys who swapped uniforms. So much for them slackening off, it appears they are once again taking out their frustrations on us prisoners.

Numerous Jews are now being hanged publicly in their lager [German word for camp], and there are also many deaths due to an epidemic of typhus amongst the Jews and Ukrainians.

26 August—One of our boys tries to meet his Maker prematurely by slitting his own throat. He's brought into hospital this afternoon and the sight is horrific, blood spurting everywhere. The men who find him are terribly traumatised and shocked, made all the more so by his seemingly passive response when he and his gruesome act are discovered. One cannot imagine reaching such a point of desperation, and it will be touch-and-go as to whether we can save him. Pray to God the poor chap does survive but, then again, he will most definitely be sent to the insane asylum at Lamsdorf if he pulls through, a place which is rapidly filling by the day. One wonders which is worse: death or insanity. I think I would choose death. But I hope it will never be by my own hand.

9 September—We receive the news that Italy has surrendered to the Allies. This has put our boys in high glee as it is indeed a major victory. About three days ago, 900 Allied men were brought here from Italy after being taken by the Italians as prisoners of war. They seem to have been rather roughly treated by the Italians and the poor chaps are not in good shape at all. It makes for quite a struggle, with the hospital now overflowing with sick men, and our camp getting so overcrowded with prisoners.

Apart from the death and funeral of our chap who cut his throat, which we have decided was for the best, very little of note has happened. We have had the concert and play *The Pirates of Penzance*. I had over 200 pages of manuscript to write for the orchestra, having had only a piano score on hand. It was a huge success.

12 December—It has been a while since I wrote anything as things remain the same in camp. Another chap is taken away insane. They, the insane, are leaving here like rats from a sinking ship and it is an eerie sight to behold when one realises a man has turned mad. The guards come and drag him out of the place. Some mental cases go kicking and screaming, while others, which are probably the hardest to witness, go quietly, their blank eyes showing no recognition of us, their fellow men, or of their surroundings.

The first batch of repatriates [refugees returning to their countries of birth] have been exchanged, and we get about 60 more men from Lamsdorf.

Nearly every Red Cross parcel brought by lorry is broken into now, and more and more contents go missing every time. We're not told where the parcels are being tampered with, and the Jerries say that they are in this condition when they arrive. We doubt that and believe this is just another lie, and we think that they are taking things for themselves.

CHAPTER 13

LIVING ON HOPE

1944

BAB 21, Blechhammer, Upper Silesia

Early January—We had a very uneventful Christmas this year. Concerts for our lads were disallowed, for no other reason than the Jerries' spite. The camp is so overcrowded that they are finding it hard to cope, and curbing our activities helps them maintain control. Conditions are now very dangerous with every man struggling just to survive. All kinds of rorts are going on, and it is becoming a very tough place indeed. With overcrowding comes disease and, as a result, I have been run off my feet at the hospital.

Mid-January—A Jerry guard is caught letting some of our boys out at night to visit the brothel through a gate next to the canal. Our men get days in the clink, but the guard gets three years' imprisonment as a 'strafe'.

A Jewish worker is murdered and left lying for two days in a lavatory. The Jerries know who the culprits are, but nothing is done about it on account of him only being a Jew. Too much work. Their lives are worth absolutely nothing—the Jews—less than the rats that infest the camp. It is now pretty common knowledge that the Jews are being killed en masse. We know that there is a camp very near here which is referred to by the Jews as 'Himmler Lager' because Heinrich Himmler is the supposed 'mastermind' behind it. Like Hitler, Himmler wants to eradicate all Jews, a desire which we are incredulous about. We have named that camp 'Heaven Camp' because no one leaves it alive. The Jews are absolutely terrified of being taken there for obvious reasons. A train goes right through the camp. Any Jew too sick for work, too frail, too old or too young is packed off there. When the Jews arrive, it is believed they are given a towel, told to strip off, and are told they are going for a bath, but there are rumours that it proves to be a lethal chamber. This mass killing is simply unthinkable to us, and it is common practice to get any Jew who can hardly walk and wedge him between two others, so he can be helped along to work rather than have him fall and have to go to that place of horrors.

Mid February—Two Russians were publicly hanged at Dorflager, and this is by no means an isolated case. Some of our boys witnessed the incident, and this is what they told me. The gallows were erected in the camp, which our boys could see from the road—no attempt to hide them. Arbeit men were made to watch. After a lot of saluting and shouting, the two Russians were marched out of ranks, stood on the gallows, had a noose slung around their necks, and were then marched back into ranks. Again, there was much shouting and saluting, and again the two prisoners were returned to the gallows, the nooses still around their necks. Each was made to stand on a box, the ends of the ropes were secured in place, and the boxes were then kicked away. One chap appeared to die immediately, but the other's legs twitched furiously; then *both* bodies trembled all over for about five minutes before they became still. They were left hanging for nine hours, having been allowed no dignity whatsoever.

We had a search by the Jerries for which we were not prepared and it proved to be disastrous for us. They found our wireless set, a distillery, two sets of civilian clothing and 100 German marks. Men were taken away for questioning, and no doubt they will face severe treatment. All of us are devastated for the poor blighters, who have not as yet returned to barracks.

1 May—I haven't written in my diary for months now, as life is simply too tedious in this place and I sometimes lack the desire. The news on the war continues to wax and wane. The Russians are continuing to advance, but our air force suffered horribly in a massive air raid on Nuremberg at the end of March. One hundred Allied bombers were shot down and hundreds of men are still missing, presumed dead. We can't get to know what went wrong, but the Jerries are in high glee and say they have new and effective spotlights and new guns that point upwards and can bring down a plane easily. They jeer and say that our RAF is 'wiped out'. One simply can't bear to hear of any further losses, never mind write of it.

I stay sane by keeping myself busy with music. We are putting on show after show for the Jerries. I am just about to complete the score of *Iolanthe*, which we are putting on in five weeks' time. At the time of writing, I have done over 240 pages of manuscript, and I have had two shows before this.

Luckily, our Red Cross supplies are still holding out well.

4 May—We have a search by the Gestapo early this morning. A cellar and still are found in our bunkhouse, two others found in another, and the suspected culprits are all marched away. My diary is still safe.

8 May—This morning some Ukrainian kiddies are outside the E3 compound wires waiting for food scraps we throw over for them. A German under-officer arrives and chases them away. The desperate kids come back again and the under-officer turns around, draws his pistol, and shoots one boy about 12 years of age in the stomach. Some of our men try to get over the wire to help the lad, who is in a terrible state, and the guard on duty fires at them but luckily misses. Our chaps are forced to retreat, and the poor lad dies about six minutes later while we stand by hopelessly watching.

29 May—I've been four years in capture to the day. This is beyond my comprehension. When will this damn war be over?

2 June—I finally receive my certificate of being recognised under the Geneva Convention, which was sent through from Blighty. This has taken such a ridiculous amount of time and, with the dire situation currently in camp, one wonders what bloody good it will do me now.

8 June—News comes through today that the Allies have successfully invaded France. A massive airborne assault preceded an amphibious attack involving thousands of ships. So much for Jerry 'wiping out' our RAF! One hundred and fifty thousand of our troops crossed the English Channel and landed on the beaches of Normandy, where they quickly advanced and liberated Bayeux. Hitler is incensed, and I'm sure he'll exact his revenge, but as far as we're concerned our boys are on their way to bring us home, and nothing can dampen our spirits. This news has raised us up no end.

15 June—As we all suspected, Hitler has ordered a retaliation against the Allied invasion, and we hear today that Jerry is heavily bombing Britain. One cannot help but worry for our families back home.

All through the rest of June we hear nothing else from the pompous Jerry guards other than that Hitler continues to take out his anger on Britain with a vengeance. They boast of their new V-1 flying bombs, which don't require a plane as they are launched from the coast of France. They gleefully enact gory scenes to upset us. *Boom! Boom!* they shout, waving their arms around simulating an explosion in an attempt to get us worked up, and then they casually pass us by, laughing their damn heads off. Their ruse works, because it is impossible for our lads to contain their anger at this mockery of our kinfolk in Blighty being blasted by their bombs, and I witness a few ugly incidents, with our lads coming off far worse, I can tell you.

5 July—We learn that the flying bombs are having devastating effects on our homeland, particularly London where we've had high losses of civilians. We feel so useless stuck in here. So much so, I could almost turn my back on music in protest and refuse to entertain Jerry.

7 July—There is an air raid at 11:00 am that lasts about one hour and ten minutes. Many incendiary bombs are dropped, which are bombs designed to start fires in the hope that they find targets of machinery plants and explosives, but they are unsuccessful. Our boys are lucky, no deaths, only two work gangs are covered with oil and grime, although one of the lads has to go to Lamsdorf Hospital with the feared loss of one eye.

11 July—One of our chaps picks up an unexploded 100-pound incendiary bomb left over from the air raid a few days ago. He is examining it when it explodes, with the result that he loses some fingers. He comes into hospital a blithering wreck, poor chap. One can't help but question the stupidity of his actions but, then again, none of us is thinking straight these days. Still, when I return from the hospital and elaborate on the poor chap's injuries and caution the boys against even thinking of such an impetuous action, I think I get through to them.

I am now busy rehearsing the orchestra for the *Mikado* production after a very successful showing of *Iolanthe*. Owing to a misunderstanding with Jerry, I only had a week to write the score for the orchestra. I had no choice but to go to the hospital cookhouse three nights and work all night long just to get it done.

Things are getting stiff with Jerry, and they are taking out their frustrations on anyone who so much as blinks in their direction. We are all consciously averting our eyes when passing them by.

7 August—We have another air raid today, which starts about 11:00 am, and it's far more severe than any previous raids. The synthetic oil refineries at Blechhammer north and south get hit heavily, putting the works completely out of action, and it will be many months before benzene is being produced again. Naturally, Jerry is very sore at this as it will severely deplete their fuel stores. We cannot get the figure of how many are killed, but it certainly is in the hundreds; many girls and Jews are among the dead, but thankfully not a prisoner here is injured. At the Reigersfeld camp, one of our boys is killed and a Jew wounded. Unfortunately, four American bombers are brought down by Jerry anti-aircraft.

Mid August—The Poles have been very excited about an uprising by their home army against Jerry. They believed they would receive backup from the Ruskies, but sadly we hear today that Russian aid did not arrive, and the Germans have conducted a shocking mass slaughter of the Poles in Warsaw. The massacre was by order of Himmler, and tens upon tens of thousands of innocent Poles, regardless of age or gender, have been slaughtered in their own homes. The uprising is still in progress, but the Polish prisoners around camp are beside themselves with grief for their losses, and we cannot think of any way to console them.

22 August—We have another very heavy raid this morning. Fortunately for us, we are not the main objective, but Heydebreck and Reigersfeld, which are south of here, get hit heavily. It lasts for nearly two hours, and many of our boys who were out working are killed and another 50 severely wounded. Scores of men are suffering from nervous breakdowns. No wonder; this is nerve-wracking hell, and it doesn't look as if we are going to be moved anytime soon. Our air-raid shelters are mere shallow trenches and we are sitting ducks. The Germans have started a smokescreen for their protection, but we are inside the ring, and we think that, contrary to Jerry's belief, this will only attract bombers; a smokescreen being like a bloody arrow pointing to a target.

Twenty-two American airmen are brought into camp this afternoon after their planes were shot down.

26 August—More bombs are dropped today, making us hopeful, because as long as we can continue to avoid a direct hit, we believe that we will soon see a finish to this war. Our boys in the air know that these are prison camps, and thus far the planes appear to be targeting mainly Jerry supply plants. We pray that continues to be the case.

27 August—We have an enormous air raid, which starts about 11:45 am and lasts for over an hour. Seven hundred and fifty large American bombers are in on this. Because we receive no proper warning, many chaps can't flee the hotspots where they are working, and sadly many are killed. Fortunately, once again, the boys of our camp escape, but plenty have terrifying experiences. The nerves of everyone are in a very bad state, and if we are not moved soon I am afraid that more men will be mentally affected. I understand that the boys at Reigersfeld get it heavy again and one or two are killed.

28 August—We get word that Paris has been liberated and the Allies are moving further through France as Jerry retreats. We are still being heavily bombed. No sooner do I make an entry in my diary than the forewarning siren goes off about 11:30 am and streams of civilians and some of our boys come into our camp for shelter, which is outside the bomb action, from their work out in the country. Fortunately for us, once again the bombers do not come here, and all of the chaps are now going back to work.

The uprising in Warsaw is still underway, but the Polish Resistance is said to be in a terrible state.

11 September—Great news. The Allies have entered Germany and have also liberated Luxembourg. Can this be the beginning of the end of the war? Perhaps 11 September 1944 will be a day to remember? We pray to God that this will be the case.

18 September—An order has come in that we each have to be issued with two Red Cross parcels, and all tins are to be opened and the contents eaten. This is a German order for all prisoners, and they tell us that they have no further parcels in store and neither do they expect any more to be delivered under the current conditions. They say they will not be giving us any of the regular rations until our Red Cross parcels are used up. We can only surmise that this is to try and pull us down to their level or even lower. That is impossible!

Last week an order was issued for all theatrical shows to be stopped. We think this order came from the upper echelon of the Nazi Party because the Jerries are under so much pressure that they need to remain on high alert and keep their focus on maintaining control. From what I witness during the concerts we put on for the hedonists their minds are only on pleasure, but I will not describe their unruly behaviour here.

However, my musicians need to play to retain their sanity and the troops need the entertainment at rehearsals for the same reason. So we decided to carry on and I held an orchestral concert practice this weekend. Up to the present time, nothing has been said about it.

As I predicted, more and more men are being affected mentally after experiencing very narrow escapes. It is frightening to witness them become mere shells of the fine men they once were as they wither into shattered souls and are taken away to the asylum at Lamsdorf.

We have had three massive air raids just this last week. We hear that the Ruskies are progressing in Poland and, as a result, Jerry is in a right old mess.

Early October—We learn that the Jerries have completely shut down the Warsaw uprising, I'm sad to report. The Poles fought on fiercely, but the Ruskies never turned up to help. One can't imagine the

Polish Resistance's desperation and certainly their fellow countrymen around our camp are beyond despair.

There have been many blackouts, and our water supply is sporadic. Jerry supplies are scant, our parcels are all used up, and our daily soup is very meagre. All we are living on is hope.

14 October—We have the heaviest air raid to date. Bombs are dropped all around the camp, and one drops on one of our three company barracks. Four men are taken away to Cosel Hospital seriously injured. It is terrible in the small trenches we have for our supposed protection, and many lads just flip out, their minds snapping with terror, and then they lie there inert, their faces devoid of all emotion. Sixty men are now living in the concert hall and of course all music has stopped.

Once again, there's no water and no lights. We are all hoping for the best—that we can survive this onslaught— but with all the carnage that surrounds us daily, it is exceedingly hard going.

Mid November—We are having so many air raids now that the boys are getting into terribly nervous states. My impression is that we will soon see many more mental cases going from here.

Jews are now being engaged by Jerry as spotters, meaning they have to lie on their backs around the factories and watch where delayed-action bombs land and then mark the spots. It is an extremely perilous job indeed, and for risking life and limb, they only receive an extra bowl of soup and four cigs per day, but of course by doing so, they hope to stay as strong as possible and avoid being sent with the weak and infirm to the extermination chambers at Heaven Camp, about which we are now hearing more and more horrors.

My stomach and chest have been giving me a lot of trouble lately.

29 November—I have been so ill that I go in front of the German medical officer for assessment and am ordered away to notorious Camp Lamsdorf for hospitalisation. Having heard nothing but shocking reports of the place I am not happy at all, but my medical officer assures me that the hospital facilities are the best of all the stalags. Let's hope he is correct.

Stalag 344, Lamsdorf, Upper Silesia

1 December—I arrive at Lamsdorf today, which is about 50 miles north-west of my old camp at Blechhammer, and my heart sinks. It is far worse than I expected, if that's at all possible. This is a terribly big camp holding all nationalities.

There are no beds available to me at what Jerry calls the *lazarett* [hospital], so I have to wait in my assigned barracks until such time as one becomes available. One of the chaps in my barracks offers me a very warm welcome and tells me that I could be in for an exceedingly long wait to get into hospital. He also warns me not to expect anything at all here; it's every man for himself and not even Red Cross parcels get through. I very quickly realise that he's not exaggerating one iota; we're almost back to 1940 conditions. It is frigidly cold, and many boys here are suffering mentally, including, I soon discover, my new 'mate'.

It is the day after my arrival. I can see hundreds of our planes passing over in the direction of the place I have just left. Pray to God my mates back at Blechhammer remain safe. I think of them huddling together in those ineffective bloody trenches, and my blood curdles. To have suffered through this long, harsh war only to be killed by one's own bombs, surely this could not happen.

I go before the medical officer this afternoon and am told I have to have an X-ray. My results show that my stomach and chest are worse than ever, and the medical officer has put me down for the next commission to hospital on 9 December.

3 December—I hear the news I had most feared. It's shocking to be told that 30 of the boys in my battalion have been killed as a result of yesterday's air strikes, and many more are seriously injured. My mind tortures me with images of men who may have been killed. I must be careful not to slip into deep melancholy though or I may be taken away to the asylum, which is at this very stalag. From what I've seen of those who have gone insane, I will be no use to anyone. And I hear from fellow inmates that the insane here are treated with the utmost cruelty, the worst cases shot. I must concentrate on getting well so I can return to my remaining pals and play music for them to lift their spirits, for life is more fragile than the thin ice now covering the multitude of puddles outside my barracks.

CHAPTER 14

A LONG WAIT

1945

Stalag 344, Lamsdorf, Upper Silesia

15 January—I am still waiting to go into hospital. I have no musical instruments with me and, even if I did, I would have no opportunity to play. Music of any kind is not allowed here, I'm told. We didn't even have a Christmas service. In fact, Christmas was completely ignored at Lamsdorf, and we have had no mail for so long I have not even been able to hear how Mabel and the girls celebrated Christmas. I can hardly recall when any mail was last delivered. Only the well-worn photograph of my wife and our daughters keep me remembering their pretty faces. I so pine for my Mabel—her beautiful face with its delicate English complexion, her rosy-apple cheeks and smiling eyes. Yes, I miss the wife something terrible, with a physical ache more painful than my stomach ulcers. I constantly dream of my return to our cosy home, my wife falling into my arms, the delicious scent of her—lavender and violets—my girls all chattering on excitedly.

Dreaming is the only thing that sustains me now—dreaming of home and dreaming of music—because this is truly a terrible stalag with over 15,000 men of all nationalities crammed in. We have very poor rations, and what rations we manage to get are often stolen. Rackets of every description go on and so by the time rations reach us there is not much to get. This is also the case with the coal briquettes we need for heating, with the result that only about 20 briquettes per week reach a barracks, which holds about 200 men. With the weather being so severe and the very heavy falls of snow, we are freezing, but somehow, we make do. Many chaps around have made things called 'blowers', the idea brought here by Italian prisoners. A wheel is turned which is connected to a fan made from old tins, driving air to a small fireplace. One can boil a large tin of water in about three minutes with hardly any wood.

Lamsdorf Hospital, Upper Silesia

16 January—I am finally sent into the hospital today to be assessed by the medical officer who gives me a very lengthy examination, and I am admitted. I'm lucky to get a bed, because many men who have been sent here from outside camps are on waiting lists as the hospital is so full. As soon as I settle in, I'm given the wonderful news by another patient that a massive number of Russian troops and tanks have entered East Prussia. It is amazing how well informed some are, but I know from past experience that there are many ways of getting information filtered through. And some of it comes from the most unlikely sources, but I must say no more on the subject.

With this latest news, perhaps we will finally soon see this war coming to an end. Jerry is in trouble, that much is clear, so pray to God this remains the case, although one can't help sometimes wonder where He is. There are also rumours going around regarding the Japs' extremism; their use of suicide planes for example. One wonders what type of person would be up for such a task—flying a plane right into a target. The Nips are extremely fervent in their quest for world domination, and apparently 'self-honour' is all that matters to them. We patients have a lot of time on our hands and we discuss this. One chap tells us that in Japan suicide pilots are held in great esteem. Sounds right daft to me, being held in high esteem when you're dead.

19 January—I have only been in hospital for two days but early this morning I am discharged from the hospital and sent to a hospital barracks that is for gastric cases only. When I arrive at this barracks, I am in serious doubt as to that, it being for stomach cases, because there appears to be many patients in here who are not stomach cases at all, and neither do they appear to be very ill. But hospitalised men at least get fed, and I imagine this is the reason some have wheedled their way in.

21 January—Startling events arise this afternoon. Five blocks of sick men are ordered to get ready to march with only two hours' notice. I wonder how they will possibly survive as it is awful weather to have to march in. It is 32 degrees below zero! This is sheer bloody madness. And where are they to march to? There's nothing but barren wilderness for miles around. However, they have no choice but to do so, and we watch on as the poor chaps march past in deep snow, heavily supervised by armed guards who are well covered in warm clothing, while some of the prisoners are barely even clothed. There's a blizzard blowing outside, and one look at the poor men's grim expressions and one knows that they don't hold out much hope of survival.

22 January—More blocks of men leave today, all in a similar condition to those yesterday. Then, many of the sick who left yesterday come back in again because of the horrific weather conditions, and, as expected, they are in a frightful state. The Jerries just seem to be in a daze and appear to have no direction whatsoever.

And now it is our turn. This same day, in the afternoon, the men in my barracks are told to be on standby for marching. The mind shudders at the thought. We are getting ourselves prepared as best as we can, and then we hear that the order has been withdrawn. We can hear gunfire and there is a great deal of aerial activity. We are now left with 4700 men in the camp and all of us are very sick, some desperately so. God only knows how we will make it on a march.

24 January—We are still here, having heard nothing further about marching, but things are in absolute chaos, and we are practically on our own. Jerry has run out of German bread and there is no soup. We are 'subsisting' on only four German Knackebrot biscuits a day. These are brown, wafer-thin biscuits, and they are absolutely awful. They taste like thin boot leather and are hardly worth eating, but one must eat if one is to march out of here. I realise that I have no chance of returning to my mates at Blechhammer. I am now left to my own devices, and I will have to have a will of iron to survive.

25 January—The water supply was cut off early today and we are down to using melted snow. The situation is now extremely dire, and many men around me are already falling like flies due to sickness, disease and starvation. The Jerries are completely confused and utterly useless. This we do not need. For while we are full of hope for the end of the war, and to see the backs of these bastards, we are dependent upon them to keep us alive.

Then, we receive word that about 30 miles away from here, there are over 300 of our now desperately ill chaps lying out in the open, many with frostbite. I cannot imagine how they must be suffering. My heart is sick for them as the weather is the coldest I have ever experienced. How can any man survive in temperatures less than 32 degrees below zero, let alone men who have been prisoners of war for so long, men who are starved, men with no coats or boots? This is absolute insanity! And it certainly doesn't bode well for us when our time comes to leave.

29 January—Once again, hundreds of sick men arrive back here, and they are in an absolutely shocking condition. Many have severe frostbite with their extremities and even faces blackened and numb. As we have few medical supplies, little food (we are still only receiving four Knackebrot biscuits a day), no heating, and the water supply is still critical, there is little we can do to help them. I doubt if many will live. We do the best we can for them, but that is of little comfort to the poor chaps. We are all in a dire state here, and I doubt many of us can survive for long under these extreme conditions, never mind having to soon be on a march and face what these poor men have had to.

Two enormous explosions occur during the night, and we hear very heavy gunfire in the distance.

3 February—We have had no word of a move from here. Our rations are cut to three Knackebrot biscuits a day, and there is no water again. As suspected, many who returned here a few days prior have died, and many more are gravely ill. The place is like a mortuary with bodies piled up outside in the snow. No possibility of a funeral.

We can hear a great deal of activity all around us, sometimes to our east, but more so in a south-easterly direction, around the Carpathian Mountains. The Jerries are absolutely terrified, their faces as grey as the clouds above, and some of them verbalise their fears to us in regard to the Russian army making such a rapid advance. Of course, we ignore them. As if we give a damn about their welfare!

And then we hear rumours that the Ruskies have entered Auschwitz, of which my old camp at Blechhammer was a sub-camp. I pray that it's true and my pals have been liberated. With this news, those of us who have not quite stepped over death's doorstep are staying hopeful and trying to keep in good spirits, despite our stomachs begging for more food.

4 February—A thaw set in early and the weather became a lot milder, which will make our eventual march less arduous. We received no rations of biscuits at all but, at the time of writing, this evening, each man receives three ounces of flour, which is about a small cupful, and at least the water is now trickling in.

A large fire can be seen in the distance tonight which lights up the sky.

5 February—All day long there has been very heavy fighting to our north, around Breslau, and this evening, as I write, it is still going on to our south-east. We have been given no food whatsoever.

All through the night very heavy gunfire continues with many explosions.

6 February—Thank God, today we are each finally issued with a third of a Red Cross parcel. From where the parcels came we have no idea.

This afternoon, Russian fighter planes fly very low over our camp, and we hear they have been machine-gunning the roads. The Jerries are in a right state, and rumour has it that we are on the brink of being rescued. We are all so tired. More men are dying, many of us now seriously ailing, and all are starving. But we remain relentless in our determination to soon see our long-awaited victory.

11 February—Yesterday it was, and today it still is, comparatively quiet with hardly any noise of gunfire. The Germans here say the Russians have been pushed back about 15 miles, but we don't believe it. The Jerries are certainly very skittish. We note they are sparse in number. Then, about 80 of our former German guards arrive back this afternoon from Gorlitz in Germany. Rumour has it that's where they took some of our chaps who left here some three weeks past, but the Jerries won't confirm it and we still don't know why.

12 February—We receive an issue of bread today—eight men to a loaf—and we are now getting a small quantity of water every day from a well which has been fitted with a hand pump. Having had no food since our piecemeal Red Cross parcel days ago, this is hardly enough to eat.

We are often getting Russian fighter planes strafing the aerodrome, but Jerry seems to be able to deal with them pretty easily.

The skies open this afternoon, and rain falls in bucketloads.

14 February—At dawn we wake to a terrific barrage which continues all day. We had nothing to eat yesterday, and our stomachs growl louder than the sound of gunfire surrounding us.

We hear via the BBC news on a secret wireless set that many of the camps have been liberated. This includes our camp—Stalag 344, Lamsdorf—but as we are still here the news is received with much cynicism. If only. Pray to God we are soon to be freed as many of our men are close to death. The Russian planes return, but finish with the aerodrome after a good half-hour of giving us their full force.

Once again, we retire for the night on achingly empty stomachs.

15 February—It is quiet again today and, when we plead for food, we are told that the bread has completely run out. This is our third day without anything at all to eat, and the starvation is hard to manage. All we can do is lie around, and it's just as well we're not marching as we haven't the energy, and plenty of rain these last few days is making the ground a complete quagmire.

It seems by the news that the chaps who left here for Gorlitz will be liberated before us, yet they are 150 miles to the north-west of us. On the other hand, they may be on the march again. It is hard to know what to believe and where the Russians actually are.

I'm told that the British officers in charge here wrote a letter to the Protecting Power a while ago with regard to our position, advising that they had applied to the German authorities to have us moved as we are in a danger zone, but nothing was actioned. However, we assume that the Protecting Power has now had results, as the Germans today say they will move us soon if they can get the necessary transport to take us to the railways, because it is now too perilous to march due to the constant attacks by the Russians.

18 February—This morning our officer-in-charge issues orders with regard to a move later today if the transport should come, and this afternoon we are advised that the camp is now being made ready. We have only had two Knackebrot biscuits a day for the past three days.

19 February—It is now evening as I write. We men are very disappointed as there has been no sign of transportation. It seems to be a case of 'so near but yet so far'. We know that many camps have been liberated, but the sector where we are situated seems to be at a standstill. The Russian planes keep coming over and doing a little bombing or strafing. If we are to be moved by rail, which appears to be the plan, it will be pretty dangerous as the railways are regularly being bombed.

The only good news is that the weather is clearing and temperatures are rising slightly.

20 February—Two thousand men leave here today and are to travel by train. This afternoon various blocks are detailed to move off at 7:00 am tomorrow by train to a destination supposedly somewhere in Bavaria. My block is not one of them, and I wonder if this is a good thing due to the danger of trains being easy targets for the Ruskies. Still, we cannot just stay here and starve to death, which will soon become the case as we are now only eating one biscuit a day.

21 February—Gunfire starts early this morning, although it is not close by. Later in the morning, more blocks of men leave, after which the noise gets nearer. Then all through the night quite a battle rages, and it's so loud it seems as if it is right outside our camp.

22 February—We wake to complete silence. Then the weather starts to deteriorate and, as the day wears on, the rain becomes torrential and the roads get in a terrible mess.

This afternoon we get word that the 2000 men who left two days ago were stopped by the Gestapo at Neisse and were made to alight the train and march. Many negative rumours regarding their fate are flying around, but none have been confirmed at the time of writing; however, it is to be hoped they are false.

The good news is that we are receiving bread again, if only in meagre portions.

23 February—We have just heard that Turkey has declared war on Germany. Another country joining in to fight Jerry. Then we hear that Posen has fallen to the Russians, and we hope that Breslau will soon fall as it will certainly liven up this sector.

25 February—The guns start up once again in our vicinity this night. They are very loud and near, and we can distinctly hear machine guns. It is a terrible night, blowing a gale, and tons of rain falls as we wait for an outcome. I hear men whispering prayers throughout the ghostly night, myself included. All of us hoping that we will survive this.

26 February—We wake to find the gunfire has abated somewhat, but we can still hear it to our west.

We hear that Egypt has also declared war on Germany, and the Jerry guards are in a state of disbelief. Our blokes are in high glee at this news, but we must be careful not to show it, as the Jerries are looking for any excuse to release their frustration.

This afternoon, as I am writing, the guns are getting louder again. The weather is still bad, and the guns continue all through the night. We are going crazy waiting for news of our departure.

27 February—A number of German doctors come into the camp today and start an examination of all the men for the purpose of seeing who is fit to march and who is to travel by train. It appears they have changed their minds about all of us going by train, and it could be very possible that the Gestapo are stopping all trains. I wonder how many of us are going to survive, myself included. For I'm sure I will have to travel by train as I'm not in a good state of health at all, and another long march across the wilds of Poland will surely kill me. Even though it was nearly five years ago, thoughts of the horrific march towards Poland still haunt me. Still, by train or by foot, I just want to hit the road—the long road back to my loved ones.

CHAPTER 15

GERMANS IN RETREAT

1945

Upper Silesia to Austria

2 March—Fifteen hundred of us men finally leave Camp Lamsdorf this morning. As all of us are sick, we are to travel by rail. We are told by Jerry that we will be travelling 30 men in a rail carriage, and each carriage will have a stove in it, but when we arrive at the station, we find there are 42 men to a carriage, no stove but plenty of dirty straw. This is so reminiscent of the nightmarish journey to Poland that I feel I could vomit. Five long years, and here I am doing it all over again. At least I'm comforted by the thought that I am heading in the opposite direction away from the hellish places in which I've been forced to live during this endless war.

The train doors are locked, and off we go about midday. We travel to Neisse in Lower Silesia where we have our first stop, and we are allowed to get out of the carriages for a short time. We receive a loaf of bread per man which we are told must last us the journey. We then travel to Czechoslovakia and stop at Prague, which is a wonderful city—a treat for anyone's eyes—although we can see that the city has been knocked about quite a bit by air raids. We are not allowed out of the carriages.

Then we travel on to Germany and stop at Munich. It is here that we hear Jerries shouting and arguing amongst themselves on the station platform. Some of our men get off the train, but no one from my carriage is ordered to alight.

3 March—It is late in the afternoon on this our second day of travel and we are now having a job with water. The tub they provided for excreta is overflowing, and along with the stench of rotting human flesh from festering wounds and sickness, and the acrid fumes of unwashed bodies, mine among them, these conditions are practically unbearable. Many men are now lying around in disgraceful states, covered in their own excreta, some barely alive, and a few I'm sad to say are dying around me. No doubt it is the case in other carriages.

We travel on to Bavaria where we again stop. Once again, there's a lot of shouting and more of our men are ordered out of other carriages and are marched off to who knows where.

4 March—It is our third day of travel and they finally let us out of the putrid train carriages for 10 minutes while they search the carriages for the dead. I'm not sure where we are. We run out into a field and manage to scramble around and get some drinking water before we are herded back into the carriages again with the aid of rifle butts and kicks.

The next stop is Regensburg. This place has got an awful bashing, and at night we hear our planes going over. Something is going on, because we seem to have travelled in a loop since arriving in Germany, and at each station men have been ordered off the train and marched away.

We then travel into Austria and we stop at Salzburg, but no one is allowed out. We head off again to Wels, where we also stop and once again we are not let out.

We arrive at Linz and again we stop. Linz is another place that has been given some attention by our air force and is terrible to see. Streets are flattened, the station is in a complete mess, and a Red Cross train has caught it bad. We wait, all of us now in an appalling condition. We are starving, and one's mind simply begs to be let out of the squalor. But no. We take off again and narrowly miss another air raid on Linz.

Stalag XVII-B, Krems, Austria
7 March—We eventually arrive at a place called Krems in Austria. This has been a terrible six days, all of us ill, and we have only been allowed out twice. The weather is bad and snowing practically all the

time. When we are finally allowed out of our carriage, we notice there are much fewer of us now. Some have died, but we find out that the reason this journey has taken so long is that we have dropped off men at different places throughout Germany. We have been travelling in a circle trying to get camps to take them.

We're marched to a stalag, about 3 miles north of Krems. It's a huge place and we are later told that it holds around 15,000 men, only 200 of whom are British prisoners of war. The rest are Serbians, Russians, Poles, Greeks, Bulgarians and French.

On our arrival the few hundred of us who are left from the 1500 who started this journey are crammed into two small huts with no bedding. There is no heating whatsoever, and the water, of which there is no hot, is of a shocking quality and in very poor supply. We are advised that the water is turned on only three times during the day for two hours at a time and, with that, we are left for the night. No food, no water. Because we cannot get any drinking water, we have to be content with drinking melted snow. We then collapse on the hard floor, squashed together in our putridity and attempting to sleep.

8 March—This morning we are marched out to bathe and get fumigated. We are very fearful, our thoughts on Heaven Camp for Jews, which we now know with certainty contained extermination chambers. After standing to attention for about four hours we are told that there is no water available and we have to go back to our cramped huts. Then, at about 3:00 pm, 200 men are ordered back to the bathhouse while the rest of us are told to be ready in two hours. At 5:00 pm we are told to be ready at 7:00 pm. Then we are told that the water is off again and there will no bath, and also no fumigation until the following day. But at 11:00 pm we are ordered out again, and this time we are on the move.

The first thing that happens is we have all of our hair shaved off. Then we are doused in cold water in large baths and marched naked to a room which is about 30 feet by 100 feet. We stand there, packed together like matches in a box, our naked, malnourished bodies just as thin as matches and freezing cold, until in the early hours of the morning, about 2:00 am, when the first batch of clothing is thrown in. This continues until all of us are finally clothed in threadbare outfits. It is 8:00 am the following morning before we are marched back to a new hut. This hut is larger than the last one, which was practically standing room only, but there are nearly 500 men among us and bedding for only about 200, so the rest of us have to sleep on the floor, me included.

I soon learn that there is also a compound of about 5000 American soldiers at this stalag; they are near us but wired off and kept under strict segregation. We are told that the Yanks get food parcels every six weeks, but we will not get any and we are to subsist on only a small loaf of bread between eight men per day.

I am happy to come across a Geordie pal of mine named Jack Ritchie, and we have a good old crack about our beloved homeland. The news he offers regarding the war is very positive, and he tells me that there's been a massive bombing of Germany by thousands of Allied bombers and that many more European countries are now declaring war on Germany. Ritchie and I believe it's only a matter of time before we are liberated from this plague-ridden hellhole.

18 March—I have been settled in our new camp for nearly two weeks now, although 'settled' is hardly the word for it. This camp is the worst I have ever experienced and I'm told that is also the description given by the Protecting Power. The place is alive with bugs, and many of the chaps who were delighted to have found beds for themselves discover very quickly that they are infested with the little creatures. So nearly all of us are now sleeping on the floor. Although we are getting a small cup of soup a day, it is terrible, and contains very little substance. We have complained, but it seems to be to no avail. Not being a British-dominated camp, the French seem to hold all the sway. And very much like it was back when I started on the Nightmare March five years ago, the Frogs are well dressed and have plenty of food parcels. We Brits look a pathetic bunch in comparison, and the only people who seem to be in the same boat are the Russians. The Krauts despise the Ruskies because their troops are advancing daily. It is rumoured that the Americans have offered to let us take some of their supplies, bless them, but the Germans will not allow it.

There is a barracks next to ours and at night it is a proper bazaar with all nationalities collecting there to barter. I was in it the other night with my pal Ritchie when the lights suddenly went out, and there was a terrible scramble of bodies in the dark and plenty of shouting. When the lights came on again, there were many free-for-all fights on account of stuff being stolen, and razors and knives were used freely. Ritchie and I made ourselves scarce, but I later heard that that this 'turning off the lights' business is a regular occurrence and an organised affair.

We sick men have been put on an invalid diet but it is appalling and meagre, and now news has just come in that the rations are to be cut further next week. That seems impossible as they are practically non-existent as it is.

We are subjected to harsh barracks inspections, the Germans confiscating anything they can. The bastards appear particularly focused on our personal items—diaries, letters and photographs—so I am careful to hide mine well, and so far, so good.

Every day now we see large formations of planes going over. We are situated right on the River Danube, so I imagine we are an easy target.

When it is discovered that I'm a musician, I am invited to play the piano for the camp orchestra. Despite not feeling at all well, I jump at the chance, and head off to my first rehearsal to take a look and have a tinkle on the old keys. I cannot wait to play and hear music again. It's been so long since I've played any instrument, and it will take my mind off my ailing stomach.

When I arrive, I find it is a 16-piece band, consisting of all nationalities, but mostly French. The music of the camp is looked after by a Frenchman, who is a Parisian professor. I find that the band is pretty good, but what surprises me is that the professor does not get the boys properly in time. I'm itching to take over, but although the professor is quite a decent chap I find him to be very excitable and as highly strung as a new violin, so I think it best if I keep my mouth shut and simply play the piano.

The rations are now getting smaller each day, and things are getting even more desperate. I'm afraid that our two officers-in-charge are incapable of dealing with the situation. They seem to be too fearful of standing up to Jerry and, despite our constant pleas to do something, they prefer to turn a blind eye to our plight. We are all sick and need more sustenance, but that doesn't appear to matter to them.

There is no room at the hospital and many of us, myself included, are now in need of hospitalisation. I hear that there's a barracks vacant which has long been planned to be an extension of the hospital, but very poor progress is being made in getting it equipped for use. Then the invalid diet is stopped completely, and we stomach cases have to eat the terrible soup dished up by the Germans. I call a meeting of the men and am chosen to head a deputation of the stomach cases to see the captain, but I'm told not to expect much as a result. I go to see him and try to get him to press the Germans to get all the gastric cases X-rayed, but, once again, my pleas fall on deaf ears.

28 March—The news now coming in regarding the war seems to be bright, and the boys are quite excited about it and contemplating a finish to the war any day now. Japan is being bombed heavily by the Yanks, and the Germans are getting it from all sides.

About 30 of us gastric cases and a few surgical cases move into the hospital extension which has now been equipped. There seems to have been a pretty big wrangle to get it ready, because, once again, as was the situation in Camp Lamsdorf, when I arrive I find there are many patients in here who are not proven stomach cases and are simply here for the relative comfort and extra food.

30 March—Typhus has broken out around camp, which doesn't surprise me given the conditions here, and it will be hard for many to fight the disease.

A wagon and trailer arrive, and we all pray it contains Red Cross parcels for us, but we are wrong again; it's for the French. We Brits are practically living on the good news we're getting regarding the war. The latest news is that our boys and the Yanks have crossed the Rhine River, and the Russians have entered Austria, so they are bearing down on us from all sides, and I suppose it's just a matter of who gets here first.

Although I'm still very weak, I'm allowed out of hospital to play in the orchestra today. It's progressing very well despite our bandleader's odd temperament, and I'm pleased to say that we have plenty of rehearsals. I have now had the pleasure of playing at a series of concerts, which takes my mind off my state of health and starvation. I find that playing in an orchestra is a pleasant change from being in charge of one, even though the professor is still a bit of a hack in my humble opinion. It's also wonderful to be playing for fellow prisoners again, rather than entertaining Jerry, and it relieves the monotony for everyone, players and audience alike, although trying to work out how to kill the bed bugs that are still as active as ever appears to provide enough amusement for some.

1 April—The fact that it's April Fool's Day does not escape us when this afternoon we are required to attend a lecture given by our senior medical officer on—contraception. If he were a fraction as good at 'fighting' Jerry with his tongue, it would be better for us, rather than having to listen to this claptrap. It is a right old laugh. Farcical. Why in God's name do we need this advice given our current situation? The poor man stumbles through his hilarious presentation, his face the colour of beetroot due to the cheeky comments flying every which way, and I'm not certain who is more relieved when it's over—the captain or his audience!

2 April—It is now Easter Monday. We hear that there are over 2000 invalid parcels in store, but we cannot get any word out of Jerry as to when they will be distributed. We sick ones are practically getting no medical attention at all, and my stomach and my chest are suffering terribly.

There are in excess of 100 Allied bombs dropped over Krems today, and it takes the townspeople by surprise as this is the first time Krems has ever been bombed. From our camp, we have a perfect view and we can actually see the bombs leaving the planes without the slightest opposition from German anti-aircraft or fighter planes. At about the same time, we can hear more bombing in the distance, and about two hours later a flight of American 'Lightning' fighter planes come over. Now, at 4:00 pm, we can see great columns of smoke in about five places on the horizon. We later hear that 300 civilians and 100 soldiers were killed and many more injured.

3 April—The weather today is just like summer. Many Russian prisoners are leaving the camp, their destination unknown. The rations are still very poor, and many of us sick chaps are suffering from shocking hunger pains, yet the invalid parcels are still not distributed.

5 April—Today is about the worst for rations ever. It's four o'clock in the afternoon before we get a thimbleful of potato soup to eat. Then at five o'clock, we get a ninth of a loaf of bread. Many of the boys are becoming very ill due to the lack of food, and another deputation goes to see the captain but receives little sympathy. We would be well and truly riotous if we weren't so damn sick.

6 April—We have reached our limit, and our captain has quite a shock this morning when he arrives at the hospital barracks to be met by all us men and told a little more than the truth in soldiers' language. Only when the men develop a seriously threatening attitude does the captain climb down from his high horse before gingerly heading off to see the Jerry authorities. When he returns, he tells us that we are all to get an invalid parcel per man tomorrow. About blasted time.

7 April—We get our invalid parcels today, thank God.

I'm still playing in the band; it is absolutely necessary for my sanity.

Many French and Russian men are coming in from working parties and tell us that in Krems things are in proper disorder.

The state of affairs here is once again similar to that at Lamsdorf in so far as the Russian troops' advancement is concerned, and they are said to be coming towards us along the River Danube. Let's hope we have more luck this time and can be liberated soon so we can set out for home. We are aware that the Jerries are in a state of fear, and then we hear that they are burning all records. They have *much* to hide.

Rumour has it that we'll all be marched out of here soon. If we have to go on a march, this time we will have very little in our kits to carry, as almost everything we owned has been traded with the French and Serbs in return for food and smokes. We are then told that, as of today, potatoes have stopped being issued, which were the only vegetables our soup contained.

8 April—Today, Sunday, things are in a complete turmoil; the

Jerries start flying around in a right panic. Then the Americans who are in the caged compound near ours are warned to be ready to march very soon, and they start throwing clothing over the wire, and all nationalities scramble for it. It seems that the Yanks will be the first to march and the weather is now absolutely atrocious.

9 April—The Americans are ordered to march out straight away early this morning, and they do so. As they march past us, a Romanian who's watching is shot and badly wounded in the thigh by a German guard for being too near the wire.

We Brits are told we're to also leave here soon, but we have no idea where we are to march, or why, but there are many theories. One is that we are to be used as human shields, and another that we will provide bargaining power for the Jerries when they are surrounded by Allied forces. Another idea thrown around is that the Jerries have no more food and as many of us will die on the march they will be relieved of their burden of feeding us during their retreat. I have to say that none of the alternatives delights me too much.

This afternoon eight dead Russians are brought out of a hut opposite ours. They had died during the night, most likely from starvation and the freezing cold. Just when their own troops are so close by. What a tragedy.

A very bright glow in the sky can be seen from our barracks tonight. It is said to be an oil refinery going up in flames. With things being so hot around here, I wonder whether we sick ones will march out soon or whether we might be liberated by the Ruskies? The latter is not an option any of us like to think about as the Russians are an unknown force. The truth of it is we would prefer our own troops or the Yanks to liberate us, but in any event I'm hoping we will find out soon as this camp is evacuating fast. Like all the lads, I'm desperate to reach home.

CHAPTER 16

ANOTHER LONG MARCH

1945

Krems to Braunau, Austria

This morning, 10 April, we are ordered to evacuate the camp in groups of 500. All of us in the hospital barracks are in a bad shape. We are told that we will first be examined by the German medical officer but this is not done and my group start the march, a sick and sorry lot indeed. We have an invalid parcel each and our kits which, even though greatly reduced due to past bartering, are still a terrific weight for ill men like us to carry. We are accompanied by heavily armed Jerry guards, who make it perfectly clear that they intend to make it back to Germany—which we learn is to be our destination—with or without us.

We march up mountains, exceedingly tall mountains, and at night we sleep right on the top of one. Some men have not made it through this first day of marching and, just as the Jerries threatened, they have been left behind—or shot. A brutal reality indeed.

This night I am all in and feeling very unwell. I think back to the Nightmare March from France when I was captured nearly five years ago and wonder how I can have survived five years next month in captivity, only to be forced to face this awful ordeal once more. I will surely perish this time, and my guts are churning with despair at the thought of being so near yet so far from seeing my loved ones again.

I am mucking in with a Londoner, and a New Zealander named Rees, so pray to God we can keep each other alive.

11 April—I start off the day vomiting. We get no drinks from the Germans, and my purged stomach is screaming for water, but somehow, I manage to stay the distance, and I keep up the march alongside my new mates, until, finally, we sleep the night in a barn.

12 April—Only God knows how, but I find that I am a little better on this the third day of our march. However, we have to leave the Londoner in a village as he simply cannot carry on. It is either that or have him shot by the ever increasingly impatient Jerry guards. I trust that he will be well cared for by the locals who seem to be a good lot, and I have to cling to the hope that he will be liberated when our troops arrive.

We know our liberators are near and men who are able to do so are escaping all along the route. The Jerries appear to take no notice; fewer men to give rations to I assume, and it makes their retreat all the faster. But then we hear that the SS are swarming all around and are shooting to kill any escapees, and we realise that's why our guards are not too concerned with runaways. I pray for the men who have taken off; they are taking a terrible risk, but I understand their desperation, and if I weren't so ill I would probably have joined them.

It starts raining, but we struggle on. Well, some of us do—there's no need to elaborate on the fate of those who cannot—and we finally reach Muhldorf. Rees, the New Zealander, is now sick, and we are wringing wet through but we manage to get in a barn where we get four raw potatoes a man. I am keeping okay and even managing to provide some assistance to my ill friend.

Each day is a repetition of the last, only harder. Too many deaths by far. Some chaps who had escaped previously return to join up with us again and confirm reports of the SS who they say are running amok—stealing, destroying farms, evicting landowners and shooting prisoners. As a result, many refugees are now on the road with us.

16 April—On we march. We can hear bombing in the distance.

17 April—Today is the eighth day of our march. The weather now is fine and warm. We have been sleeping in barns since the second night. The civilians [Austrians] are very sympathetic to our plight, but unfortunately, they have very little food themselves otherwise I am sure they would give us anything they could.

The country is beautiful but climbing mountains and marching in this difficult terrain with our packs takes it out of us. This is despite our packs only containing our limited kits and the few tins of almost finished Horlicks, Bengers and Nestles condensed milk and other drinks that we had received in our invalid parcels, along with a blanket and overcoat. But I am keeping okay and if I can get enough food I think I can go on for a long time yet. I have had a job keeping Rees going since he fell ill, but I managed to get his pack on a German wagon and I have been like a wet nurse looking after him and doing the little cooking there is to do. Luckily, wood to make fires is plentiful, and I am pleased to say that at the time of writing Rees seems to have come good. We have now just passed through Grein and we're having a short break.

All the villages we have passed through are lovely little places. We're keeping in good spirits and sing going through the villages. No matter how tired we are we remain in unison. For once, I'm not leading this singsong, and I'm grateful to the boys for keeping me going with music. It's balm to my aching soul.

I'm told that we are now about 35 miles from Linz.

18 April—Today will be a day to be remembered. It rains like hell and we struggle on like drowned rats although we do manage to pinch a few spuds from the fields along the way. Finally, we stop for the night in a barn, drenched through. We get the same thing to eat we do every night: a small cup of thin watery soup along with four Knackebrot biscuits. Our invalid parcels are just about finished. I strip off everything and attempt to sleep under the straw despite the cold.

19 April—My clothes are still wet this morning but they soon dry on me as I walk in woefully wet and broken boots. We pass through Naarn and arrive at a strafe camp which is full of all nationalities. I believe the work here is mining granite. Every man has his head shaved down the centre. We are ordered to remove our caps to be examined and treated for head lice before we are allowed to stay the night.

20 April—This morning those of us who are able to do so start off towards the town of Linz. Some men we have to leave behind and my heart aches for the poor blighters.

We just get into the Linz suburbs when the air-raid alarm goes off about 11:00 am, but we march on for another half an hour until we come to a halt between the main road and the railway, and more planes pass overhead. We're out in the open like sitting ducks and are told by the guards that if anyone moves they will shoot to kill. The guards are sheltering nearby, watching over us like bloodthirsty wolves, either hoping we'll take a direct hit from above or waiting for any excuse to pounce—and kill—but luckily the planes continue on with no bombs dropped.

We start off again at 1:00 pm and reach Linz, which is in a terrible condition. It is practically in ruins, nothing but rubble and twisted metal, and hardly a building standing. We are just going over a bridge across the River Danube when the air-raid siren goes off once more and once again we are lucky and there's no raid. We carry on for 10 more miles and sleep the night in a barn.

21 April—We begin our twelfth day of marching when five Red Cross lorries pass us on the road but, despite our shouts for food, they don't stop, and we march on for roughly four miles before halting for a day's rest.

As I write, I can hear our planes bombing further down the Danube. Then, I hear men shouting and see them jumping up and down, wildly waving their arms around, and I look in the direction they're facing to see two more Red Cross lorries coming towards us. Thankfully they hear us this time and they stop, and we receive two French Red Cross parcels each man. These are not very good parcels, having no milk or butter in them, but regardless everyone is very happy to have some food again and God bless the Red Cross.

23 April—It started teeming down yesterday and it is still raining today. We're wringing wet and marching up to our knees in mud, making it hard going.

25 April—Today is our rest day. For the last three days we have had a very rough time of it. Men have been collapsing all along the route and have been left to face their fate. I'm ashamed to say that we simply have to accept the situation. It is a matter of survival of the sturdiest, and if one stops to assist a man who has dropped one is shot. The weather has not helped those of us who remain upright with continuous rain causing thick mud. My boots have completely fallen apart, and I have had to tie them together with rope. My feet are constantly wet.

However, now, at the time of writing, the sun has come out and, although quite chilly, it's pleasant enough and I decide to remove my saturated boots in the hope that they will dry out a little. It is a risk and something we rarely do during long marches for fear of not getting the boots back on again due to feet swelling, but I simply must remove them. When I do so, I see that my feet are an abomination, as are everyone's, and I am shocked at the sight. They immediately start to swell up. Realising my folly, I immediately force my feet back into the wet boots and, thank God, I manage to get them back on.

26 April—Nothing of any great importance happens today, other than another gruelling day of marching and air raids. We must have marched nearly 25 miles and we are all dead beat when we land at a barn. My stomach has been giving me hell, but I'm determined not to give in as the German officers in charge of our party are very inefficient and disinterested in the sick, and I know only too well what my fate will be. We can all starve to death as far as they're concerned, and many among us are not far off granting them their wish.

27 April—We start off about 10:00 am. We are nearing our destination, which we have finally learnt is just past Braunau, here in Austria. Braunau is Hitler's birthplace, or so the Jerry guards boastfully tell us, as if we're in the slightest bit interested. To a man, we ignore them, keeping our thoughts to ourselves of what we'd like to do to bloody Hitler if we had half the chance.

I'm writing during our midday halt. We are about 8 miles from Braunau, but we have just received word that we're only going another few miles today and then on to our destination tomorrow. I believe the Americans have broken through in our sector and have taken Passau, which is only about 30 miles north of here. On hearing this, the Jerry guards become very flustered and a complete state of disarray ensues—shouting and a frantic waving of arms. No one seems to be in command. They start pointing every which way, and an argument breaks out as to which direction we will continue to march. Some of our chaps say that we will soon be marching on our own, and there are more than a few laughs about this.

We recommence our journey. I continue to place one painful foot in front of the other, compose music in my head, and try to concentrate on the scenery. I have noticed on the march through Austria that there are a great number of shrines at almost every road end. Many of them are kept in very good condition, but I have not seen one actually being used during our 18-day march. No doubt the locals are avoiding the Germans.

We arrive at another barn for the night and I just finish writing when a Red Cross lorry pulls up. We are given a food parcel between four men and soon discover they are Indian food parcels supplied by the Indian Red Cross. There is no meat or cigs in these parcels but lots of spices! Still, they are gratefully received nonetheless, as we have not received anything from the German guards for days now.

28 April—Nothing of importance to report today, only another long, arduous march.

29 April—We start our twentieth day of marching in the pouring rain and it continues all day. We pass through Braunau, and then we find we are lost.

The Germans lose control altogether; some march away by themselves to the nearest lager, only to come back. One wonders who is leading who? Still unable to reach an agreement, they break up our party of men and lead us in different directions. I am left with about 40 men and we are now out in an open area with no cover at all. We march back again for a couple of miles and enter a forest where we find a barn to stay the night. We're all wringing wet, we have had no German rations for a long time, and we have had to survive on only the quarter of the Indian Red Cross parcel we got two days ago.

Braunau, Austria
30 April—We are still at the barn, surrounded by forest. I'm

feeling very unwell. The 20-day march has been absolutely punishing. Many, many men have not made it, and I cannot believe that I'm not one of those to have been left behind or shot. We have marched approximately 175 miles, in a westerly direction from Krems to Braunau. I have recorded many of the places we passed through on the march, which are:

KREMS, STIXENDORF, MAIGEN, LOBENDORF, MUHLDORF, TRANDORF, HEILIGENBLUT, LOIBERSDORF, POGGSTALL, OSTRONG, YSPERTAL, SANKT OSWALD, GREIN, KLAM, BAUMGARTENBERG, MITTERKIRCHEN, NAARN, NEIDERZIRKING, MAUTHAUSEN, LANGENSTEIN, STEYREGG, LINZ, WILHERING, ALKOVEN, FRAHAM, POTTING, NEUMARKT, TAISCHKIRCHEN, ANDRICHSFURT, MEHRNBACH, ZIMETSBERG, LANGDORF, MAIRING, RANZING, GURTEN, GEINBERG, ALTHEIM, MINING, SANKT PETER, BRAUNAU.

This afternoon the Jerry guards erupt into a state of heightened panic when they learn that the Yanks are very close by us. They simply don't know what to do or where to go. I, for one, find it highly amusing to see these once-arrogant men at a complete loss. They have no orders to follow and it appears they are incapable of making any decisions. However, the fact that they have no food and we are starving is far from amusing. It is starting to snow.

1 May—The guards' faces are as pale as the snow outside. Surely it must be sinking in that all is now lost? I have not an ounce of sympathy for the bastards after what I've seen in this bloody war of the consequences of German cruelty: deprivation, death, suicide and insanity. I would laugh and spit at the guards if I had the strength. Thank God it is nearly all over, and may we never see another world war again.

2 May—We awaken to find there has been a very heavy fall of snow overnight. We are still at the barn near Braunau where we stopped two days ago. Braunau, it is just announced, has fallen. It is across the other side of the River Danube and we are waiting impatiently to see if the Yanks cross the river and release us.

Yesterday there was, and today there still is, a lot of artillery action very near to us. In fact, during the night some shells landed very near the barn.

Though some of our Jerry guards are still with us, and I believe they have the choice of going or staying, they remain at a loss as to what to do. They sit in a huddle, whispering and wailing, discussing their options from all angles. We couldn't care less. We are beyond hungry and some of us, myself included, are now so ill we couldn't march another step if we were threatened to do so at gunpoint.

As I write this diary entry it occurs to me that I've been five years in capture at the end of this month and I'm still not in the clear. I lie here in semi-darkness feeling awfully sick and waiting for freedom. There are no German rations left now, not even for Jerry. A few of our stronger chaps have been going out on their own, pleading with the farm folk for eggs, potatoes and anything else they can get, but now this has been stopped on account of some British chaps being found beaten up by the SS. The bastards are all around us and they are a marauding pack of trigger-happy sadists.

3 May—We wake to be told by Captain Kay, one of our medical officers who arrives at our barn, that we are no longer prisoners of war. He has been scouting the area for his men and tells us that the 3rd American Army has passed us by. Their infantry has crossed over the river, but until bombed bridges are rebuilt, he assumes that no transport can get over to assist us, the desperately sick and infirm. When we are told that we will have to provide for ourselves for perhaps another 24 to 48 hours, I wonder how we can do so? I see that our German guards have left us, fleeing into the night. We have no food and no means by which to obtain any. I am so very weak and my stomach is giving me hell, but I have no choice but to get down to it to try and get some more sleep and pray that we are rescued—soon.

4 May—I wake shivering with cold and see that heavy snow has covered everything outside. The ghostly trees are veiled in it, the ground a thick carpet of white, and inside the barn I can see no movement, only the huddled shapes of men lying around. It's hard to tell if they are sleeping or dead but, regardless, I honestly don't have the strength to assist anyone and, even if I could do so, I have no food to offer. There's no sound of gunfire, no Jerry guards and no chatter. I realise that I have never woken to this—the sound of complete silence—in nearly six long years. It is an eerie feeling and I have no choice but to remain still and try to sleep in an attempt to mask the gnawing hunger, which is only overridden by the chest and stomach pains now racking my body.

Now I can hear the rain teeming down. It becomes a constant drone in the background as my mind starts to wander in and out of sensibility, and a feeling of utter hopelessness settles over me like the shroud I fear it may become.

The night that ensues is a terrible one. I can hear only the slightest of rustling of men, an occasional groan escaping from lips obviously in deep trouble. Visions of my dear wife's face blur in and out of focus as I try to hold onto my own life.

Where are the Yanks?

5 May—This evening will be etched in my mind forever. An Australian, who says his name is Duffey, rouses me out of my stupor. I don't know where he came from, but I can see by the expression on his face that he realises I am in a terrible state, and he gives me some much-needed water and stays by my side. Then, at around 4:00 am the next morning, he encourages me to accompany him out in the forest to forage for food. 'C'mon, cobber,' he says in his strange singsong accent, 'you need to get up and shake a leg.'

I know not how I do it, but I manage the task and it turns out to be quite an experience, despite the risk of being shot by the SS. Duffey thinks they may have fled the area. I hope he's correct.

Not far from our barn the Aussie finds a sword and I find a revolver, both Nazi weapons, and I shudder when I realise just how close the SS were to finding us. We manage to get quite a bit of food, but the highlight for me comes when, all of a sudden, I see a duck darting out in front of my new mate, and the Aussie kills it by taking its head off with one swift swipe of his sword. He grabs the headless bird with a loud 'Gotcha!' and we return with the rest of our supplies to the barn where I collapse into my bed of hay again while Duffey begins preparing a right royal feast for everyone.

I can now smell the duck cooking; the mouth-watering aromas reach my nostrils and cause my mouth to salivate. Duffey beckons men to come and eat, and those who cannot do so he feeds like babies. Needless to say, I enjoy the duck and accompaniments immensely, as does everyone, and we all thank the Aussie profusely for cooking the food. Unfortunately, most of us bring up our food shortly after gobbling it down—a side effect of starvation. Still, day after day, Duffey goes back out to find more food for us, and each time we take it a bit easier when eating.

CHAPTER 17

IT'S OVER

Liberation

8 May—Today is a day I shall forever remember. Some Yanks arrive in the morning and tell us that it's VE Day [Victory in Europe Day]. Oh, how long I have waited to hear this news. This description makes me weep tears of happiness and I blubber like a baby. Their long-awaited words are music to my ears. I have survived this war!

We're told we're to be moved by lorries, along with other survivors, to a factory in Braunau where more Yanks are waiting for us to be brought in.

At 10:00 pm, a very sore and sorry lot indeed, we're taken to Pocking Air Field, where we sleep the night on the aerodrome on concrete, expecting to fly the following morning.

9 May—We are terribly disappointed to find that we're not flying back to Blighty today, as only the Americans are scheduled to fly out, but we are assured it will be tomorrow. We watch on longingly as the Yanks take off, but there's a bonus as we're able to sleep in the Yanks' billets, and we're delighted at the level of comfort awaiting us when we arrive at the huts nearby. Four of us share a little room and we muck in well together. There's a South African, a New Zealander, the Australian Duffey—my nursemaid, who is still looking after me and offering his hilarious jokes which have us all in stitches of laughter—and myself.

10 May—There are not sufficient planes to take us today.

11 May—No planes arrive at all today, but we have to learn patience, and we remind each other that we are now free men. There's always time for a good crack with the other fellows now amassing around the place, and news comes in thick and fast.

We learn that the Nazi Party is no longer. Hitler is dead by his own hand. Praise be! He was trapped by the Ruskies in his place of hiding in Berlin, an underground bunker where he'd been since January this year and killed himself and his new missus before they could reach them. Goebbels, his wife and six children also committed suicide the day after Hitler. Apparently, the Nazis made a pact to do such a thing if they were to lose this war—death by cyanide capsules. Weak bastards they are. After what we prisoners have seen, they need to be made accountable. It also appears that Hitler's mate Mussolini met with his death at the hands of Italian partisans. At least we still have General Goering, who was captured by the Yanks a few days ago, so I guess he won't be elevated to the next Fuhrer after all! And Amen to that, I say.

We are once again assured that our planes will arrive tomorrow.

12 May—This morning Duffey and I are ordered to different sections to await the arrival of our respective planes. I embrace the Aussie and thank him for all he's done for me. I fear I shall never see him again, but I shall be forever in his debt. Duffey pats me on the back, breaks free of my grasp and drawls in his lyrical accent, 'No worries, mate. Now, off you go to Limey Land. You get back into life, back to playing your music, and back to that good lookin' missus of yours, eh?'

He walks away, stalls and turns to face to me, his eyes glinting with what I believe are tears, as he offers his final words. 'Til we meet again in heaven, cobber.'

I am now writing aboard an impressive transport plane, the C-47, which we have nicknamed the Moon Sucking Rocket. I have a platoon of 52 men alongside. We had a hell of a rush to board as the planes arrived earlier than expected. I believe our destination is Reims in France, and then ... on to Blighty—and my darling wife and our girls.

This will be my final war diary entry. It's over.

CHAPTER 18

BLIGHTY!

May 1945

France to Britain

The war might have been over, but our army days were not it seemed. We were still enlisted men. I can guarantee that this thought had not occurred to any of us ex-POWs after liberation; all we could think of was getting home. We were soon to be met with a harsh reality.

At Reims, France, we lined up and got fumigated front and back with a flit gun before 24 men at a time boarded a Lancaster bomber, one of many such planes arranged to evacuate ex-prisoners of war out of Europe in accordance with Operation Exodus. The look of pity on the faces of the crew spoke volumes. We were a bedraggled bunch: our filthy 'uniforms' a mixture of clothing and nationalities; our footwear, if we had any, was more often than not mismatched and clogs or worn-out boots. Our bodies were the only thing in unison—each wasted away to skin and bone.

Like that of every other chap on that plane, my heart was bursting with pure joy when I first caught sight of my country's coastline, particularly when the pilot flew over the white cliffs of Dover, which found us breaking into Vera Lynn's song of the same name. The crew had trouble restraining us as there were limited viewing positions in a Lancaster bomber!

When we landed, you cannot imagine our elation as we took our first step on our beloved soil, or aerodrome, I should say. I fell to my knees and kissed the ground, unabashed tears of emotion rolling down my cheeks, and I was not alone on that score.

The first thing that happened on our arrival was that we were taken to a reception and receiving centre in Southern England and given a cup of tea and biscuits, which were served by delightful young ladies from the Women's Auxiliary Air Force. Only a Brit could understand what that first cup of tea tasted like after five years without one, but any ex-prisoner of war of any nationality would have appreciated the experience of conversing with real women who spoke in gentle voices in their native tongue. Then came hot showers, shaves and clean clothing. Heaven. Feeling refreshed, we got free telegrams to send home, simply stating: *Arrived Safely, See You Soon.*

Then we got down to business. There was an exceedingly lengthy 'Prisoner of War Liberation Questionnaire' to fill out, many questions of which were too difficult to answer, given our state of minds in terms of memory.

Then came the medical examinations. Men who were deemed medically fit were granted leave, after which they would have to return for repatriation and await their demobilisation papers. Those who did not pass the medical had to go straight to a repatriation centre, one of many arranged by the War Office, in order to undergo the healing and reassimilation process. I was in the latter group.

I was placed in a military hospital at the repatriation centre. Some men couldn't accept it—having to go through this rehabilitation 'process' and they took off. To be honest I don't know what became of them, but I do know that those who were caught in the act faced disciplinary action. I couldn't blame them for escaping or trying to; we were wild animals in an unlocked cage, but I had to accept the process as I was in no condition to run.

Imagine my shock when I finally made contact with home only to be told that Mabel was too ill to visit me. The wife was in hospital herself with heart problems. This did not help my unsettled nerves but upon hearing that she was on her way to recovering, I resigned myself to doing the same, and I endured many weeks of being poked and prodded by doctors and put on treatment. I won't complain, because many men had to undergo operations in an attempt to remove old shrapnel and, much worse, to rectify the speedy hack jobs that had been carried out under perilous war conditions by questionable regimental aid personnel like me.

We had to attend lectures to prepare us for our 'assimilation' back into society. We had to learn what we could expect on our return to our loved ones. How society had changed while we'd been caged up behind barbed wire. What our wives and children had been going through in our absence. How women's roles had changed as a result of the war. How they dressed in new fashions and something about them having become independent, which was not something we boys particularly liked to hear. What our womenfolk knew of our lives during war. How our children might not recognise us. How they might resent our authority when we returned to our role of father figure, and how we were to deal with that.

Technical experts were brought in to talk about new types of industry and gadgets and to discuss 'modern life' as they called it. We were updated on the economy and how we would find employment again, and we were given all sorts of advice on our future career paths or, for some, pension plans. On and on it went until I, like most of the chaps, just sat blank-eyed through these lectures. We sighed and rolled our eyes at each other, giving a wink here and a conspiratorial whisper there. Our lives and wives would be just fine, thank you very much. Just let us get home to them, and we'll show you.

Of course, I am referring to those of us who hadn't been seriously affected mentally. There were some at the repat centre who were in terribly poor states of mind. The severe cases were kept in a compound for the insane. I didn't like their chances of ever returning to normal life, and I shuddered to think what the authorities were going to do with them. You see, it wasn't the thing to do back then to send a notice home during wartime saying 'I'm sorry to inform you that your father/husband/son has gone completely barmy.' Families were simply informed that their loved ones were prisoners of war and in an unknown state of health or told that their men were receiving hospital treatment as a result of unspecified injuries, when in fact they were suffering from serious shell shock, mental breakdown or lunacy as a result of hardship and torture. And although our troops had managed to get some men suffering from shell shock back to Blighty for treatment during the early part of the war, many were not so lucky and were taken prisoner only to have to endure further torment.

Besides mental afflictions, there were those at the reception centre who were physically maimed. Men with blindness, deafness, missing limbs, scarred and fire-ravaged bodies were in abundance. And then there were the ones who were disfigured facially. Oh, they were the hardest to look at and, of course, the poor chaps worried what their wives and girlfriends would think of them. Some had even decided not to return home at all, and various madcap schemes to disappear into the abyss when they got out of repatriation were underway, despite the doctors trying to persuade them otherwise.

To be fair, our doctors and officers in charge had a lot to contend with and they did their best, I suppose. We even got lectures on sexual health and contraception, and I laughed at this, remembering the time when our poor old captain had given a lecture on contraception in Camp Krems on April Fool's Day earlier that year. I don't think the chap ever forgave us for our lewd comments, which continued long after his lecture had ended.

At the end of May 1945, we heard that Heinrich Himmler had also committed suicide via a cyanide capsule. This incensed us all, as we recalled his many monstrous actions during the war, particularly towards the Jews. We were only now beginning to learn of the truly sadistic treatment of the Jews who were so savagely targeted by a crazed leader and his elite group of madmen. With so many others in the upper echelon of the Nazi Party dead by their own hands, we had all been looking forward to Heinrich Himmler having his day in court—and what a day that would have been. Not to mention how he would have been made to suffer in prison. But Himmler had taken the coward's way out. My heart wept for humanity.

And then we heard about what the Yanks had been up to in Blighty during our absence, and it was at this point that some of the lads completely lost their heads, particularly the younger chaps. It appeared that old GI Joe had been spreading more than just good cheer around our country since the Yanks had arrived on the scene in 1942. They had enticed our women with their new dance moves, candy, sodas, chewing gum, cigarettes and nylons; and their salaries being more than five times than the likes of us, British soldiers, they'd had plenty to splash around. We were told that we had lost tens of thousands of our women to the Yanks: War Brides, they called them—GI Joe War Brides.

This did not go down at all well with us chaps. It was exceedingly demoralising to think that our women had been playing up with the Yanks while we were away fighting for them or locked up dreaming of them. Some chaps received 'Dear John' letters while they were in repatriation. We renamed them 'Dear Joe' letters if a Yank was involved. That was hard to witness. Seeing the poor lads struggling to improve their health only to be told that no one would be waiting for them on their return home. No, it wasn't easy to stomach, although while I sympathised with those lads who'd been so heartlessly discarded, I wasn't overly worried about the wife. I knew my Mabel was a loyal wife and, besides, I think she would have agreed that, being in her forties, she was past the age of getting all heated up over another man. But I still felt slightly uncomfortable in so far as my daughters were concerned. I hadn't seen them since my 48-hour furlough in March 1940 before I headed off to France, and it was July 1945. I knew my girls would have grown a lot since then. The eldest, Nelly, was 24 years of age and Mabel had told me in her letters that she was still a contained sort of young woman and not too interested in messing about. Mona was 22, although I knew I didn't have to worry about Mona because of her physical difficulties. As for Betty, she was 20 years old and she had certainly enjoyed herself during the war from what Mabel had written. Joan, of course, was still too young to attend dances. However, I simply had to believe that they'd all behaved themselves.

We men also had a bit of leisure time to have a good old crack among ourselves. We were free men, well, almost. We were relatively comfortable and well fed. And we had survived, and that's all most of us really cared about, apart from getting home. Of course, we were still eager for news about everything that was going on elsewhere in the world, and this was readily supplied to us. No hidden wireless sets and no Jerry propaganda, and I'm pleased to report that the news was mostly favourable as far as Europe was concerned. The Ruskies were liberating many countries. The Red Army had also entered Prague and then liberated it, and of course more concentration camps were being discovered and liberated.

Unfortunately, in South-East Asia the Allies were still hard at it. The Nips were still giving us trouble, but we were pleased to hear that the Aussies were making ground and had fought many a grand battle with the Japs, with the aid of the Yanks, who were bombing the bejesus out of Japan. We hoped Emperor Hirohito would soon announce surrender. We held our breaths and waited for positive news. The Allies must have been exhausted, and there had been far, far too many lives already lost in this war. Here, in Britain, we were only now learning of the actual death toll. It stood in the hundreds upon hundreds of thousands, but there were many, many more injured, their physical and mental scars running deep. Indeed, there was not a family that had not been affected by the war.

Our commanding officers kept repeating the words 'Well, we've won, chaps, so let's just get on with it, eh?' Stiff upper lip and all. But I wondered what we had actually won? We may have won the war, but we'd lost almost everything else.

In the first week of August, after spending many weeks at the repatriation centre, my physical condition having been in far more of a mess than even I thought, I was told that I was to be released into civvy street very shortly. I had been categorised as needing to be 'invalided out' and no longer fit for further service in the army. It was explained to me that I was being given a priority discharge. I was to receive 56 days' pay and allowances, along with a post-war credit of sixpence a day, dating back to 1 January 1942. This I was happy with and although I was deemed an 'invalid' by the army my stomach was feeling much better and I felt my body was stronger with the food I'd received in repatriation. My mind was calmer and, for the first time in a very long time, I felt like a whole man.

It was then that I heard the news. The Yanks had dropped an enormous bomb on the Japanese city of Hiroshima with devastating consequences. Reports were flying in thick and fast—the city had been flattened, hundreds of thousands of people had been killed and similar numbers shockingly injured. When the bomb hit the ground, a massive strange-shaped cloud billowed to the heavens, after which a fireball erupted and an ensuing firestorm radiated throughout the vast city. My God! The bomb was nicknamed *The Little Boy*, which sounded absurd considering the results. I had to wonder what the next one would be named—as the word was that there would be a next because, despite the Japanese people begging the emperor of their country to surrender, Hirohito wasn't having any of it.

I was so very blessed to have a loving family to go home to and I had been deluged with mail from them all telling me as much. Mabel had been released from hospital a few weeks prior and was getting stronger by the day. I spent a lot of time wondering how Mabel had managed during my absence. She had sounded tired and a bit flat in my last phone call to her, but she had said that she and the girls had been saving their coupons and were putting together a lovely welcome home dinner for me. She told me that she and Joan were going to meet me at Bransty station, while our other three girls would be preparing the dinner, following their mam's strict instructions. This made me laugh. Mabel sounded just like my old mam, Eleanor, used to with her airs, graces and strict schedules.

The day of my departure I was given all my certificates of clearance, along with a final account from the regimental paymaster, a free rail pass to Bransty and a complete set of civvies, right down to new underpants. I dressed in my new outfit—shirt, tie and suit—and went to put on my shoes but found they were two sizes too small. I was considering wearing my old army boots, when I donned the trilby that they had also supplied and took a look in the mirror. I looked bloody ridiculous, just like a bleedin' American gangster. So, I immediately discarded the lot and dressed back in my baggy uniform. I might have looked a bit of a ruffian, but at least I didn't resemble a ponce.

CHAPTER 19

HOME TO WHITEHAVEN

7 August 1945

I was on the train travelling home to Bransty, Whitehaven, and my thoughts were firmly on my future. I would soon be home. I would be a 'free' man. But strangely, as excited as I was to become such a person, the closer I came to my destination the more my stomach began tying up in knots, seeds of doubt sowing in my overly-fertile imagination. I could not quell anxious thoughts as to whether things would ever again be 'normal' for me. Could I step back into my old life simply by placing my feet back into the comfortable old slippers that had been awaiting my arrival for nearly six years? Could I pretend I'd just popped out to the pub for a beer with the boys and had come back to sit at my table, my dinner placed before me by a devoted wife? Would Mabel and I be able to resume the loving relationship we'd once had, despite the fact we had been living two very different and separate lives? Would Mabel resent me for leaving her to fend for herself and deal with the girls? Would those girls accept me as the head of the family once more? And would Mabel press me for information on what I'd been through?

The officers in repat had advised us not to discuss our war experiences with our loved ones. They said that we couldn't possibly expect anyone who hadn't personally gone through such indescribable horrors to identify with them. They told us to forget the war—to place it into a padlocked box and shove it in the very back of our minds. Said we should forget what we'd witnessed—the horrors, the losses of our mates, the mental strain, the deprivation and the torture. Well, that was all very well for them to say, but how did one ever get over such a thing? How did one simply forget? Oh, I wanted to. I really wanted to and, like most of the chaps, I had vowed to never again talk about the war, but reminders were all around me.

I looked around the train carriage through the blue haze of smoke hanging in the air from the chain-smoking troops on board—a carriage packed to the brim with returning soldiers, many of whom I knew. And I can tell you, we weren't a pretty sight. I imagined that, just as I was doing, every man on the train was getting more and more anxious the closer we got to our final destination; acrid fumes of sweaty apprehension began to permeate the air and compete with stale smoke.

A few poor chaps were not returning to welcoming arms, their divorce papers or applications for same stowed away in kitbags. Others were maimed, some horribly. Others had kinfolk who would not be returning: fathers, sons, brothers, uncles, cousins. And all of us had mates who would not be returning and we knew we would have to face their heartbroken families and sweethearts. We would have to offer them empty words of condolence and platitudes such as those we'd been brainwashed at repat into repeating: 'He was so very brave' or 'He died in the line of duty' or, worse still, lies such as: 'He died peacefully in my arms'. No one dies peacefully at war. *No one.*

A deep hush descended over the carriage as the train began to slow, the hooter blasting to signal our approach to Bransty Railway Station in Whitehaven. We were nearly home.

The train pulled up at the station, plumes of grey-white steam filling the air and blurring our first sight of loved ones. And then it cleared a little and I saw my Mabel and Joan. None of Mabel's family were there. Mabel had already told me that the Cranstons had decided to give us time to settle in as a family. Neither was my band playing, as it had done when I'd set off to war, and I wondered how many of my former band members were left; whether the band was still in action; how many of them had followed me to war; and how many were dead. Perhaps some had been called up when conscription had ramped up in 1942 and had been extended to 51 years of age. This type of information had been censored by Jerry in letters from home.

Oh, my Lord, our Joan had grown up; she was a young woman now at the age of 15. I had last seen her at this very station, a youngster of nine. She had left school two years ago and was serving a hairdressing apprenticeship, so Mabel had told me. I waved from the window. Joan saw me and she started jumping up and down, pulling at her mam's coat to get Mabel's attention as she was looking further up the platform towards the front of the train. Something got caught in my throat when I realised how much of our youngest girl's life I had missed out on—on all their lives—but I would have known Joan anywhere, even with her shoulder-length red hair now set in a new style.

And then I feasted my eyes on her beautiful mother, and my eyes welled up with pure emotion. Mabel! My Mabel! I had waited for this day for so very long, and it had finally arrived. I took a moment to scan the wife from head to toe. She had aged, there was no doubt about that; the strain of the past six years was telling in her pale features, thin frame and wisps of silver now threading through her hair. I noted her hair was set in a wave similar to Joan's. Gone was the victory roll and headscarf I had long been used to seeing her wear. The wife was now 46 years of age and would be 47 in November. But to me, she was still the most beautiful woman on that train station platform.

Mabel saw me, and I couldn't contain my happiness as her eyes came alive and sparkled with emotion. I had to keep calm until the train completely stopped. All the boys, who I noticed were trying to wipe away tears of their own, started reaching for their kits in overhead luggage racks in readiness to alight the train. Of course, out of respect, we all contained our excitement long enough to allow our crippled men to alight first, able-bodied men assisting them off the train. Complete silence descended over the crowd outside as they did so, only to be followed by barely contained gasps of disbelief at the sight of men returning in such confronting physical states.

Finally, my feet hit the platform, and I ran to my wife and daughter, fighting my way through the throng of embracing bodies amid shrieks of welcome and tears of happiness—and, sadly, wrenching sobs of grief. I found my girls, threw my kitbag down on the ground, and wrapped my arms around Mabel before lifting her high into the air, twirling her around and around, despite my weak body resisting such an impetuously impassioned move. But damn it, I had rehearsed this scene over and over in my mind, just like a nervous groom anticipating his first kiss after he says 'I Do' on his wedding day.

When I placed the wife back on the ground, Mabel offered an embarrassed giggle and made some silly woman-like reference to her age and being too old for this type of public display. But I could see that she was secretly delighted and didn't mean a word of it. She was tickled pink. I could feel our Joan cradling my back in an effort to get in on a bit of the action, and I patted her before holding Mabel at arm's length. Studying the wife's face, I saw the fine lines around her eyes, the years of sadness causing them to droop a little at the edges, and my heart turned over in my chest. What had the war taken from every one of us?

'Come on, love,' Mabel said, fussing over me, fiddling with the lapel of my uniform and wiping away invisible specks of lint. I knew what she was thinking; how much I had changed. I was practically a bag of old bones, only held together by an ill-fitting uniform; the khaki colour matching the skin tone on my haggard face; my once ginger hair losing a battle to grey.

'Ready?' Mabel continued. 'The rest of the family are waiting for you at home.'

Home…

I looped my kitbag through my arm, and it dangled over one shoulder as Mabel took my hand to lead the way. Her long efficient strides were purposeful as if she were taking a stray dog home—which she was, I thought wryly—and Joan took hold of my other hand, she now the adult leading the child. The three of us walked for 10 minutes along the road leading to what was to be my new home; our hands were firmly interlocked and swinging as we chattered on about everything but nothing at all—inane matters, stilted questions and answers, for we still had to become familiar again.

Mabel happily babbled on—I needed fattening up, and she had just the thing to fix that waiting for me at home; she'd prepared a roast with meat, spuds, vegetables and Yorkshire pudding with lashings of gravy; the three eldest were at home tending to dinner and waiting anxiously to see me again after so long. I thought the wife was talking too rapidly, but I took it as her nervousness at seeing me after so long apart. I knew this would be a bittersweet moment for Mabel, her mind no doubt turning over thoughts of our future life together.

I was soon to discover the real reason behind the wife's heightened anxiety.

The walk actually took a bit out of me, and I realised that I was far from healed, both physically and mentally. Even trying to take in so many familiar sights confused me somewhat; people waving or peeking from behind curtains; landmarks and scenery; the rows of houses—all of it overwhelmed me after having spent the war locked up in sparse barracks in a cold, hostile and unfamiliar land.

We entered our street. Our new place of abode was only a few doors from where Mabel's parents lived. I lowered my head as we passed the Cranstons' door as the thought of being bombarded by Mabel's family the minute I had stepped on Whitehaven soil unnerved me. The only thing I wanted to do after seeing my own little family again was to visit my poor old dad's grave. And I wanted to do this alone to pay my last respects to a man I didn't get to see buried and tell him all the things I had wanted to say for so long. Only then I would be ready to meet the Cranstons, who I knew had certainly not escaped the war. Mabel had told me all about her siblings' involvement in the war effort over long telephone conversations while I was in the rehabilitation centre—

All of the Cranston boys bar one had been in the forces. Geoffrey and Bert joined the army, but after eight months Bert had been invalided out due to stomach ulcers. I was pleased about that, knowing only too well what it was like to suffer from the wretched condition and not receive adequate treatment. William, Ernie and Bert's twin, Jack, joined the Royal Air Force—Ernie and William in the Military Police division. Unfortunately, Jack drew the short straw and was sent to the Pacific where the poor chap had been torpedoed while on a boat in Singapore Harbour. He'd been captured and, like me, Jack had been a prisoner of war—in Changi Prison Complex. The family had been informed that Jack had been horribly wounded in the head, resulting in a metal plate having to be inserted, but other than that they hadn't had any further news of his condition. However, with what our chaps heard in Poland regarding the Japs' treatment of their prisoners, I didn't like to consider what Jack had suffered at the hands of the Nips, if in fact he was still alive.

William was due home soon, along with Geoffrey. Ernie was still in India where he'd been stationed for most of the war, but I was particularly looking forward to having a crack about music with my favourite brother-in-law over an ale or two when he returned.

As for Mabel's sisters, only Betty had enlisted. She had joined the Women's Auxiliary Air Force and had made it to sergeant, and what a surprise it was when I heard that Betty had met a chap in the forces and was engaged to be married. Good for Betty!

Another Cranston girl, Mary, had had a rough trot though. Before war in the South-East broke, Mary was living in Malaysia with her well-to-do and well-educated husband, John Sumner, who had decided to expand his career horizons by taking a job as an electrical engineer at the Central Electricity Board in Kuala Lumpur. Mary had been lapping up her lavish lifestyle in the tropics, a life consisting of servants, Mah Jong and pink gins. All that came to an abrupt halt when the Japs invaded, and all men were ordered to stay put and defend the country. John Sumner was no exception. Mary fled to Australia, getting out of South-East Asia by the skin of her teeth, thereby avoiding the shocking end that befell other women and children who had not been so expedient. Mary had been pregnant at the time of her narrow escape and gave birth to a daughter in Perth, Western Australia. She and her daughter had arrived home to Blighty recently, having taken advantage of our government's assistance of a free passage by ship under military escort, despite the perils. Mary had not had any word regarding her husband's fate since her escape from Malaysia. I said a silent thank you that we prisoners of war in Europe had at least had our details passed on to our loved ones. What a horror-filled existence it must have been for women like Mary, having to endure the terrible long wait, not knowing if a husband was alive, injured or dead.

As soon as I walked in the door of a home I had never seen, I was rushed from all sides, my three daughters all vying for my attention, their unfamiliar womanly scents, a potpourri of perfume, make-up and hair-styling products, invading my nostrils. After a while of rocking to and fro amid kisses and words of welcome, Mona with her height disadvantage hugging the back of my legs so tightly I could have toppled over were it not for Nelly and Betty holding me upright in their vice-like grips, I untangled myself from their collective embrace and asked Mabel where our bedroom was so I could put my things down.

The wife was having none of it. 'Don't you go getting yourself all worked up about silly things like that, Harry Jackson,' Mabel said with a dominant wag of her finger. 'Come and see what's waiting for you!'

She took my kitbag into the dining room and beckoned me to follow. I must admit to taking a long and hungry look at the wife's enticing backside wiggling in front of me in a new-style, straight and tightly hugging skirt. It had been a very long drought and I couldn't wait to get her inside the aforementioned bedroom.

The table in honour of my homecoming was set beautifully: a glass bowl holding colourful flowers sat with boastful pride in the middle of a pure white, well-bleached and heavily ironed linen tablecloth; plates and cutlery and even glasses for celebratory wine were in magnificent alignment, so much so that I imagined Mabel had made the girls take a measuring stick to them.

'Sit! Sit!' cried Mabel, directing me to the head of the table as my girls all shot off in the direction of the kitchen to check on the dinner.

'You go and join Dad, Mam!' said Mona. 'We've all got this under control.'

Mabel offered a proud smile as she took her seat next to me.

Mona then let out a long sigh of annoyance. 'Oh, you can go and sit down too, Joan,' she ordered her younger sister. 'You'll only get under my feet like you always do!'

With a sigh to match her older sister's, young Joan plonked herself on a chair, her mouth in a sulky pout, and I winked at my youngest daughter. Despite being only four-foot-nothing, it seemed that her sister Mona still wore a sturdy pair of bossy boots on her little feet. Mabel rolled her eyes in agreement with me, as if to say *I told you so, there's nowt wrong with our girl that a few inches wouldn't fix.*

The meal was a grand feast, fit for a king, and my eyes nearly popped out of their sockets when I saw dish after steaming dish laid before me. I forced away a memory of the watery soup and wafer-thin tasteless German Knackebrot biscuits I had been subsisting on for the past five years; forced away the image of starvation and invalid food; of wasted bodies and skeletal faces as men toiled in the snow under threat of death. 'Flashbacks' we'd been told these images were called, and we'd been warned to expect them. I blinked hard in an attempt to refocus my thoughts, just as we'd been shown how to do during repatriation, and then I offered a weak smile as the waft of roasted meat and gravy entered my nostrils and threatened to engulf me with nausea. The truth was that I wasn't at all sure that I could eat even a few forkfuls of the meal. The explanation the doctors had given for my lack of appetite was that my stomach had 'shrunk', and they advised that rich food needed to be avoided and bland food taken in small quantities for a while. Still, I sat by compliantly and watched on as Nelly piled my plate high.

'Sorry love, it's only meatloaf, and there's not much meat in it at that,' said Mabel, pouring out a small glass of wine for each of the adults at the table, Joan further sulking for not being included in the ritual due to her being underage. 'We've learned how to add fillers to meat to make things go further, and the mince is a bit fatty and gristly but, you know, what with rationing and all...' Mabel's apologetic voice fell away, and I realised that she thought my grim expression was due to the poor quality of the fare. Oh, if only she knew, but of course, I would never tell. I made up my mind then and there to keep my diary away from prying eyes. I made a decision to hide it away in the attic just as soon as I had time.

'It's wonderful, Mabel,' I assured and took her hand, giving it an appreciative squeeze while I **waited for** everyone's plate to be filled.

'There's plenty more roast spuds, and mashed spuds, and parsnips and peas, Dad,' said Nelly as she sat herself down on the other side of me, assuming her rightful place as eldest daughter. 'Oh! And look at that wonderful Yorkshire pud'. Hasn't it risen beautifully?' she said, handing me the gravy boat.

The plates full, I looked around the unfamiliar room and wondered when I would be taken on a tour of my new home. I noted with satisfaction that Mabel had got my old piano hauled in and I determined to play for the family when dinner was over. My fingers were tingling at the mere thought of playing again.

A nod from Mabel to all and I took up my knife and fork, staring at our best cutlery as if they were foreign objects, my hands trembling somewhat at having to relearn such basic social habits. Jerry hadn't been in the habit of offering silver service in the prison camps.

'Dad!' Joan screeched as I took the first forkful of mashed spuds dipped in gravy to my mouth, her green eyes flashing in admonition. 'We haven't said grace yet.'

I dropped my cutlery and stared at Mabel, my eyes questioning her as to when this ritual had started.

'We've been saying it regular like, Henry,' the wife responded, using my formal name and again sounding very much like my late mother, Eleanor. 'Grace, I mean. You know, I thought while you were away a word or two to Him up there wouldn't go astray.' She winked at me.

'We also said our prayers for you every night, Dad,' Joan added proudly before bowing her head reverently to lead the offering of grace. Perhaps the girl was rather long-winded and dramatic in her sermon-like offering, but I let her go. 'Amen!' Joan finally trilled and, after her superior nod to her sisters, we started the meal.

In an attempt to disguise my lack of appetite, I asked questions of the womenfolk as I pushed my meal around the plate. What had been happening in their lives while I'd been gone? What was the latest crack around the traps? How were their jobs going?

They all responded in a gaggle of excitement, each vying for one-upmanship.

'And have you all been behaving yourselves with the lads while your old dad has been away?' I teased.

Silence descended. It was then that all eyes lowered, and a lot of shuffling about occurred, heads bobbing up and down, napkins folded and refolded, and rapid sips of wine taken. A sound from down the hallway reached my ears—a little mew like that from a kitten. My eyes darted in its direction.

'Gone and got yourself a cat, love?' I asked Mabel, whose face I noticed had turned the colour of the bleached tablecloth.

The wife gave no answer and resumed her meal. The mew became a wail. A distressed wail. Louder and louder it grew, until it was plainly obvious it wasn't a cat. It was the wail of—a baby.

CHAPTER 20

NOT THE EXPECTED HOMECOMING

'What the hell is that noise?' I asked the wife, my voice strangled, almost a whisper. But I knew what it was, of course I knew.

Mabel stared blankly straight ahead, her meal now discarded, her cutlery resting carelessly on her plate, her wine untouched.

'It's the baby,' muttered our daughter Joan and jumped to her feet to run to the next room. 'I'll see to him, Mam.'

Him?

Our other three girls remained silent and seated, their expressions as frozen as their mother's, and I could tell that they were mute with terror, awaiting my response.

I persisted in my enquiry, my intense gaze never leaving Mabel's face. 'And who might *he* belong to? The *BABY*.'

The wife shrugged her shoulders as if it were nothing; then her frame became rigid, her back erect, and I recognised Mabel's stubborn streak coming to the fore. But still she held her tongue. Nelly turned pleading eyes to her mother, who shook her head in response and waved her away.

'Well?' I asked. 'Am I just to sit here and be ignored? Or shall I go and see for myself?' I took a long sip of wine and waited.

Finally, Mabel spoke. 'No, you will not, Harry. He is ours now. The baby. I'll not explain here and now, but I will have you know that he is staying.'

I nearly choked on my wine. The wife dared to speak to me in such a tone? I stood to go and investigate, forcing my chair to scrape along the floorboards, and it released a spine-chilling screech, as if to say: *I will not sit here and be taken for a fool!*

'Harry, love, please don't be angry. He's a little cherub. We named him after you…' Mabel stalled mid-sentence.

I stopped dead in my tracks. I could feel the blood charging through my body. My head was whirring and whirring around, a horrible ringing and buzzing noise getting louder and louder in my ears. What in the hell was my wife trying to say? I spun around in confusion. 'Ours? Whatever do you mean *ours*, Mabel?'

Mabel now also stood and took two steps towards me, her shaking hands held out to me. 'Please, Harry. If you'd just calm down, I will explain… later.'

I shook the wife off, the veins in my neck swelling and pulsating, and I knew they would be forming blue-black tracks, as they always did when I got myself into this state. Nothing could have prepared me for this. I heard something explode inside my skull, and it was then that I knew that the little bastard in our bedroom was Mabel's baby. My eyes widened in disbelief. Nelly was sobbing, Betty trying to console her, as Mona sat with her head hanging down, her eyes shut tight.

My hand balled into a fist and I held it up to Mabel. 'You bleedin' tart!' I said, willing my hand to control itself. I was no woman beater but every man had his breaking point and, God knew, I was very close to mine. I heard my shocking accusation but once again the wife said nothing to prove me wrong. And in that very moment, all my years in hell amounted to nothing compared to this news. Suddenly the roar inside my ears stopped and everything became deathly quiet.

I left that house and I was never, ever returning. I slammed the front door so hard I nearly took the brass doorknob with me. The only sound now coming from the house which was to have been my new beginning was the taunting wail from *that* baby through an open window.

It began to shower lightly as I stormed along the road in the direction of the nearest pub. I was still in the uniform I'd worn on the train. It was a mild day, despite the drizzling rain, and I was sweating, but it was more from the rage inside me than the outside temperature. I imagine anyone looking on would have seen the steam blowing out of my great red lugs, I was that angry. My brain was frazzled, my thoughts jumbled, as I walked on, talking to myself and using words of blasphemy worse than any I'd ever heard in the prison camps. I swear if someone had approached me I would have punched them fair in the mouth.

Dear John, I regret to inform you that I've met someone else… Oh dear Lord, how many times had I advised chaps in prison camp to overcome their feelings of despair? Of rage. Of downright hopelessness. All the time smugly clinging to the belief that *my* wife was loyal and true. How many times had I watched on while those who could not come to terms with the betrayal had descended into insanity? Had taken their own lives? And here I was…

Half a mile down the road, about a five-minute walk for me given my frantic pace, on Whitehaven harbour, I found the destination I was looking for, and stamped my way in with heavy boots straight to the front bar of The Queens Arms in Bransty Row and ordered a stout. I searched my pockets for coins, having left my money in my kitbag, and found enough to buy me a few pints of the warm amber liquid. After not having much alcohol for six years, I doubted I would need too many drinks to reach my goal of getting well and truly drunk.

The barman was a newcomer to me and thankfully, after serving me, he left me in peace. I was pleased to find my cigs in the upper pocket of my uniform and, along with the free matches at the counter of the bar, I had all I needed as I made my way to a secluded seat.

The first stout went down a treat and, by the time I sat back licking the froth off my thin ginger moustache, I could feel some of the tension leaving me. I *was* a free man, damn right I was, and I could sit in my local pub and have a pint or two, now couldn't I? God knows I'd spent many a day pining to be at Whitehaven harbour again, and there I was. So close, I could have jumped aboard a boat and taken off to sea. Left all the treachery behind me. But for that moment, that afternoon and night, as long as everyone stayed out of my bloody way, I was on a mission to destination oblivion.

It didn't go that way, of course. I was soon aided in my quest by the very people I had thought I wanted to avoid—my old pals. A few chaps wandered in, caught sight of the khakis, and then recognised me, and I didn't have to worry about my lack of funds then because everyone began celebrating my homecoming and buying me round after round of stout. I became swept along with the tide of renewed friendships and I darted, ducked and wove my way past any questions relating to the wife and family with more efficiency than I'd outmanoeuvred Jerry bullets. And if anyone thought it odd that I was not like most recently returned soldiers, celebrating my homecoming with my *appreciative loved ones*, no one commented. Even when time was called at 3:00 pm and the pub was due to close for the regular two-hour afternoon break on account of the law, my friends persuaded the longstanding, good-hearted old publican, who'd returned from his dinner break, to let us hang around sinking ales in the back room until five o'clock, on the promise that we'd have all the chaps in the district drinking with us from five until final closing at nine that night—and beyond if that's what he agreed to.

'Aye, and I don't see why not,' old Thomas replied in his broad Cumbrian accent. 'But it'll 'ave to be in t' back room, like. We've a lot of celebratin' to do 'ere in ol' Whitey, what wi' all our lads comin' back from war to be reunited with t' likes of us, eh? Anyroad, I want to hear all t' crack, Drummie, me marra; yer a bleedin' hero, ye are, Harry Jackson!'

If I weren't so tipsy, I would have told old Thomas that I was no hero, but the drink and the attention from the lads was puffing up my previously deflated ego and I was happy to ride my high horse for as long as I could. I knew the people of this town and it wouldn't be too long before gossip had spread regarding the wife's and my troubles. And then the spirited steed I was riding would be brought to a halt with a sharp *whoa there!* and I would be questioned on Mabel's new brat.

'Another one, lads?' I asked. 'It's my round, if Thomas will extend me some credit.' With a nod from Thomas, who brought over his slate for me to sign, we all crowded into the back room and before long we were just one big happy family. Bugger my real family; this was where I belonged—with the lads. *They* had never deceived me.

'Play us a tune on the old piano, Drummie,' one bloke called out, but Thomas the publican was having none of it.

'Not within closin' hours, lads. Ye'll get me in trouble with t' ol' fuzz, ye will.'

We knew that this was an exaggeration. For what policeman would charge a publican with breaking rules at this time in history? He'd have to be a right cow. The war was over in Europe, and the whole country was celebrating. Still, we obeyed Thomas and stuck to his rules regarding playing music, right up until the very minute the clock struck 5:00 pm, and then we all piled into the main bar again and I began to tickle the old ivories.

Oh, I soon got the lads all worked up, with songs like: 'We'll Meet Again', 'There'll Always Be an England', 'The White Cliffs of Dover' and 'I'll Be Seeing You'. One chap asked for 'It's a Long Way to Tipperary' and I played it, but the lyrics reminded me too much of my capture when that cocky Jerry officer spat the words in my face before holding my own revolver to my head during my capture. The memory still haunted me and so I decided to lighten things up a bit as we were all becoming a bit maudlin.

'Here's a good one for you, chaps… this will get you all going,' I called out with a grin and began playing a parody that I had marched to with my battalion before I was captured. The ditty was a send-up of the Nazis and based on the rumour that Hitler had lost one testicle in the Great War at the Battle of Somme. It's to the tune of 'Colonel Bogey' c.1916, with the words:

Hitler has only got one ball,
Goering has two but very small,
Himmler has something similar,
But poor old Goebbels has no balls at all.

I had all the lads in stitches of laughter after a few rounds of that song. We even changed the lyrics to past tense when it came to Hitler, Himmler and Goebbels, seeing as the little bastard and his notorious mates were now dead. Yes, we were having ourselves the kind of homecoming we all needed. No need to think about how we'd been deceived by our women: just us lads releasing our frustrations of having suffered through a war the likes of which we hoped we would never see again. I knew we Brits said that after the last one, but this time we bloody well meant it.

When the word spread around the traps that there was a great time to be had at The Queens Arms—a blinding night, all right—I was delighted when many more lads turned up, both in and out of uniform. Crack spread and jokes abounded, particularly in regard to wives allowing their men out on a loose rein. Once again, I kept my mouth shut; my personal life, or what was left of it, was not up for discussion on that night.

I cannot recall what number pint I was on when last drinks were called and a roar of objection resounded throughout the bar, but I do remember that I was having trouble with my balance and was feeling exceedingly dizzy.

Mabel's younger brother Bert strolled into the pub, and I went to run to him and wrap him in an embrace, when I completely lost my footing and came crashing to the floor. I hit my nose so hard it began bleeding. Bert picked me up and sat me on a nearby chair, tilting my head back and covering it with a handkerchief.

'I thought I'd find you here, Harry. The sister's right worried about you, she is. I think the night has come to an end, mate,' he said and I thought the lad sounded ever so grown up.

'Just one more glass of stout. And one for you, eh Bert?'

He shook his head and sat down beside me. 'No, it's closing time, Harry. Time to head home, eh?'

Old Thomas turned up with a wet rag and placed it over my nose, said I'd survive and I replied something to the effect that I'd survived worse. 'Get us another pint on the slate, eh, lad?' I tried to persuade the bartender, but he wasn't having any of it, and he told me that he was no lad. And this time, he said, he had to abide by the law and close up the pub or he'd have the fuzz down here doing it for him with the assistance of a cold pair of handcuffs.

'No great damage done to that ugly mug of yours, me marra,' said Thomas. 'Now, it's been grand to see ye again, Drummie, and ye've entertained us like t' fine musician ye are, but I think it's well past due time for ye to return home to t' wife, like. T' war's over, marra, and ye've plenty more days left in yer life so as to come back 'ere and have a drink with t' lads. Hey, perhaps ye could have a tinkle on t' ol' piano regular like? I can pay ye. Say, one night a week. Like I said, there's no one who can play music like ye!'

Wife be damned!

'I'm the Kapellmeister, do you know, Thomas?' I slurred.

Thomas looked at me strangely, and I felt I had to explain. 'The Germans called me the Kapellmeister. It means "man in charge of making music". But my mates in the camps called me the Music Maker.'

Thomas nodded his head and hoisted me up, Bert taking my other side. 'Well, I'll never have owt good to say about t' Jerries, Harry, but I will admit to 'em bein' right on that score. Ye are certainly t' Music Maker in my books, me marra. Goodnight now, time to be off with ye, Music Maker. We'll talk later about ye playin' here regular like, eh?'

I don't know how Bert did it, but the lad got me home in one piece. Well, to be precise, he got me to *his* home in one piece, and I collapsed into his bed beside him in a head to foot position, and it was lights out for me.

Bert was gone when I awoke, the harsh light of day hitting me seconds before a bolt of nausea, and I ran to the washing bowl in the bedroom and brought my guts up. And I mean it in the literal sense, for whatever progress I'd been making in terms of my stomach ulcers had been undone by last night's antics, and I felt very sore and sorry for myself indeed. But if I thought that was the worst of it, I was very much mistaken.

I crept down the stairs of the Cranstons' house, fully dressed in my uniform, praying to God that the noise of my heavy boots on the creaky staircase wouldn't alert anyone. And when I say anyone, I was referring to Matriarch Elizabeth Cranston. I had no such luck. My time had come and it had been far sooner than I'd predicted.

There she stood, all five-foot-nothing of her. But to me that morning my mother-in-law appeared a giant—her hands crossed, one foot tapping and a face like thunder. Without her saying a word, I knew I was in for a hiding, and no bloody Jerry could have put the fear of God into me like Elizabeth did that morning.

She ushered me into the parlour and, like a lamb to slaughter, I followed her strident frame into the very room where I'd first met the woman who took no prisoners.

'Sit yourself down there, Henry Barnes Jackson,' the mother-in-law ordered, pointing to her husband's rocking chair and using my proper name, as one would when chastising a child. 'I have a thing or two to say to you!'

Now you might have realised by this stage that I was no mouse. I'd stood up for myself with Jerry when I'd felt it had come to being necessary. And to be fair to myself, I did try and get a word in edgewise with Elizabeth, but as soon as I sat and opened my mouth to protest, the woman shot me down in flames with more precision than a missile.

'Don't you start on me, Harry Jackson!' she said. 'You may have been able to railroad my Mabel, but I'll not have you thinking I'm as easy a touch as my lass. I *will* have my say if they are the last words you hear. And looking at you as I am now, sitting there in my good rocking chair with a face that looks like it's your last day on Earth, my words might very well be the last thing you hear, my lad!'

A lad I felt, all right. A small, small lad. Elizabeth was still standing and, with me swaying around and feeling nauseous in the silly unstable rocking chair, good one or not, I was her captive audience. Even if I'd wanted to escape from the woman's claws, I hadn't the energy to do so. I sighed and slumped back into the chair, which set me off on a dizzy ride, Elizabeth's angry face blurring in and out of focus.

Have her say she did.

'I know everything that went on yesterday, Harry, and I'm telling you that you've got the wrong end of the stick. My Mabel is in a complete state. The poor lass made every effort to give you a right royal homecoming and off you go storming out of the house before you'd even so much as taken a bite out of the meal my girl had to go without for many a week in order to provide for the likes of you.'

I couldn't hold my tongue any longer. The nerve of the woman. 'And I suppose me coming home to face the fact that your poor "lass" has been having it off with another bloke while I've been locked up in labour camps in the wilds of Poland for five long years is your idea of a welcoming homecoming is it, Elizabeth?'

Fists balled, Elizabeth lunged at me and she held those fists so close to my face that I thought she was going to wallop me one and bust my nose open again. 'Oh, don't you go banging on to me about your being locked up, Harry Jackson. What do you think we women were doing while you were gone, eh? Do you think we were sitting around twiddling our bleedin' thumbs?'

This was the first time I had ever heard Mabel's mam swear, and I knew she had plenty more to say, so I hung my head and pretended to look interested. Hard life or not, she was kidding herself if she thought she could pull on my heartstrings in order to justify what her daughter had done.

'Let me tell you what we've been doing while you've been away, eh? We've been feeding our children food scraps. We've been lining up for hours to buy those food scraps, only to find when we get to the front of the line that everything is sold out and then we've had to go home to give the youngsters bread and dripping for yet another night. We've taken on other women's children after them being evacuated following bombings. We've been looking after the sick— my husband and *your* father. We've been volunteering for the war effort late into the night, knitting and sewing things for the likes of you until our fingers bleed and our bones ache. We've been waiting every minute of every hour of every day to hear news of our loved ones who were away fighting. And then, when that news finally came in the form of a telegram advising us of a death, we've been falling to our knees and praying to a God that we no longer believe in to make it not be true. We've reduced ourselves to pathetic nobodies begging the telegram boy to check and recheck his paperwork in case he'd got the wrong address. We've been cut to the core when we saw neighbours receiving those very telegrams. We've seen men coming home with missing limbs and impaired or no eyesight and even ones with no bloody sense, like the condition in which I'm still waiting for my Jack to return to me. The lad has a steel plate in his head, Harry. The doctor told me the poor thing will be without his marbles. A laughing stock around town. A village idiot, no less. And I will be the one to look after him. So, don't you tell me about how bloody hard you've had it, Harry Jackson!'

'I'm not trying to tell you anything, Elizabeth. But the… baby… I cannot and will not accept that.'

She clicked her tongue with impatience. 'Oh, you are as daft as you look, Harry. The baby is not Mabel's. When would the lass have had the time to lift her skirts to anyone, eh? She's been working her fingers to the bone raising your daughters, keeping house, working all hours. She's been walking the streets trying to sell insurance to women who are so desperately poor they feign illness rather than answer the door when they see our Mabel coming! She's witnessed them being evicted from their homes, and she's even put her hand in her own pocket for some to save it from happening! My God, you are a right idiot if you think that your wife has been acting like a slag in your absence!'

'But…'

'Don't you dare "but" me! I'm telling you it's not Mabel's baby. Good Lord man, haven't you any nous at all? Mabel is nearly 47 years of age. She couldn't fall pregnant if she wanted to, daft bugger you are. Mabel hasn't had her courses for going on four years now, probably brought on by all the worry you've caused her.'

That was a subject I didn't want to be discussing with my mother-in-law. Women's issues should be left to womenfolk. I shook my head in discomfort, but Elizabeth ploughed on.

'Mabel has gone through the change, Harry. You know…'

I sat forward and the rocking chair lurched, causing my pickled brain to shift inside my thick skull. 'Yes! Yes, I know what you're referring to, Elizabeth. I know, but I don't want to know, if you get my meaning? I'm not stupid…'

She snorted out her derision. 'You could have fooled me, Harry Jackson.'

I closed my eyes in confusion, my hands covering them. I was shocked with the serving I was getting, shocked by Elizabeth's profanity and an evil thought appeared in the recesses of my mind: Elizabeth would be saying quite a few apologies when she next visited the house of her Lord—if she still visited Him. But I was also very confused. Elizabeth's mention of women's business had brought a flush to my pallid cheeks, but then I realised that the woman was in fact making sense. Mabel *was* too old to conceive. Of course she was. What *had* I been thinking? I uncovered my eyes, eased myself out of the rocking chair with some difficulty, and offered Elizabeth my hand in surrender.

'Perhaps I am, as you say, a silly old bugger, Elizabeth, but be that as it may, would you please tell me why I have a baby in my house?'

Elizabeth accepted my hand and led me to a nearby settee, where she sat her weary bones down beside mine and released a long sigh.

'No, I will not, Harry. That is not my place. It is your wife's place and I have given my word to Mabel that I will not interfere. All you need to know for now is that the baby is not Mabel's.'

I swallowed back my response in reference to her not interfering. Elizabeth Cranston made interfering a full-time job. Then realisation hit me.

'It's one of my girls', isn't it? Why didn't I think of that? Well, Elizabeth, I'm sorry to have accused Mabel but when I was away— and I won't go on about that ever again after this, believe me, I want to forget as much as you do—I thought of my girls as the age they were when I'd left. I couldn't imagine them all grown up. And as for Mabel… well, many of the lads got letters from their girls saying they'd met someone else. Others got letters from their own families who'd had to tell them of the goings on between their wives and other men. And about illegitimate pregnancies. It nearly killed some of the lads. In fact, it *did* kill some—they took their own lives. But I remained adamant that my Mabel was faithful to me. I suppose I just snapped yesterday, Elizabeth, because Mabel wouldn't tell me about the baby.' My eyes watered like *I* was the baby in question.

Elizabeth nodded in understanding and then withdrew her hand from mine. She handed me a delicate lace-edged handkerchief, her initials embroidered in blue in one corner. I took it gingerly and blew my nose loudly, trying to reconcile this gesture of generosity with the blasphemous old woman who'd just dished me up for her breakfast.

'So, which of my girls got pregnant? And who was the bastard who took advantage of her?' I asked when I had composed myself somewhat.

But the true Elizabeth had returned to the room. 'I did not say the baby belonged to any of your girls, Harry! I told you before; it is not my place to divulge such information. I'll leave that to Mabel. I *will* say, however, that your wife is a paragon of virtue, indeed I have lost count of how many times my lass has come to people's aid during the war years. Mabel took in nearly every lost dog in the area.' Elizabeth sniffed, her nose held high in the air just like a dog. 'As I said, that included *your* father, Harry.'

I felt the direct hit. She'd more than made her point. My body slumped further in the chair and her voice droned on while my mind searched for answers. Perhaps Mabel was caring for the baby while its mother was ill? No, she had said it was *ours*. Perhaps the baby was an orphan and Mabel had taken it in for a while? If that were the case, why hadn't she just said so?

Elizabeth was still talking. 'Because I care about my daughter, I have arranged for the two of you to go on a short holiday to Blackpool. To discuss things. You are to leave this very afternoon in fact.'

My eyebrows raised in shock. I'd just got home after a bleedin' long time in prison camps and she was sending me off again.

Elizabeth mistook my expression for gratitude. 'Please don't thank me; I'm not doing it for you.' She paused at last and I thought she'd finished. But no…

'If I may have a last word, Harry?'

Who was going to stop her? Not me.

'Please make the most of this holiday. You may think that you're God's gift to my lass, returning home to reinstate your dominance over your family and your meek and mild wife, but believe me you'd better pick up your socks from now on as the world has changed, Henry Barnes Jackson, and we women are no longer the frail little serving girls we once were.'

Oh, my Lord, I had to snap my mouth shut that very second before I laughed so loud they would have heard me back in Poland. Elizabeth Cranston a frail little serving girl? Never.

CHAPTER 21

STILL PUZZLED

I was a slightly different man who returned home to Mabel later that morning. And while I can't say that I'm a humble sort of chap, rather a man who leans towards brooding when the chips are down (and I'd spent long enough in prison camps practising my brooding skills), I had the good intention of apologising to the wife. With flowers I'd pinched from one of the neighbour's gardens on my way home in my hand, I knocked on my own front door and waited to see if it would be opened to me. I didn't even have a key to the house.

Mabel opened the door and released a long sigh of exasperation. I had the distinct feeling that she also intended to brood, and indeed her face said as much. 'Come in, Harry,' she said, releasing a tired sigh. No kiss. No 'Harry love'. No 'Happy to see you'. I knew I had my work cut out for me but, still, I *was* a man and I did have my pride— and I still wanted an explanation. But Mabel simply walked away and I had no choice but to follow like the bedraggled specimen I was.

I was confronted by the object of my dissent—the baby. Mona was sitting in the parlour feeding the little fellow a bottle, her stubby little arms straining to hold him. I guessed he was a few months old; he was certainly no newborn.

'Hi Dad,' Mona grinned, as if I'd been a regular part of her life these last few years and was just returning home from work. 'I'd get you a cuppa, but I'm busy with Harry here. My baby is a lot of work, but I do love him so.' She met the young lad's eyes and starting cooing, talking in that silly way womenfolk do when addressing babies. 'Don't I love you, Harry Jackson? Don't I just love you, eh? Who's my beautiful boy then? Yes, you are. Yes, you are!'

I stood rooted to the spot. They'd named the child Harry Jackson. Mabel had already told me that, but it sounded so strange hearing Mona calling the lad by my name. Why would they do that? Mona!

The baby was Mona's. That's why Mabel had been so secretive. But the doctors had said it was unlikely Mona would ever conceive a baby, and certainly not carry one to full term. And as far as I was aware, she'd never even had a fellow. But then again, it seemed that I knew nothing. Nothing at all. You could have blown me over with the slightest of breaths as I watched on. Mona was consumed with the young lad. It was as if I wasn't in the room.

I heard Mabel in the kitchen, banging some pots and pans around in a none too discreet manner. Yes, as sweet-natured as the wife was, Mabel had some of her mam, Elizabeth, in her when she was angry—and when I entered the kitchen, I could see that she still very much was. I knew I would have to tread warily if I was to get the truth out of her, although I thought I had it—the truth—as incredible as I found it to be.

'I don't suppose you'd be putting the kettle on, Mabel love?' I asked gingerly.

The wife let out a sigh of disgust. 'I would not, Harry Jackson. I am very busy and I have a lot to do if *I* am to make it on the afternoon train to Blackpool.'

I put the flowers on the bench, filled the kettle, lit the range and plonked on the kettle. 'And am I still invited to be on that train to Blackpool, love?' I asked timidly.

Mabel wasn't giving me an inch. 'I can see my mam's spoken to you.'

'She has, pet, and I think it will do us the world of good, going to Blackpool. Now, I'll make us both a good strong brew and then perhaps you can tell me all about it, eh? The baby, I mean. I can see the girl is over the moon with him, Mabel. I can now understand why you had to protect her and keep it quiet from the neighbours, and also from me—until after I settled in, that is. It doesn't mean that I'm at all happy with the situation, Mabel, and if I find the lad who took advantage of poor Mona, I swear I will kick his arse so hard he won't be able to sit down again.'

Mabel stared at me as if I'd lost my marbles—and she said as much. 'What a lot of bloody rubbish you're talking, Harry Jackson. Did you go getting yourself that kaylied last night that the drink has pickled your brain? The baby is not our Mona's.'

'What? Then, in the name of God, will you tell me whose baby it is, woman?'

Mabel's whole body drooped and I could see that I had pushed her too far. She began to cry. And, in response, Mona began to cry and, in response to that, the baby began to cry—and then he began to wail his lungs out.

'Oh, for Christ's sake, I'm getting out of here,' I sighed and removed the whistling kettle from the range.

'Where are you going this time, Harry?' Mabel asked through her snivelling. 'To the pub again?'

The hurt in her tone made me calm down a bit. I was never one for tolerating women's emotional upheavals and I was exceedingly uncomfortable when they turned on the waterworks. 'No love, I've had enough of the stout to last me a good while, although I have to say it is tempting at this very moment. No, I'm off to pay my last respects to my dear old dad and while I'm at it I'll have a chat to Mam. I'll ask her what on earth you womenfolk are thinking, although I imagine that is an unanswerable question. Do you mind if I take these flowers, seeing as you won't be needing them as we're to be heading off to Blackpool soon?' I asked and picked up the now-wilting flowers.

That got a smile out of the wife. 'Will I pack your clothes, Harry?' asked Mabel, mopping up the last of her tears on a dishcloth. 'For Blackpool?'

I nodded. 'Yes, you can pack for me, but I'm not sure whether I'll fit into my old clothes. Anyway, I'm not too worried what I look like. I've looked worse over the past few years, I can tell you.' With that, I set off to see Dad and Mam.

I stood awkwardly at the foot of the side-by-side graves of my parents, overcome with grief, but not willing to show it lest I made a spectacle of myself. But I soon realised that I was not alone in my sorrow and many a person around me was unashamedly shedding a few tears. Some were returned soldiers who, just like me, were probably confronting the death of a loved one that had occurred while they'd been away at war. I couldn't find any words, so I sat on the side of my dad's grave and softly sang to them both. I knew Mam would enjoy it and I convinced myself that Dad would too. They had been so very close, my parents. Even in their later years, they had been inseparable.

When Dad had been laid off due to the economic downturn, he was already suffering from consumption as a result of years working in the coalmines. My mam had fought hard to get my dad a pension, which was being denied to him by the owners of Whitehaven Pits. Mam went to court and took out a Relief Order for 12d a week, which cited that my dad was disabled, very weak of body and deeply spent in consumption after 26 years of loyal service. To no avail. That didn't stop my mam. She went back to court to get an Order of Demand and I'm pleased to say that Dad finally received his pension.

Mam died before the war, in 1937, but she died content in the knowledge that my dad would be okay. She was 66 when she passed, not a bad innings, but it still came as a shock to us all as poor Dad was the one whose health had been failing. Dad took her death really hard. He was lost without his beloved Eleanor, so much so that Mabel immediately moved him into our home. Dad seemed to come good again, being surrounded by my raucous family. To the wife's surprise Dad even got himself a lady friend and he toddled off to stay with her every weekend. Mabel wasn't too impressed with his choice; she thought the woman was a bit of a money-grubber. Thought she was after his pension, but my dad wouldn't hear anything bad said against the woman, and he continued his stubborn pursuit of her, despite his illness. I suppose she was a comfort to Dad—he missed my mother so much.

I sat silently, my throat in a tight knot, before I could say anything further. Then I gave my final offering: 'I love you, Mam, and you, too, Dad. You're together again. Rest in peace, now, eh?'

I laid down the wilted flowers on Mam's grave, told her I would return with a proper vase soon, and walked away. I'd made it back from hell; my parents now knew I'd survived another war, and I had paid my last respects to my dear old dad.

It was time to look to the future, whatever that may hold.

CHAPTER 22

BLACKPOOL

I'm a hard-headed old man, no doubt about it, and while both Elizabeth and Mabel had sworn the baby was not Mabel's and, as Elizabeth had pointed out, the odds were statistically stacked against it, I could not get it out of my mind that Mabel had deceived me. Therefore, our train trip to Blackpool, a seaside holiday town on the Lancashire coast in North-West England, was rather tense, and I muttered less than four words to the wife throughout the journey. I was uncomfortable with everything—my thumping headache from the drink the previous night, my confusion at stepping into a new life, my silly-looking civvies that were hanging off me like those on a scarecrow, and my loss of authority. Mabel was in no mood to chat either, and we even ate the egg sandwiches that she had made and wrapped in wax paper in silence.

The train finally pulled up at Blackpool Central Station in the early evening, and we alighted and headed off, carrying our one well-worn suitcase, following the directions Mabel had that were to lead us to the boarding house where we were to stay. If the wife was excited at being in Blackpool, she didn't show it and even the bright lights of the large hotels and attractions failed to bring a lightness to her step as we trudged on through the dimly lit streets. I suppose Mabel would have liked to have stayed in one of those fancy hotels on the promenade, such as The Imperial Hotel with its hundreds of suites complete with private sitting rooms where rich folk took high tea—thinly sliced cucumber sandwiches and the like—but that wasn't in the budget of the likes of us, even though Elizabeth had contributed to the holiday. Our boarding house had meals included in our tariff, but I was hoping that I could at least treat my girl to a meal of fish and chips on the promenade, or one of the piers, during our short stay. That might have cheered her up.

The landlady of the boarding house greeted us with all the warmth of a Cumbrian winter, giving me an intense questioning regarding my marital status prior to showing us to our room. An interrogation by the Gestapo would have paled in comparison to the grilling Edna Smythe put me through. She'd had far too much 'hanky-panky' going on behind her back in her reputable establishment during the war years, thank you very much, she said by way of explanation. I had to hold my tongue or else I would have asked her if she would have preferred it to have been in front of her back, but I knew my Mabel wouldn't approve of that sort of talk. Offering practically all the information I could provide, short of producing a marriage certificate, we were finally permitted entry. We followed the landlady's stout bottom up to the top floor of the boarding house where we were given a rundown of the strict routines, rules and regulations of the place before she left us to it.

Mabel looked at me, her eyes crinkling at the sides with amusement, and as soon as we heard the landlady's retreating footsteps clomping back down the stairs, we both started to laugh. Oh, it was good to hear the wife laugh again. My Mabel had always had a wicked sense of humour before the war. I suppose most of us Brits had, come to think of it.

After a quick look around the poky room, consisting of four discoloured walls, a lumpy old mattress on a tarnished-brass bedframe, a faded picture of our King George VI above, an imposing set of drawers and one window with a fancy frilled curtain hiding a view of the building next door, Mabel unpacked our meagre possessions, and then we sat on opposite sides of the bed, our backs to each other as we stared at those yellowing walls.

I finally stood and walked around to Mabel. 'Well, love, I think we should make the most of our first night on holidays, eh? You've just heard the landlady say that we've missed her scheduled Wednesday tea of black pudding on a pea mash.' I pulled a face to show my distaste. Despite being a Cumbrian, I'd never managed to get a liking for black pudding with its dried blood squashed into intestines. 'So, let's throw caution to the wind and go and take a nice look around town. I'll find us a local chippy and get you some lovely fish and chips, eh? How long is it since you've had hot cod and chips saturated in salt and vinegar and wrapped in yesterday's newspaper?'

I saw the doubt reflected in Mabel's eyes and I knew what she was worried about. Money. I assured her that I had some money from my discharge from the army and that won her over. Mabel smiled, asked me to give her a couple of minutes to freshen up in the shared bathroom down the hall on the landing below ours, and she was back in no time.

As we exited the front door, much to Edna's disapproval if her loud tut was anything to go by, and stepped into the street, I could hear the landlady's shrill voice calling out the time of her 'establishment's' closing.

The sea air hit my nostrils as soon as we got a few streets closer to the shore, and I inhaled deeply. Oh, it was grand, strolling through Blackpool with my girl on my arm again. We took in as many sights as we were able to, given the time of evening and being mindful of Edna's curfew. Then we dashed to the promenade to buy the promised fish and chips and we sat on Victoria Pier to eat our fare. I nibbled at mine but my wife appeared very satisfied with hers. She finished every scrap and then licked her greasy fingers clean.

'It feels a bit greedy to be suppin' on the likes of this,' Mabel said, and I assumed she was referring to the difficulties of obtaining food during war rationing.

I chuckled. 'Perhaps so, love, but the war is over, and may we never have to go without again, eh?'

Mabel nodded and then turned to me with affection. It was a pleasant evening, despite the sea breeze, and it was certainly not cold, but I moved closer to the wife in a pretence of keeping her warm. Mabel did not resist; she leant her head against my shoulder and said, 'It's been hard for you too, love. I know it has been. There were times when I thought I'd go mad if I didn't hear from you soon. The time after you were captured was the worst. Months and months not knowing.'

Her tears fell freely and I handed her a handkerchief. 'Come on, love. I'm here now, eh? Queer-looking old man that I am.' I gently patted the wife's back, as if I were burping a baby, and she shook her head, her mouth upturned at the sides indicating she didn't agree with my description of my less-than-dashing looks, bless her. 'It must have been hell for you, pet. Not only worrying about me, but having to endure deprivations during wartime,' I said. 'I know a little of the difficulties you faced while I was away. Your mam certainly filled me in on a few aspects of the hardships when she was giving me a good dressing down this morning.'

I grimaced and Mabel laughed. 'Oh, well. I suppose we've all had our crosses to bear, Harry. But our lasses have been wonderful. You would have been proud of them.'

I realised that we were now on safe ground. Common ground. Our daughters. 'Tell me about our girls, Mabel.'

Her eyes lit up and a happy flush appeared on those lovely cheeks I'd spent so long yearning to see again. I sat mesmerised, watching her delightful lips dancing around as Mabel spoke with animation regarding our daughters. Nelly had been a trooper; she'd worked long hours in a textile factory making parachutes for our lads and had helped Mona out around the house while Mabel had been at work. Her boss was a marvellous man, very wealthy, and he'd taken a shine to Nelly and had introduced her to his wife and daughters, who Nelly had been thrilled to meet. It seemed the feeling had been mutual and when the end of the war was in sight and the factory began making textiles for fashion again, Nelly's boss had asked her if she would like to move into his mansion to care for their three girls. His wife had a 'delicate' disposition, and she had wanted only Nelly. Well, our girl had jumped at the chance and now lives in grand style six days a week.

'Oh, she still comes home to her mam, very regular like,' boasted Mabel. 'Full of stories of a life that folk the likes of us will never experience, Harry.'

She continued. Even Mona had found work cleaning offices in town two evenings a week. And Mona had been the one Mabel had turned to when she'd been worried sick about me, Mona not having any social life to speak of. The girl had proved to be Mabel's rock.

As for our youngest, Joan, she loved her job at the hairdressers and had moved on from sweeping floors, washing towels and fetching cups of tea and lunch orders, and was now helping with hair washing and permanent wave-setting. Mabel held her hand to her new wavy hairstyle, patting it in an upward motion before releasing it to show how the curls fell back into place.

'Joan created this, Harry. You should have seen the concentration on the lass's face while she was doing it. Her boss was keeping a keen eye over her while she did my hair. Poor Joan's hands were shaking something terrible. Apparently, mine was her first ever permanent wave. Guinea Pig Perms, they call them!' She threw back her head and laughed, and I could have placed my mouth on that trilling throat. Oh, she was beautiful.

'Joan starts on haircutting soon. Her boss is a grand woman and she really thinks our girl will make something of herself.'

My wife's pride in our daughters was infectious and it also got me going. We sat on that pier, feeding the demanding seagulls my leftovers, swinging our feet, reminiscing and laughing about the fun times we'd had when the children were little. The clear night sky displayed only a silvery moon and a dusting of stars: no fighter planes, no bombs being dropped, no flashes of light in the sky and no tongues of flames in the distance. And the sounds—only the swish of a silky ocean whispering back and forth in peaceful rhythm—no wail of air-raid sirens, no gunfire, and no screams from men doing battle. Life was back to normal and I for one wanted to embrace it. As long as my Mabel was with me, I could do anything. That's how I felt. Invincible. I leant in to kiss my wife—really kiss her—and I was rewarded by her tender response.

Mabel released a soft sigh of contentment. 'I suppose we'd best be making tracks, eh Harry? Get back for curfew?'

I took that for *I'm looking forward to being wrapped in your arms tonight, Harry,* and I eagerly leapt up and offered Mabel my hands to lever her up. Then off we went, heading back to our boarding house, arm in arm and in synchronised step.

It was only then that I realised Mabel hadn't told me about our other daughter. 'And how did our Betty get along in my absence, Mabel?' I asked jauntily.

I felt the wife's body tense up. No doubt Betty had been her wilful self and caused her mam a few moments of anguish while I'd been away.

'Oh, our Betty's…' The wife sucked in some air.

I stopped dead in my tracks. 'Mabel? Are you crying? Whatever's the matter, love?' Taking her by the shoulders and squeezing them in support, I turned her to face me. 'Has Betty been all right, Mabel, or did something happen to her?'

Mabel looked at me mournfully and then told me what I should have guessed all along if I'd had my head on straight—the baby was our Betty's.

I stood rooted to the ground. I must have looked like a silly bugger and, if the stares from other couples strolling past us were any gauge, I was correct in my assumption. I guided Mabel to a nearby bench and sat her down next to me; a wailing sound began building in my ears, like an air-raid siren going off after a bomb had been dropped.

'If Betty was here right now I'd bloody pull shreds off her! Just wait until I get home!' I finally shouted into the night air.

Of course, this was the very reaction Mabel had been fearful of at my homecoming dinner and, between gulps and sobs, she told me as much.

'You weren't around, Harry. And I was busy; the whole world was busy, just trying to make ends meet, and my mothering skills were a bit lax, I suppose…'

I wrapped my arms around her. 'No, Mabel. This is not your fault. This is Betty's doing and I'll make certain that she answers for it just as soon as we get home!'

Mabel broke into further tears and I had to contain my anger towards my daughter until she composed herself. 'Harry love, I don't want our Betty getting upset. She's been through enough. The baby wasn't something I could have written to you about, not where you were…'

I nodded my head, although I didn't exactly have sympathy for Betty. However, I did sympathise with my wife and I listened patiently while she explained.

'Betty took off from home in early April last year. I remember the date because our Joan was planning on having a small gathering for her fourteenth birthday on 6 April. It was an afternoon tea with just the immediate family and a couple of her friends like, but it was important to her. Well, Joan was terribly disappointed when Betty said she was leaving town beforehand. Betty said she'd found a terrific job in a factory down south somewhere. She was very vague on details, but she did write to me regular like, and everything appeared to be okay. But when Betty returned at the beginning of November with a bulging lump in her belly and I saw that she was due to give birth at any moment, I did my calculations. Oh, I knew straight away that she'd fallen pregnant before she left Whitehaven. I suppose she had gone away in the hope of getting rid of the child, but it isn't that easy and it's very dangerous…'

Mabel started shaking at the very thought so I patted her hand and urged her to go on, even though I found the topic of conversation uncomfortable. Women's stuff—monthly calculations and terminating pregnancies—were not things I cared to hear about.

'Anyway, our Betty pleaded with me to help her. And what sort of a mother wouldn't do so, Harry?' Mabel looked up at me, her face challenging me to disagree with her, but it was not the time for doing so. Even a silly chap like me knew that much.

'The baby was born on 19 November last year. In our bed. I delivered him. I was too afraid to even call for a midwife, for fear that the neighbours would find out and bang on about our family shame. Oh, there's nowt as funny as folk, Harry.'

I smiled on hearing Mabel's well-used colloquialism. A Cranston family favourite.

'It was a terrible night. Our Betty had a hard time of the birth. I had my mam with me, and between the two of us we did all right. Our Mona was up and about, fetching hot water, rags and the likes as I instructed her to do. Our Joan woke up too, wanting to know what all the shouting and running around was about, but Mona shooed her back to bed quick smart, she did. And in the morning, Joan just stared at the newly born wee mite and went off to work as if nothing was out of the usual like.'

I knew Mabel was getting herself worked up as her Cumbrian dialect was coming to the fore, just as Elizabeth Cranston's did when she got herself in an anxious state. It seemed the apple didn't fall far from the tree in that respect. However, I could not contain myself any longer. 'And who is the bastard who did this to our girl?'

Mabel shook her head. 'I don't know, Harry. God knows I've asked our Betty that question many a time. She says it was some bloke she met down south, some soldier, but I know that's not true. The baby was born in a ripe old form; he wasn't a premature wee thing, that much I do know. Anyway, our Betty is not telling.'

I stood up too fast and felt the blood draining from my head. 'Well, she will bloody well tell me. I'm her dad, and I may not have been around to prevent this from happening, but I am around now, Mabel. And I'm telling you right now that I will get the rotten cad's name out of Betty if it's the last thing I do, and then I'll…' I swayed, feeling rather unwell.

Mabel pulled me back down to the bench seat and took my hand. 'You'll do nothing of the sort, Harry Jackson. Look at you, you're in a right old state. Your face is as green as the ocean over there. That's why I didn't tell you as soon as you returned home. I knew you'd carry on like this. I know it's only natural for a father to want to be protective of his lasses, but, Harry love, our Betty won't be at home when we return.'

'What? Where is she off to?'

'Betty has met a really grand chap. He's not from Whitehaven and he's asked our Betty to marry him. Our daughter has a chance for a better life now—don't you see, pet? She can start over again, as a married woman. Bill—that's her new bloke's name—loves the lass. He'll take care of her and give her everything she wants, although I'm not sure our Betty really knows what that is. Anyroad, Betty has left home to go and live with Bill's parents until they wed. Took off early this morning, she did, like I told her to do… without the baby.'

185

'Is *he* the father of the baby?' I asked, still hoping for answers. 'This new fellow of hers?'

'No, he's not, Harry. I know that to be a fact.'

My chest deflated. 'Well, does this lad—what's his name again—Bill? Does he know about the baby?'

Mabel shrugged. 'Our Betty says yes, but I wouldn't go believing anything she tells me—not ever again will I be that daft, Harry. Anyway, I think that's for them two to sort out and I'll not be sticking my nose in where it's not wanted.'

As ridiculous as this seems, I laughed out loud at the absurdity of the wife's statement, drawing further attention to myself from passers-by. One chap waved at me and called out something about the war being over and said all was grand with the world. If only he knew! I turned back to my wife.

'Well, I don't know about that, Mabel. I think our noses have been well and truly ground into the mud. Anyway, what, may I ask, do you intend to do about the baby?'

Mabel had it all worked out and I realised that a conspiracy had long ago been connived, probably between Mabel and her mother. It now occurred to me that this was the very reason I had been brought to Blackpool.

'The baby is going to stay with us, Harry. I can't let him go. Not now. He's won a piece of my heart. And our Mona has come to love the lad like her own. She fawns over the wee thing. She's the one tending to him now while we're away. Betty truly doesn't want the baby, I'm sad to say. But she'd have been a poor mam to him, Harry. Our Betty hasn't shown so much as a slight interest in the poor lad since the day he was born.'

'The baby is to stay with *us*?' I asked. 'In what capacity? And don't I have a say in the matter, dear wife? What will everyone think of me as a man, coming home from war to face an illegitimate child?'

Mabel offered me an indignant stare. A glare, more like. 'The lad will not be illegitimate, Harry. I want to adopt him. I've already started the process.'

I stood again and began to pace, my thoughts addled with confusion. 'Oh, *you* have already started the process, have you, Mabel Jackson? And what about me, eh? Am I not the head of this family?'

The sad look my wife gave me answered my last question. No, I was not the head of the family any longer, it seemed, and her reply confirmed the fact.

'I'm sorry, Harry. Yes, I would love for you to lead this family once more. But I could go it alone, if necessary. I have before, although to be perfectly honest with you I cannot adopt young Harry myself as I need your signature on the papers. The authorities won't allow a *single* woman to adopt.'

So, there we had it. We had come to the very crux of the matter. A *single* woman, she'd said. Mabel had been living life as a single woman for six years now. She'd headed a family and she was now making it patently clear that she could continue to do so.

It was all too overwhelming for me. 'I need a drink, Mabel, and I think you could do with one too. Do you still like a wee drop of brandy?' I asked.

Mabel smiled. I liked to think it wasn't a smile of triumph, because I certainly was not going to give in that easily. There remained many questions and I intended to get every single one of them answered. However, it was not the time to force the issue. I extended my hand, the wife graciously accepted it, and I led us off in the direction of the nearest public house. Damn the bloody landlady and her rules, regulations and lockout laws.

CHAPTER 23

DANCING TO FORGET

Mabel and I were eating our breakfast of kippers on toast (with a side of sliced black pudding left over from yesterday's tea by the look of the dried-up specimen I scraped on to Mabel's plate) in the dining room of our boarding house. The hostile glare from our landlady bore into me, having been the rogue who'd woken her up the previous night to allow us entry after closing time had well and truly passed.

It had all been worth it, and although nothing further had been discussed in relation to the baby at home, whose fate was awaiting my decision, Mabel and I had had ourselves a merry old evening at a pub. I'd persuaded the band to allow me to join them in a tune or two and Mabel's eyes had lit up when I did so. I suppose I got a bit carried away with myself, playing on all the different instruments, but the wife had always encouraged my musical activities, and she'd been among many in the audience who'd given me a royal cheer when I finally got off the stage. God knows, it had helped to ease the tension of the last couple of days.

Mabel had fallen asleep the minute her head hit the pillow on our return to the boarding house last night, me two seconds after her. No thoughts of lovemaking. We were no spring larks anymore. But I can tell you, we made up for it when we woke up that morning. Oh, it was wonderful being intimate once more with the woman I loved more than life itself—like swimming naked in the refreshing ocean after spending years in a… well… a prison. And afterwards, we'd even had some time spare to have a bath, which we did together, albeit in tepid water due to us not having enough coins for the water meter. Yet we'd still made it downstairs in time for the scheduled breakfast to be served.

We had plans to do some sightseeing that day. Armed with brochures and a packed lunch of sandwiches from the boarding house, which I prayed did not contain any dried blood, we hit the streets of Blackpool to discover the place in daylight.

I had the wife laughing like a young girl when I told her what Hitler had once planned for the tourist town. It was rumoured that Hitler had dreamed of making Blackpool his headquarters after he'd conquered Blighty. He'd wanted to put his swastika on top of Blackpool Tower and own the place. Make it a playground exclusive to him and his men. Our chaps based in Blackpool said this was the very reason that the seaside attraction had remained relatively unscathed during the war, despite it having two airports used by the Royal Air Force, a radar site on top of the tower, and having been home to thousands of troops for training purposes. It was due to Hitler's dream of using it for his own entertainment. The little man had been enraged when Goebbels had ordered and carried out a couple of bombings on one of the airports, but luckily the factory next door where the twin-engine Wellington bombers were constructed missed being struck. Hitler must have eventually got his way after that because no further bombings ensued. So, fortunately for us Brits, Hitler not only inadvertently saved Blackpool from destruction, he never got to have his free holidays.

Mabel and I took our time wandering through the Winter Garden, taking in the magnificent sights of the floral hall, grand pavilion and fernery topped by an amazing glass and iron roof housing a myriad of exotic plants. The wife was wide-eyed and said that her dad would have adored the sight and smell of all the colourful blooms, and she cheekily stole one to dry-press for the poor old man. We then caught a tram out to Stanley Park, about a mile out of Blackpool town centre, and marvelled at the scale of the place with its boating lake at the heart, surrounded by tennis courts, bowling green, cricket pitch and golf course.

My eyes lit up when we arrived at a bandstand and a band began setting up, but Mabel shook her head knowingly and pulled me away. 'You can be just a spectator for today, Harry Jackson,' she joked half-heartedly.

I feigned hardship but conceded defeat when she suggested we sit in the shade under a nearby tree to eat our lunch and listen to the music.

Mabel brought out our fare and I made some smart comment about it being a black pudding sandwich. Well, imagine the laughter that ensued when Mabel opened them to reveal just that? I satisfied myself with eating only the bread and crusts, and afterwards I stretched out my body and lay on my back, the music from the band drifting in and out with the light breeze as I stared sleepily up at the cornflower blue sky above with its white puffy clouds.

Mabel looked down at me lovingly, her finger lightly trailing my face. 'It must be marvellous to see our Blighty skies once more, love, after you being locked away…' She faltered and I could have wept tears of sadness for the concern in her voice. All the times I'd craved this very moment.

However, I did not have any intention of telling Mabel about the concentration camps. How could any chap explain to his wife what it had been like? And why would any decent person want to do so? No, I would never do that. It was enough for me to know that the wife understood some degree of my pain. Mabel had commented on my restless night that very morning—she'd heard me ranting and raving and had felt me thrashing about. Nightmares. We'd been told in rehabilitation to expect them, although, to a man, we knew every last detail of those nightmares as we had them so frequently. It was like reading and rereading the same horror book.

'Try it, Mabel,' I encouraged her in an attempt to change the subject of conversation. 'Lay back with me and look at the grand skies above us.'

Mabel swatted me playfully. 'Now, Harry, I'm not a young girl any longer. I'll not be so fanciful as to engage in such frivolity.'

I sat up, wrapped my arms around my wife, and eased her gently to the ground. 'Oh, is that correct, Mabel Jackson? Well, let me tell you something. You're as young as my eyes tell me you are. And there is no reason in the world why a woman as beautiful as you cannot allow herself a little pleasure!'

She did not resist, and she lay on her back beside me, a small chortle of embarrassment escaping from her lips as she modestly pulled her skirt down over her knees.

'Tell me about it, Mabel. The pleasures you've lacked since I've been gone.'

'Oh, Harry, love. You don't want to hear about all that. Look at what *you've* had to endure.'

We were back to that; both of us attempting to divert the topic of conversation, like two opposing tennis players. However, I was determined to hit an ace.

'Ah, that's where you're wrong, love. If I hear what you've been through, it would take my mind off the… places I've been. I'd like to hear, pet. It might help me readjust to normal life, eh?'

I had her game, set and match. Mabel and I lay there as she told me of how life in Blighty had been over the past six years—a life that had been denied to most men. She explained how the world had changed during the war in so far as women were concerned. Women had had to take over men's work, in 12-hour shifts six days a week. They did work such as filling shells with high explosives in munitions factories so that we men could use them to kill and maim; the chemicals causing lung complaints, staining and burning skin on hands that had once been so soft and resulting in horrible rashes. Women had built much of our new infrastructure: Waterloo Bridge in London, railway lines, ships and motor vehicles. They'd driven public transportation: trains, trams and buses. Women had joined the armed forces or had been conscripted. Women in the Land Army had toiled on the land: growing vegetables, building fences and undertaking many other types of backbreaking work, day in and day out. Nurses worked on the front lines in field hospitals or at home trying to repair soldiers who were in irreparable states. Women in the Auxiliary Territorial Service had served in anti-aircraft command operating searchlights and manning anti-aircraft guns, although they weren't allowed to fire them. Women had run the Women's Royal Voluntary Service and built bomb shelters and provided support during evacuations.

'And on the home front, local women took in other women's children who had been evacuated following the bombings in London and other places that were hit hard. Oh, Harry, you should have seen the tiny wee bairns. Scared silly, they were, the clothes on their backs shredded to pieces, the poor young mites so terribly thin and shaking with fear and cold as they stood in their little bare feet. Some of them were motherless and many had witnessed siblings, relatives and neighbours killed. Our women gathered them up in their arms like they were their own children and took them back to their homes to feed and clothe by scrimping and begging for supplies, often receiving donations from women who could ill-afford to give.'

I turned to face my wife and lifted a stray tress of curls away from her damp eyes. 'The world has changed, Mabel, and you women have changed it for the better.'

'Oh, I wouldn't know about that, Harry. But I'll tell you one thing I do know. We supported our men to the bitter bloody end. We women picked up the shocking mess men left in their wake, and we dusted those pieces off, and we tried to make them whole again.'

She reached for my hand. 'Please understand that I'm not criticising you, Harry. God knows I am so proud of what you did. I know you went to war to protect what's yours and I hate that bastard Hitler and his band of savages as much as the next person. My heart bled for you every second of every day that you were away. But now that you're back—men, I mean—the government has asked us women to return to our domestic duties and forget that we ever discovered what we are capable of. They have told us to take a back seat and I'm not sure we can do that anymore.'

I nodded. The wife was, as always, correct.

'Harry, I want us to keep him. The baby.'

Ah, we had come full circle, so to speak. I could see that Mabel was awaiting my reaction. She sat up and fiddled with her outfit, running a hand anxiously through her hair and looking far into the distance before returning her brown-eyed expectant gaze to me.

I also sat up and held her gaze. 'How do you anticipate we do that, Mabel?'

'Well,' she began warily. 'Like I said, I'd like for us to adopt him, love. He's a lovely little thing, Harry. He's full of beans and he's very intelligent. Even at his age, he practically talks to me and I know he understands everything we say, especially our Mona. He's—'

She sounded as though she was touting for business outside a shop, but I was in no mood to be manipulated into caring for a child who was not mine. I allowed the wife's voice to fade into the background while I concentrated on the feel of the warm sun on my face.

She finally finished her spiel and coughed. Loudly.

I turned to her. 'Mabel, I'm no youngster, love. Neither are you. I simply can't imagine being a father again at my age. Nappies and bottles and all that stuff…'

Mabel laughed and swatted me playfully. 'Ah, get away with you, Harry Jackson. You've never, ever had anything to do with those kind of things, baby rearing and all. If you're concerned about an extra mouth to feed, I intend to keep working, you know. Our Mona is more than capable of taking care of the baby's needs. She loves him like her own; surely you can see that.'

I shrugged. 'I'll not agree to any such thing as adoption, not yet, Mabel. I have a lot of thinking to do on that score. But for now, I suppose we shouldn't let this sunshine pass us by, Mabel love. How about an ice cream down on the shore, eh? We can kick off our shoes and walk on the sand. I've been dreaming of doing just that very thing with my girl for so long now.'

Mabel sprang to her feet, and I not-so-nimbly followed suit. 'You have yourself a deal, Harry Jackson,' she trilled.

'Oh, I didn't make any deals, love. For that, you would have to reimburse me in kind, Mabel Jackson,' I teased.

'And just what did you have in mind?' she asked knowingly and started to run away.

I followed hard on her heels. I was getting a kiss from my girl if it was the last thing I did—and, after that, I intended to get more—much more. I loved the wife and I was like warm toffee in her hard-working hands.

The ice cream was like tasting a little bit of heaven. Sweet, creamy and cold, the vanilla mixture slid down my throat delightfully, and it took away any further thoughts of the baby and what to do about the situation our daughter had landed us in. Mabel though seemed to assume I was coming around to her way of thinking, and she kicked off her shoes and frolicked about in the sand like a young girl.

I lay on the warm sand and watched her. It brought back memories of days long past, when I'd courted her. Mabel would dance in the sand at St Bees Beach: her joy, her wonderful smile, her eyes, all indications of her happiness.

I was a lucky man, indeed, but there lay the problem. Our girls were adults, and Mabel and I should enjoy our last few years of life. *My* last few years, in any case. The doctors had told me at repatriation that after what I'd been through, I wouldn't lead a long life. Of course, I wasn't going to burden Mabel with that news but, to me, it made all the difference in terms of what I wanted out of life from there on in. I wanted things to be easier than they were before the war started, not harder. I wanted to enjoy more times like these, not be saddled with another child. Another *man's* child.

Mabel lifted her skirt and waded barefoot in the shallow water. Her satisfied smile strengthened my resolve. The wife also deserved more from life than to be stuck with a baby, no matter how delightful she thought he was. I made a decision there and then. I would speak to our Betty and force her to tell me who the baby's father was, and then I would travel to the ends of the earth to find the man in question and make him shoulder his responsibilities. If that meant spoiling my daughter's new life with this Bill fellow of hers, whoever or whatever he was, then so be it. If Betty couldn't (or wouldn't) name the father, then I would demand that she take the baby. Tell her that she couldn't just waltz out of the picture and leave us holding the picture frame. Tell her that her new bloke could take the child on. I, Harry Jackson, was no easy touch. I would not be treated like a fool or a man who'd lost his marbles. I had fought hard to retain those marbles and I was not going to relinquish them supporting a child who was not mine.

My decision made, I turned my full attention back to the wife. We still had another two nights and one full day in Blackpool and, as God was my witness, I would treat my girl to a night of dancing at the Tower Ballroom that night. Then the next day I would take her to the new open-air baths that I'd read about in one of the brochures I'd found at the front desk of our boarding house. The baths sat in grand style between Victoria Pier and Pleasure Beach, and it was the largest such facility in the world. We would have been mad to miss out on all that fun. I was desperate to see my Mabel in her best dress as I swirled her around the dance floor but I was more than desperate to see the wife in a bathing suit.

Mabel carried on a bit when we returned to the boarding house and I told her of my plans to go out dancing that evening. She had all the usual female objections—none of her outfits was up to scratch, her shoes were too shabby, her hair needed setting and she'd forgotten to bring her hair rollers—but I waved away her concerns with a flick of my hand.

My own outfit was also rather worn and hung loosely on my shrunken frame. I tried it on to show Mabel and she shook her head sadly.

'Now, lass, there's no need for that glum expression. We're in the same boat as all post-war folks. No one cares!' I reassured her. 'Life is short, love. Look how happy we've been today. Besides, no one will know us. We'll be just like any other couple, just old Harry and Mabel having ourselves a merry old time at the Tower Ballroom.'

'Less of the old, thank you,' Mabel laughed. 'But…'

'But?'

'We'll have to get a late pass from the landlady.'

'Oh, don't you worry about Edna, Mabel. I didn't survive the Germans' stronghold without learning a trick or two. I happen to know that the old dear is rather partial to a tot or three of brandy. I've smelt it on her breath a couple of times, so I think she'll be delighted with my offering.'

Mabel's eyebrows arched. 'You mean your bribe, Harry.'

'Call it what you will, love. Believe me, Edna will be happily ensconced in her inebriated dreams by the time we get back from the ballroom… and I will be holding a key to the front door of her grand *establishment* in my hands. Now you go and get yourself ready, Mrs Jackson. Here's a few coins for the hot water. And take your time, love, because time is now on our side.'

I was correct. The landlady was a pushover. Edna Smythe and I happily swapped merchandise. With a furtive glance around to check the coast was clear, she took the proffered bottle of brandy and I pocketed the spare key and returned to my room to dress and await the arrival of my girl.

Mabel did not disappoint. In a simple but elegant, long sleeveless black gown, two rows of faux pearls around her neck, earrings to match and long black gloves, my wife was glowing.

I paled in comparison, but the suit was passable. Not as smart as a tuxedo, which was mandatory attire in pre-war days, but I knew it would do because I'd checked on the dress code at the Tower ticket office that afternoon. I was also delighted to be offered half-price tickets, seeing as I'd served in His Majesty's Forces.

I handed Mabel a pretty corsage I'd purchased and my girl's eyes welled up in gratitude. 'Thanks, love. It's beautiful. I think I'll pin it in my hair to dress myself up a bit, eh?' she said, and I assisted her in doing so. I could smell her heady scent. It was still her favourite fragrance—a mix of lavender and violets—and again it evoked memories of our courtship days. I felt like a young chap once more.

The wife wrapped an elegant shawl around her shoulders. I offered her my arm, and we strolled down to the oceanfront venue like two toffs from London.

Mabel's eyes stood out like rosebuds on stalks when we entered the Tower Ballroom. The place was simply breathtaking: a hand-painted ceiling covered in rocaille panelling depicting Baroque paintings of beautiful women dressed in their finery; and a glass dome skylight featured in the centre so we could see the stars in the night sky.

Crystal chandeliers were sprinkled throughout, hanging like clusters of sparkling diamond earrings. They gave off enough light for me to see the wife's prettiness—and she was so very pretty that evening despite her former worries of being underdressed—but the lighting was dim enough to set the mood for romance. Galleries for spectators, faced with rocaille moulding on two levels, took up three sides of the ballroom. Red carpeted steps led to an opulent stage with a painted backdrop of the Mediterranean Ocean, red velvet drapes either side held together with heavy gold rope and large tassels. And of course, for me, the pièce de résistance was the Wurlitzer organ, one of the finest instruments I had ever seen.

I led Mabel to the mahogany, oak and walnut dance floor, polished to perfection, and we joined the masses of fellow dancers to await the band's arrival. Drinks were served on silver trays and I took two crystal champagne flutes filled with sparkling rose gold and handed one to Mabel before taking a bow in honour of her. She giggled like a young girl as we clinked glasses and toasted to ourselves and our future. When the wife took her first sip of champagne, she threw her head back in laughter as the bubbles tickled her nostrils. My heart turned over; my Mabel was as happy as the day I first asked her to marry me and, as I had done then, I felt like the luckiest man alive simply to be in her presence.

When the band came on stage, the place erupted with excited applause and off we went, twirling and whirling our way around that dance floor. We were a bit rusty but dancing is similar to riding a bicycle—one never forgets—and we were soon mastering the steps to the slow two-step, foxtrot and waltz before moving on to the cha cha, salsa and polka.

When the band took its first break, I was well and truly exhausted and we headed to seats nearby, accepted another glass of champagne and did some people-watching—Mabel's favourite sport.

'I wish I owned a Brownie to take a snapshot, Harry. Our girls won't believe their old mam and dad attended such a fine place. Oh, and take a look at that one over there dressed like a flapper. I think she's forgotten what era we're in, eh?'

I nodded my agreement. 'I can remember you wearing one of those dresses, pet. Cut a fine figure back then, you did,' I replied and quickly added, 'as you do tonight, Mabel love.'

As the band prepared to start up again, a man came on stage and took the microphone, his expression austere. The room went quiet after he held up his hand for silence, all eyes firmly focused on him. He announced that the Yanks had dropped a second bomb, which we now understood was an atomic bomb, on the city of Nagasaki. This bomb had been named *The Fat Man* and so one could only assume it was larger than the monster dropped on Hiroshima named *The Little Boy*. Following the announcement, there was not a sound in the room as we all took in the news and considered the impact on the war in the Far East that the Yanks' latest move would have.

Then someone called out, 'War all over the world must surely be over! Let's dance!'

A roar of cheering erupted, and the band started up again, this time to an upbeat ragtime tune. Mabel and I looked at each other, shrugged our shoulders, drained our flutes, and nodded as if to say *Why not*? We took to the floor and I'm delighted to report that we did okay. The music then increased in tempo and we danced a Charleston. Then came a tune to a recent dance called the Lindy hop. My eyebrows lifted in question and Mabel explained that the Yanks had brought the dance to our country during the war. It was apparently a dance that our daughters favoured. Well, we gave it a go but, after only a few seconds, we both knew we were far out of our depth. I was in no condition to throw the wife in the air, let alone catch her on her way down! By tacit agreement, Mabel and I conceded defeat and happily retired to our seats to watch the whirlwind of younger (and far more energetic) dancers show us how it was done.

I lit a cigarette and took in the electric atmosphere. Whilst I was in awe of the moves, I was shocked because women's thighs and even knickers were fully exposed. I certainly had reservations about my daughters flashing their private parts on a dance floor. I told Mabel as much but she laughed and replied that it had been like this on VE Day in Britain on 8 May this year: bands playing and people dancing such wild dances as this in the streets.

I had a 'flashback' of being stuck in a barn near Braunau in Austria and being kept alive by a chap named Duffey when we'd heard the news that was music to our ears. For a short moment, I thought of Duffey and I hoped the young Aussie was now back in his home country and also dancing merrily with his girl—but perhaps in a more sedate fashion!

Times had certainly changed, it seemed, and I supposed I should make an effort to move forward a little myself. One thing hadn't changed though…

I pulled my girl closer and kissed her on the lips. 'I love you, Mabel Jackson.'

CHAPTER 24

BACK TO FACE THE MUSIC IN WHITEHAVEN

The Japs conceded defeat shortly after Mabel and I returned home from Blackpool. Emperor Hirohito issued a broadcast to his people announcing Japan would surrender. On 15 August, VJ [Victory over Japan] Day celebrations began in earnest after a two-day public holiday was announced by our new prime minister, Atlee, who had defeated Churchill in the last election. We celebrated in true Blighty style: champagne, parties, fireworks and dancing in the streets. On witnessing such revelry, I understood what Mabel had described of VE Day. We now knew that our lads in South-East Asia would be coming home soon and Blighty waited, as did the rest of the Allied world, to welcome our troops back into our fold.

Mabel's mam, Elizabeth, was anxiously making preparations for the return of her injured son Jack, who she hoped was still alive. Our lads had not yet been liberated, but no amount of telling Elizabeth that would settle her down. We realised a lot of this was due to her anxiety regarding the seriousness of Jack's condition. With a metal plate in his head and a suspected brain injury, Elizabeth was facing a difficult road ahead caring for who could be her man-child. And at the age of 69 and having borne 11 children, the family matriarch didn't exactly have an eternity left to her. Certainly, her son Jack, being only 28 years of age, could outlive his mother. We all waited with bated breath to see if Jack would return and we prepared ourselves for the worst if he did, whilst praying for the best possible outcome given his head injuries.

Unfortunately, something did happen to bring a smile to Elizabeth's lips. I say unfortunately because Elizabeth Cranston's amusement often came at the cost of someone else's misfortune. Her daughter Betty Cranston, Mabel's next younger sister, had returned home from war while Mabel and I had been on our holiday, broken apart by her recent discovery that her fiancé was in fact already a married man. Whatever the chap had thought could be gained by placing a ring on poor Betty's finger would have had to have been in the form of instant sexual gratification. He was just lucky he was too far away for Elizabeth Cranston to get hold of him. The bollocking she had given me would pale into insignificance in comparison to what he would have received.

Betty had flown in the door in an inconsolable state and she had not stopped sobbing for an exceedingly long time. Elizabeth, however, was another story altogether, as she did not stop smiling—behind her heartbroken daughter's back, of course. For Elizabeth now had her 'Mabel replacement' back in the fold, and she had the perfect solution to the problem of caring for Jack if and when he returned home. Funny how some things work out. Poor Betty. We were all back to calling her 'Poor Betty'.

Speaking of the name Betty, I decided it was high time I spoke to our daughter Betty. Unfortunately, I told Mabel this and unfortunately she contacted Betty, who decided she would beat me to the post, so to speak, and return home to face the music before I turned up at her new place of abode and ruined her life forever by tainting her in the eyes of her fiancé. Although, according to Mabel, Betty was still saying that the chap knew about her illegitimate son and he wasn't in the slightest bit concerned. I must say, the young woman had nerves of steel.

Betty was due to arrive on the afternoon train, and I intended to meet her—alone. Mabel was as restless as her mother, and the two of them sat twittering away in Elizabeth's parlour like a pair of female robins trying to build a nest. Luckily for Mabel, she was the flavour of the week, so I hoped she would be getting some support from her mam as I'd told her to remain there while I dealt with our daughter, much to the wife's chagrin.

As for the baby, well, I'd returned from Blackpool to my home and to my marital bed, and I couldn't exactly ignore the fact that the young lad was around. Mona had moved him into her bedroom, which she shared with her sister Joan, and I'm glad to say I got some sleep, but he certainly still managed to make his presence felt. Harry Jackson Jr was a true Jackson, all right, and at only nine months of age, he already bore many of my features. He was a happy little chappie, I'll give you that much. He seemed to take to his old grandfather and he called out in a babble of excitement to get my attention whenever I was within sight. Yes, I will admit, the little mite was chipping away at my hard exterior as expertly as a woodpecker at a tree and I came to accept my role as grandfather, albeit reluctantly. However, I remained unwilling to sign any adoption papers and thereby become his father. No, another man was the child's father and I was determined to find out who that man was, and then I would make him face his responsibilities.

Betty's train pulled into Bransty Railway Station and off she stepped, as carefree as you like, dressed in a fashionable grey skirt suit, a pillbox hat perched on the side of her pretty blonde head, and Betty Grable curls framing her perfectly made-up porcelain face. She held a fine-looking leather portmanteau in gloved hands and, with an air of 'Don't you dare mess with me, Dad', my daughter offered me an icy-cold cheek, her lips slathered in bright-red lipstick held high in the air, far from the direction of my own cheek. Then she stood back in a defensive stance and we walked home in stony silence.

When I opened the front door, I noted that Mona had taken the baby out for a walk as his perambulator was missing. A smart move by the girl. Mabel, however, had returned home, much to my annoyance, and she banged around in the kitchen as Betty and I took seats opposite each other in the parlour.

I started bluntly. 'Who is the child's father?'

Betty was startled by my direct question. I recognised the same expression of fear that she used to wear when I'd chastised her in days long gone. 'I don't know,' she answered and sat up straight in an attempt to fool me with her confidence, but I noted her answer came out in a high-pitched form.

Still, her dogged reaction angered me. I was not here to fool around. 'Don't be so stupid, Betty! Of course you bloody well know who he is. Or did you wear a blindfold when the mongrel was doing the deed!'

Mabel's banging got louder, her huffs of disapproval making her position patently clear to me, but I had told the wife to give me and Betty time alone, so she could damn well put up or shut up.

'I, um… I don't know his full name, Dad. He was just a soldier.'

'Rank? Nationality? Anything, Betty?'

'An American,' she promptly replied, as if I'd just provided her with a perfect solution.

'You're lying to me. I've always known when you are lying to me! Now, you better come clean or I'll… I'll…'

Betty sat back and lit a cigarette, crossing her silky nylon-clad legs at the ankles. Her eyes narrowed as she asked, through a haze of exhaled smoke, 'You will do what, Dad? Smack me? Report me to the authorities?'

I stood and raised a fist to her. 'Don't you go getting all smarty-pants with me, my girl. I'm still your father, and I can do what I bloody well like under my own roof. We're talking about a young lad's life here.'

Betty stubbed out her barely smoked cigarette and also stood, taking one step towards me. 'Actually, Dad, we're talking about my life. Yes, I made a mistake, but I'm about to marry the most wonderful man. I want to start my life all over again…'

'Don't we all, Betty!'

'… with Bill, and I have no intention of doing so with a baby that is not his.'

I looked at her incredulously. 'Well, it's not my baby, either! Neither is it your mam's, nor your sister Mona's, but you appear to expect that we will all simply take up the slack as a result of your larking around. It's *your* bleedin' baby! *Your* son! You're a selfish girl, Betty Jackson.'

Betty sat back down and placed her head in her hands. She had always been a hard type of lass but I could see that I was finally getting somewhere. She began to cry and, as if on cue, Mabel brought us in some tea—a British panacea for all woes. The wife looked at me questioningly, one eyebrow arched, as if seeking my permission to console Betty, but I shook my head and sent her packing. Thankfully she left without another word.

'Betty, look at me!' I demanded. 'It's too late for tears. I need answers.'

Betty nodded, wiped her dripping nose with a fine linen handkerchief, and took a sip of tea with shaking hands. 'Dad, I'm sorry, but I don't want the baby. Bill … my fiancé … he doesn't know yet … and I honestly don't know what he would do if he found out.'

'So you've been lying to your poor mam about that too. You told your mam that this latest chap of yours knew about the baby. And do you mean *if* the poor chap finds out or do you mean *when* he finds out, Betty? Because I'm telling you, if you don't tell him, then I will.'

'Dad! I was horribly taken advantage of and I'm not going to live with that memory all my life.' Betty started trembling again, her face now as pale as the white wall behind her. 'Whenever I see him … the baby … I'm reminded of …' She broke into tears once more.

I waited until she had composed herself. I sat very still and drank my tea, which was going cold, my gaze never leaving her face. I felt sick to my stomach at her words: 'Horribly taken advantage of …' Betty had always been the odd one out in our family; she had a chip on her shoulders the size of Blackpool Tower. Her older sister Nelly was a sensible girl, full of airs and graces and well read. And then there was Mona, who we'd probably been overprotective of as a result of her affliction. And, of course, Joan was unexpected, and a later-in-life baby, the youngest and last, and I suppose she'd been a bit mollycoddled too. Betty had always struggled to make her mark in life. And here she was sitting in our parlour, looking as pretty as a picture, but with a tale that was like a bomb going off in my mind.

'Betty love, listen to me. If you were… ah…' I couldn't say the word aloud—raped. Memories flooded my mind. The girls who'd been raped and killed by Jerry. The prostitutes' bodies being removed from the brothel after they'd died servicing the thousands of men who lined up like hungry beasts, day and night. The poor female Poles and

Jews: spat upon, whipped, brutalised, raped and slaughtered en masse by brutish men who thought of these women as less than animals. No, I couldn't face the thought of my own daughter being taken advantage of. I knew I should have pressed Betty further for details of the father of the child, but it was all too much for me to take in. I paced the room in agitation.

Betty finally spoke, 'I will tell him, Dad. Bill, I mean. I promise you. And if he doesn't want me, then I will have to accept it. But if Bill does still want to marry me after I tell him about the baby, it will never be a package deal. I will not take the baby on. I stepped out of his life the minute he was born. Besides, Mam and Mona love the lad.'

I simply nodded. 'And if this new fellow of yours can't accept that you had an illegitimate baby?'

Betty's eyes opened wide in terror. 'If Bill… if Bill can't accept the fact that I've had a child, then I will go my own way. But I will never return home. Nor will I ever take on the baby.'

'And if I decide that the baby is to go from here?'

I heard Mabel dropping a dish, the sound of it shattering, followed by her shrill sobs.

Betty stood again, pointed a finger in my direction, and offered me the last words she was to say on the subject. 'Then I will apply for the lad to be adopted out to someone else.'

With that, our daughter picked up her portmanteau, walked into the kitchen, kissed her mam farewell and left the house. I heard the front door close, followed by Mabel's soft weeping.

Betty was obviously not going to stay the night. She had left and it occurred to me that she had never even mentioned her baby by name—Harry Jackson.

CHAPTER 25

LIFE AND WEDDINGS ROLL ON

In the end, and after much deliberation, I had no recourse but to agree to the adoption. It was either that or break the hearts of my wife and our daughter Mona. Or kill the bastard who had brought this situation upon Betty. And as much as that thought was constantly on my mind, I knew Betty would never tell me who that bastard was.

I signed the application forms for the young lad's adoption on 8 October 1945. Betty also signed, her name being on the papers as the mother, but at no stage did she ever verbally acknowledge the fact. We never knew whether her fiancé had been told the truth, and the subject was never mentioned ever again—not to anyone, including the lad in question. On 22 October the court granted the adoption. The lad was 11 months old and Harry Jackson Jr became my adopted son from that day forth. I was one week shy of turning 47 years of age and I'd been through more in my lifetime than most. I felt like an old man with one foot in his grave. The problem was that I could not look upon the lad as my son. And I feared I never would.

On the war front, the Japs had finally signed a Surrender Agreement by the time we applied to adopt young Harry, and the Changi prisoners of war had been liberated on 5 September 1945. We had been advised that both Jack Cranston and John Sumner were alive and we awaited their homecoming.

Jack was the first to arrive, only a matter of weeks after his liberation from Changi Prison Complex. Repatriation for those chaps who'd fought the Japs was not the lengthy process it had been for most men in the European Allied Forces. It was done in the camps. I suppose our government decided they had spent enough time and money by that stage and just wanted to get it all over with.

Oh, what a pitiful state the poor young man was in. As much as we had been praying for the best outcome, the fact was it could not have been worse. Emaciated beyond belief, his skull deeply indented and talking complete gibberish, Jack was most definitely deranged in the head. He had the mental capacity of a child; his only interest was in eating. Sugary food, mainly. Any mention of Changi Prison brought him completely undone. Elizabeth tried to do her best for her son but, in the end, even she came around to accepting the fact that he was a hopeless cause. Jack turned to the bottle and took to living rough; his invalid pension enabling him and many other returned soldiers to stay permanently drunk and living on the streets. Poor Betty, his sister, was put in charge of finding Jack and she repeatedly brought him home in a filthy state to feed, bathe and dress in clean clothes, only for Jack to take off again. His twin brother Bert eventually took over Jack's pension and handed Jack only enough to survive on while banking the remainder for his future. But in the end, many years later, the family, at their wits' end and on doctor's advice, had Jack committed to Garlands Hospital for the mentally handicapped in nearby Carlisle—I doubt he even realised where he was.

But, I'm getting ahead of myself…

Within a few weeks of Jack's return, John Sumner was reunited with his wife Mary and the daughter he had never met. Like Jack, John was skeletal, barely six stone in weight, but unlike Jack his brain was intact. John said he'd never met up with his brother-in-law whilst in the Changi Prison Complex and, in many ways, the family saw that as a good thing, given Jack's paranoia.

I took the brother-in-law out for a quiet ale one night, sensing his reluctance to talk about his ordeal in front of the womenfolk, as did most returned soldiers. We sank the first ale in one long gulp, ordered another and settled back to have a long crack. John explained why he'd never come across Jack Cranston in Changi. Besides the fact that there were thousands upon thousands of men at the prison complex spread over many different bases, after his capture, John had been interned only briefly in Selarang Military Base near the village of Changi. John explained that in the early days, life at Selarang had been relatively innocuous. Prisoners met with little interference from the Japs; the camp was organised into battalions and regiments and military discipline was maintained. Food and medicine were provided and gardens were allowed to be dug up by the troops and filled with vegetables for their own needs.

Then, in 1943, tens of thousands of men, including John, were sent to work on the construction of the Burma–Siam railway. Those men left behind, a few thousand, were too sick to labour on the railway and were locked up behind bars inside the cold and forbidding stone walls of Changi Prison. Jack had been one of them. Originally built to hold 1000 inmates, the Japs had crammed those thousands of men into tiny overcrowded cells. Disease was rampant and they were treated harshly by the Japs. No food at all was provided to men who didn't work doing forced labour, so those too ill to work had to rely on those men who were capable of working to feed them. Brutal punishment was handed out regularly. There were no medical facilities and no medicines dispensed and many, many men perished as a result of disease and starvation.

John and I looked at each other as we sipped our drinks, our silence speaking volumes regarding our thoughts on that, for surely, given his shocking state of mind, Jack Cranston would have been better off had he died.

As for John's time on the Burma–Siam rail project, well, he didn't wish to elaborate and I understood. I'd heard enough about the conditions to know that they had been hell on Earth; men slaving for up to 18 hours a day, hacking paths through mosquito and leech infested jungles in sweltering heat, and carrying backbreaking building materials amid monsoonal rains while subsisting on only a handful of rice per day. Death was an everyday occurrence. Living conditions were appalling. Japanese brutality was rife. Disease was rampant: beriberi, dengue fever, cholera and, of course, tropical ulcers (which John had contracted in both legs, following which he was returned to Changi shortly before his liberation) that caused one's flesh to putrefy and dissolve through to bone. John had been lucky to retain his limbs.

As if sensing my thoughts, my brother-in-law reached down and rubbed his leg. 'When I returned to the Selarang Prison Camp I found it to be a much harsher environment than before, but it was nothing, *nothing*, in comparison to Burma,' was all he would say on the subject.

Would any of us ever be the same again? I thought as I made my way back to the bar to buy another round. I doubted it.

As hard as it was to believe, after only a few short months recovering from his ordeals in South-East Asia, John Sumner was asked to go to Japan because his engineering expertise was needed to assist in the rebuilding of the cities of Nagasaki and Hiroshima. One simply couldn't imagine anyone doing any such thing after having endured the Japs' cruelty, but John was a mellow sort of chap. So off he sailed—but without his wife and their daughter, as Mary was also horrified at the thought of living amongst the Japs. Mary did, however, want to eventually return to her lavish lifestyle in the tropics, and she promised John that she would reunite with him in Malaysia once his work in Japan was complete.

In our household, young Harry Jackson continued to dominate and I left Mabel and Mona to it. It was all too much for me.

1946

Mabel and I hosted a New Year's Eve gathering for a small group of family and friends. The baby was asleep tucked away in Mona's bedroom, but the evidence of his existence was all around us—baby paraphernalia was strewn all over the place. As always, if anyone knew or suspected of his origins they didn't mention the subject. Harry Jr simply was. People just referred to him as 'the baby'. Not our baby, not Mona's baby and certainly not Betty's baby.

I sat in silence for a while, nursing my glass of stout as I studied our guests and thought about how we post-war Brits danced around the brittle edges of the truth. I imagined there would be many wee bundles of illegitimate life tucked away in cribs, tightly wrapped in blankets of deception on this night.

The clock struck 12 midnight, and I found Mabel, kissed her and stood to raise my glass to the New Year before I hit the old piano keys and played 'Auld Lange Syne'. Oh, how long we had all waited for this time to come. The war years were over. It was time to look to the future. A future far too many would never again experience.

The last of the Cranstons, Ernie, finally returned from war in early 1946 after spending several months getting through all the red tape in India: home embarkation, a maintenance unit and then a dispatch centre. By that time, he was eager to join my new band, which I named the Exelda Dance Band after the band I had formed in the 1920s. Ernie played the drums and we had ourselves a merry old time performing around the local traps. The band started attracting quite a following and before long we were fully booked. I enjoyed the atmosphere and having like-minded musicians around me got me away from the home front. It also gave me a penny or two in my pocket, not to mention free stout! As old as I felt at home with a toddler around my feet, I felt like a young chap again when I got to play music. Mabel attended a few of our performances. It got her away from the youngster and Mona was only too happy to take care of Harry Jr, who was now getting into anything and everything he could. It gave Mona someone to boss around, I suppose, seeing as her younger sister Joan was now old enough to attend dances (not mine!). I laid down strict rules for our Joan though. After what I'd seen her sister Betty reduced to, I wasn't going to let Joan get away with doing anything she liked. If my youngest daughter ever missed my curfew, I was on to the girl swifter than a fired bullet.

In mid-year, the first of a whirlwind of family marriage celebrations began. In May, Alfred Cranston married a woman named Rose who was 10 years his junior, and a right outgoing woman she was too. We were all surprised because Alfred was such a quiet and reserved fellow and the only one of Mabel's brothers who chose not to go to war. Still, they say opposites attract.

Then, in June, Elsie Cranston married a chap named Claude. Elsie was 44 years of age and Claude was seven years her senior. He was a bit of a queer fellow but, men being in short supply following the war, I suppose women were grabbing anyone they could. Claude insisted on wearing a Hitler-style moustache, which endeared him to no one in the family; nor I suspect would it have endeared him to anyone in Blighty. So, for the life of me I could not understand why he didn't shave the offending thing off. Elsie had always been the 'lady' of the Cranston family, or at least she liked to think so, and we all had a bit of a chuckle at her choice of husband.

Then came some news that left us all reeling. On 15 October 1946, just when the world was realising the extent of the shocking atrocities committed by the Germans during the six years of war, particularly towards the Jews, General Goering committed suicide. Goering, Hitler's second in line and the highest-ranking Nazi official to be tried at the Nuremberg Trials, had finally been found guilty of numerous war crimes and crimes against humanity. His trial had taken 218 days, during which time prosecutors brought forward witness after witness to testify to the notorious Nazi's brutality, and he had finally been sentenced to be executed. Typically, the coward resorted to the Nazi preferred method of death by cyanide pill and he died in an instant, just two hours before his scheduled execution. The world was in an uproar. Where was the justice? And how did Goering get hold of the poison? There was much speculation but no answer to the questions raised. It was indeed frustrating for us all.

Life went on. On the wedding front, my mate and brother-in-law, Ernie Cranston, came next, marrying a woman named Marjorie in Cockermouth, Cumberland in November. This decision to marry came quite out of the blue as we all thought Ernie would be a confirmed bachelor for life, for we'd never so much as seen him look at a woman. I had a tear in my eye, though. The lad had been like a son to me, and now he was off on the road to having one of his own. At least, I hoped that would be the case for him. For Marjorie was a bit of a Nervous Nelly. She twittered all through the wedding ceremony and more than a few of the Cranston clan thought that Ernie was in for a difficult ride with his new wife.

And finally came the day that I had been waiting for. In December my daughter Betty married William Byrne, or Bill as we all came to know him, and a right good chap he was too. He doted on my daughter and I was happy for her. Of course, there was never any mention of young Harry Jackson being her son and, when I came to think of it, with the lad being named after me, well, what was the point of stirring things up? I was getting the girl off my hands and I was relieved, I can tell you. I walked Betty down that aisle at St Nicholas Church in Whitehaven at a pace so fast it was a wonder I didn't trip over the red carpet. I held my breath and didn't release it until both bride and groom said 'I Do' and the vicar announced them husband and wife. I was blue in the face by that time and I wasn't shy at ordering my first stout at the reception centre before any other wedding guest came to the bar to drain the kitty I'd put down.

Yes, my black suit was well and truly worn out and it had a shiny backside to prove it. After Betty's wedding, Mabel gave the suit a good clean, wrapped it up in brown paper and stowed it away for what I hoped was to be a very long time.

1947

The year started with a bang. And Elizabeth Cranston was once again the cause of the explosion. It was her youngest son Bert's turn to experience the matriarch's wrath. Bert, the twin of poor deranged Jack, married the love of his life at the Carlisle Registry Office in January and opted for not one member of the Cranston clan to be in attendance. The reason for this? The woman Bert had chosen to marry had been married before. In his mother Elizabeth's eyes that was a criminal offence and Bert could not cope with his mother's dramatics. Made me laugh it did! And when Mabel and I caught up with the happy young couple for a celebratory drink or two a while later I must admit to all of us having a bit of a chuckle at Elizabeth's expense.

Then, in February, as if we hadn't had it up to our necks with Elizabeth, she flew into our house and told us what she thought was a wonderful piece of news. Her daughter Mary was returning to Malaysia to reunite with John Sumner whose work in Japan had come to an end. Oh, her Mary was the best daughter and so refined, boasted Elizabeth. Yes, Mary was returning to a life the likes of us could only dream of. By 'us', I assumed she meant Mabel and me.

Well, when Mary and her young daughter returned to Blighty a few short months later, did Elizabeth ever have egg on her face! Mary was pregnant to, and on the arms of, another man. 'Things hadn't worked out,' Mary had said as if she were referring to the servants she'd employed in Malaysia. Things had worked out just fine aboard the return ship, it appeared, because Mary had snared herself a major no less. Major James Robert Fairclough had been in the Indian Army and was returning to Britain on the same ship as Mary, who had seen her opportunity of climbing back up that gold-plated ladder of hers reflected in his very eyes.

Elizabeth, while impressed with the status of her daughter's new catch, was not in the slightest impressed with Mary's illegitimate pregnancy, however, and she tried her utmost to infer that the child was John Sumner's. I thought the situation was all rather murky myself, having not heard any reference being made to Mary and John's divorce. Still, who was I to talk about illegitimate children?

1948

I'd well and truly had enough of the mother-in-law and, as luck would have it, mid-year I was offered a job managing a pub called The Puncheon Inn, in Chapel Street in the centre of Whitehaven. The job came with a large flat which was situated above the pub. I can tell you that I jumped at the opportunity; it could fit our family of five (Nelly was still living with her wealthy employers) and, more importantly, it got us away from Elizabeth Cranston, who was now back to ramping up her spiteful shenanigans and causing a right ruckus between her children, which encompassed her new in-laws, both male and female. I said to Mabel when we moved in that from the position of our new flat we would have a bird's eye view of the street and when Elizabeth approached our door, being that we were to be living upstairs, I could throw a bucket of slops over her from the second-floor sitting-room window.

Mabel didn't see the funny side of that.

All things considered, life settled into a good rhythm. The only snag was that I had to dissolve the Exelda Dance Band due to my job, which kept me going all hours. But I enjoyed my job, I could play the piano onsite and I enjoyed living away from all the Cranston dramas.

1949

I finally purchased a new suit in December when Nelly, our eldest, was wed. She married Reginald Pellat; he was a decent sort, and we got along like a house on fire. All I had to offload was Joan and then Mabel and I could perhaps enjoy some freedom.

1951

My last 'offload' happened two years later. At the end of the year our youngest, Joan, married a chap in the Royal Air Force, after which they sailed off to Gibraltar, the first of her husband Clifford Smitham's many exciting overseas postings. Our Joan, out of all of the girls, was to be a world traveller. Clifford's parents were a grand couple from Carlisle. His mother Doris was a nurse and Mabel liked the woman a lot. His father Bob was a musician and there's no need for me to tell you how we got along! I couldn't have been happier. Seven-year-old Harry contained his energy at the wedding ceremony just long enough to perform his pageboy duties, before he had Mona chasing after him all over the reception venue as soon as the lad had gobbled down his share of the wedding feast.

I got into bed after the wedding and let out a long sigh of relief. 'We've done it, love,' I said to Mabel, my eyes staring with satisfaction at the ceiling. 'Now we can start doing stuff for ourselves, eh? Bob and I were discussing taking you and Doris to visit Joan and Cliff in Gibraltar when I get my next holidays. Then, well, who knows where Cliff will be posted next?'

'No,' replied the wife in a sleepy voice. 'We can't leave young Harry.'

My heart sank…

CHAPTER 26

A GOOD AND DECENT HUMAN BEING

1952

Just after New Year's Day, Mabel and Mona decided to take a short break to visit our daughter Betty, who had a three-and-a-half-year-old daughter of her own and was a bit worn out. She hadn't seen much of her mam over the past few years, so Mabel asked me if I would look after young Harry while she and Mona, who Mabel said needed a break from the lad, went to check on things with Betty. She didn't have to explain why she couldn't take the boy with her.

I wasn't overjoyed at the thought. I was to commence work at the Workington Steelworks in mid-January where Nelly's husband Reginald (who we all called Bunty) had got me a job as a storeman. I'd recently quit my job at The Puncheon Inn as I'd worked long hours which had tired me out and kept me away from music. That was the reason I wanted some time to myself over the holiday period—to re-form my band, and I couldn't do that with an overly-active young lad on my hands. A child I still resented, truth be told.

Still, I relented as it was only to be for a couple of days.

After the women left, young Harry and I stood in the large living room of our new flat in Queen Street and stared at each other for a long time; it was as if we'd only just met. I wondered what on earth I was going to do to entertain the lad, and I said as much to him, but he just shrugged his shoulders and continued watching me, his eyes wary. I was old enough to be his grandfather. God, I *was* his grandfather and I'll admit to not having the first idea about being a father to a boy. And nor did I want to be! Mona and Mabel had always had the parenting covered and I was only ever called upon to mete out discipline when they found it all too hard. *You just wait until your dad comes home, young lad,* was sung to him as often as the national anthem in schools.

It suddenly hit me how to entertain him—I could teach the young chap how to play the piano. Why hadn't I thought of it sooner?

Well, we plonked about on that piano until the lad's hands were practically red raw, but nearing the time for Mabel's return, I just knew my aspirations for him to become a musical prodigy were never going to be realised. Not even close! I'll admit to losing my temper with him a few times.

On Friday night, after feeding us a serving of chips from the local chippy, I took a long sip on my umpteenth glass of stout, released a long sigh to match young Harry's and ordered him off to bed with a vague suggestion of resuming music lessons in the near future.

Yes, I was disappointed. Yes, in him.

But the lad just stood there and hung his head, shuffling on skinny legs, his long school shorts exposing knobbly knees, blue with cold from the dying fire.

'I'm not like you, am I, Dad?' he said in such a low voice that he got my attention. 'You're the Music Maker. Everyone knows that. The lads at school are right proud of you, they are. And so am I, Dad. I'm very proud of you, I am. But I don't have it in me, do I? Music, like.'

I continued to watch him as he fumbled with his shirt, twisting it around in knots with nervous fingers. Suddenly I was transported back in time. I could see myself, just like Harry Jr, a young lad of seven, telling my father that I was a musician. Waiting for his enthusiastic response. But no enthusiastic response ever came, such was my father's determination for me to follow *his* chosen career path—down the mines.

Was this what I wanted for the young boy now standing in front of me? That he pursue *my* passion in life?

I studied young Harry. He certainly bore my features; his face, his lanky frame, even the shape and colour of his eyes were mine. But—

'Dad?' he asked. 'Am I in trouble? Dad?'

DAD. He called me his dad. Shouldn't that mean something to me? Hadn't I always wanted a son? Well, here he was.

I smiled and shook my head to allay his concern. Then I decided to call him by the title I had failed to do for far too long.

SON.

I put down my stout and stood, placing a protective arm around the lad's shoulders as my father's words came back to me. Wise words. Words *my son* needed to hear. It was well past time—

'Son, a man's passion for the arts, whatever that may be, is fine and dandy, but more than anything a man needs to be a good and decent human being. I have faith that you will achieve such ends.'

My son's smile lit up the room.

SUMMER TIME IS NEARLY OVER

SUMMER TIME IS NEARLY OVER
I'M ALWAYS THINKING OF THE SPRING
WHEN YOU WERE MY EVERYTHING
SOMETIMES SKIES ARE GREY
SOMETIMES THEY ARE BLUE
SO, TO YOU...
I BRING A DREAMER'S MELODY.

SUMMER TIME IS NEARLY OVER
SEE, THE SKIES ARE ALMOST GREY
SOON WE SHALL BE AWAY
WHERE SKIES ARE ALWAYS BLUE
THEN WE'LL BE TOGETHER AGAIN, JUST ME AND YOU

SUMMER TIME IS NEARLY OVER
ALTHOUGH THE TREES AND
FIELDS ARE SNOW CLAD
AND MY HEART RATHER SAD
BIRDS WILL BE SINGING SOON
IT WILL MAKE US GLAD THEN
WHEN SUMMER TIME IS HERE AGAIN.

Arthur Winup
Prisoner of War,
Poland
World War II

NAMES AND ADDRESSES OF MEN IN DRUM MAJOR JACKSON'S WORLD WAR II DIARY

The names and addresses listed below of some of the men who were British prisoners of war with my grandfather at various times during his internment were entered in his diary by the men themselves and some handwriting is difficult to decipher. Therefore, I offer my apologies for any mistakes that may have occurred in my transcription. Some service numbers (#) were entered in the diary, others I found on The War Forces Records website, UK. Some I could not trace. In reference to Duffey, the Australian Harry Jackson wrote about prior to his liberation, I wrote to the Research Centre at the Australian War Memorial and received information that they could find only one Australian prisoner of war in Europe surnamed Duffey. His records show that he was transferred from Italy to Germany to Stalag XVIII-A in Austria in April 1944 and arrived in Britain as a recovered prisoner of war in May 1945. I can only assume that this was the soldier that my grandfather referred to.

I hope this information brings closure to anyone searching for information pertaining to each and every one of these brave men.

ADAMS, Alexander: 12, Albion Street, Peterhead, Scotland—5th Battalion, Gordon Highlanders

ALEXANDER, RG: 195, Hythe Road, Ashford, Kent—Private, # 6288965, 5th Battalion East Kent regiment (Buffs)

ARMSTRONG, Reginald Robert Marius: 29, Elmdale Road, The

Chessels, Bedminster, Bristol. 3—Private, # 4126333, 4th Battalion, Cheshire Regiment

BARKER, J: 3, Second Street, Wheatley Hill, Durham—Private, 10th Army Field Workshop, Royal Army Ordnance Corps

BARLOW, CA: 63, Green Street, High Wycombe, Buckinghamshire—1st Buckinghamshire Battalion Light Infantry

BARNARD, R: 'Alandale', Park Street, Princes Risborough, Buckinghamshire—Lance Sergeant, # 5384254. 1st Buckinghamshire Battalion. Oxfordshire and Buckinghamshire Light Infantry (Bucks)

BELL, R: 49, Back Devonshire Lane/Street Lane, Leeds, Yorkshire—Sergeant, # 78817627, Royal Armoured Corps, Royal Tank Regiment

BENNETT, Frank William: 16, Woolwich Road, London—Lance Bombardier, # 943120, Royal Artillery, 2nd Searchlight Regiment

BIRCH, D: Barleythorpe, Oakham, Rutland—Private, # 4859144, 1/5th Battalion, Leicestershire Regiment

BOWDEN, R: 99, Exeter Road, Kings North Newton, South Devon—Gunner, # 1521326 Royal Artillery, 1st Searchlight Regiment

BREWER, FJ: Rosemont, Greaves Road, High Wycombe, Buckinghamshire—Bugler, # 5382879, 1st Battalion, The Oxfordshire and Buckinghamshire Light Infantry

BRYCE, L: 3, North St James Street, Edinburgh, Scotland—Trooper, # 7891737, 1st Lothians and Border Yeomanry, Royal Armoured Corps

BURKE, T: Middlewood Street, Gordon, Manchester—Private, # 3598654, 4th Battalion, Border Regiment

CAIN, Ed: 193, Woodthorpe Road, Woodthorpe Estate, Sheffield—Private, # 5882447, 1st Northamptonshire Regiment

CAPSTICK, W: 4, Sands Avenue, Kendal—Private, # 3600188, 4th Battalion, Border Regiment

CLARKE, L: 77, Dunkerley Street, Oldham, Lancashire—Private, # 3314823, Highland Light Infantry

COCHRANE, W: Dundee, Angus—Corporal, # 2027578, 237 Field Company, Royal Engineers

COLBOURNE, GW: 21 Sompting Street, Worthing, Sussex—2/7th Battalion, Queen's Royal Regiment

COLLARD, C: 14, Windermere Gardens, Totton, Southampton—Lieutenant Corporal, Royal Military Police

COLLINS, F: 333, Jockey Road, Sutton, Coldfield, Birmingham—Private, # 5110750, 2nd Infantry Base Depot, Royal Warwickshire Regiment

CRAGGS, A: 16, Johnson Street, Gateshead on Tyne, County Durham—2nd Battalion, Durham Light Infantry

CREIGHTON, S: 145, Graham Street, Penrith—Sergeant, # 359418, 4th Battalion, Border Regiment

DAVIDSON, Albert: 9, Ferrier Crescent, Woodside, Aberdeen, Scotland—Private, Field Ambulance Royal Army Medical Corps (brother to Alex)

DAVIDSON, Alex: 9, Ferrier Crescent, Woodside, Aberdeen, Scotland—Private, Field Ambulance Royal Army Medical Corps (brother to Albert)

DAVIES, R: The Pick Hatch, Brampton Road, Madley, Hereford—Sergeant, 6th Battalion, Durham Light Infantry

DAVIES, R: 6, Station Mansions, Finchley, London—Sergeant, # 1981021, 100 Field Company, Royal Engineers

DAVIES, RV: 50, St. Hughs Road, Anerley, London, SE 10—Private, # 6018866, 1st Battalion, Oxfordshire and Buckinghamshire Light Infantry

DAWSON, GE:188, Castlenau, Barnes, London—Private, # 6205485 1st Battalion, Princess Louise"s Kensington Regiment

DENT, W: 2, Brackenbed Lane, Halifax, Yorkshire—58th Anti-Tank Regiment, Royal Artillery

DIXON, JT: 325, Scotswood Road, Newcastle—Private, # 3600447, 1st Battalion, Border Regiment

DOYLE, G: 46, St Anthony's Avenue, Woodford Green, Essex—Gunner, # 2056063, 1st Searchlight Regiment, Royal Artillery

DOYLE, J: 37, Frizington Road, Frizington—Corporal, # 3598000. 5th Battalion, Border Regiment at start of World War II, then got transferred to 2nd Battalion, Parachute Corps.

DUDDING: Captain, Company Commander, Border Regiment.

DURRANT, L: 40, Campbell Street, Bilton, Rugby, Warwickshire—Private, # 97517 Royal Army Service Corps

EDWARDS, E: Cartref Mules, Llysfaen, W Colwyn Bay, Nth Wales—Gunner, 1st Searchlight Regiment, Royal Artillery

ELLIS, HA: 12, Duncombe Road, Highgate—Rifleman, # 6844345, 2nd Battalion, King's Royal Rifle Corps

FERGUSON, Walter H: 17, Banklands, Workington—Private, # 3601117 4th Battalion, Border Regiment

FIRTH, RR: 34, Lime Street, Barrow, Lancashire—23rd Field Regiment, Royal Artillery

FITZSIMMONS, T: 4, Roslyn Street, Tranmere, Birkenhead, Cheshire—Corporal, # 3652066, 1st Battalion, South Lancashire Regiment

FORBES, J: 28, Ainslie Gardens, Perth, Scotland—Private, # 403786, Royal Army Service Corps

FOSTER, W: 9, Crown Terrace, Penrith—Private, # 3600884, 4th Battalion, Border Regiment

FRASER, NK: 21 Cruachan Street, Carnwadric, Glasgow—Signalman, # 2328177, Royal Corps of Signals

FYNN, EW: 41, Chestnut Avenue, Bedford, Bedfordshire—Lance Sergeant, # 2568788, 140

AFR, Royal Corps of Signals

GORDON, JG: Dundee, Angus—Private, # 83058 526 Company, Royal Army Service Corps

GRANT, W: 130, Rectory Lane, Little Bowden, Market Harbour Leicestershire—Sergeant, # 3128655, Royal Scots Fusiliers

GUDGEON, J: 24, Green Gate, Kendal—Private, # 3599295, Border Regiment

HALL, J: 17, Broad Ing, Kendal—Private, # 3595185, 4th Battalion, Border Regiment

HARDY, Walter D: 5, Church View Terrace, Limavady, County Derry, Nthn Ireland—Private, # 404977, 5th Battalion, Border Regiment

HAZEL, N: 15, Villet Street, Swindon, Wiltshire—Trooper, # 320253, 4th/7th Royal Dragoon Guards, Royal Armoured Corps

HAZELDON, D: 42, Peter Street, Whitehaven—Private, # 3598084, 5th Battalion, Border Regiment

HEALD, H: 31, Alice Street, Bradford, Manchester—Gunner, # 1492778, 2nd Searchlight Regiment, Royal Artillery

HOPKINS, AJ: 15, Churchbury Road, Haddenham, Buckinghamshire—Private, # 5383345, 1st Buckinghamshire Battalion, Oxfordshire and Buckinghamshire Light Infantry

HUNTER, William H: 39, Bridge Street, Cowdenbeath, Fife, Scotland—Private, # 2755706, Royal Highland Regiment, The Black Watch (Royal Highlanders)

JACKSON, Henry Barnes: 32, The Green, Bransty, Whitehaven, Cumberland—Sergeant, # 3591894, 5th Border Regiment

JONES, HAM: 'The Lawns' Farm, Wormelow, Hereford—Driver, # 91410, 3rd Reserves, The Royal Army Service Corps

JONES, HW: Victoria—Rifleman # 6895034, King's Royal Rifle Corps, 1st Battalion, Queen Victoria's Rifles

KIRKBRIDE, Fred J: 8, Snaefell Terrace, Whitehaven—Private, # 3601145, 4th Battalion Border Regiment

LARKIN, J: 2, Mann Street, Liverpool—Private, # 1474287, 7th Battalion, King's Own Royal Regiment,

LE CUIROT, FJ (Mick): The Forge, Vermont, St Saviour, Jersey—Signalman, # 2329788, Royal Signals

LOFTHOUSE, H: 2, Cowper Road, Liverpool—Private, # 3851439, 1st Battalion, Border Regiment

MacINTYRE, M: 17, Stirling Street, Renton, Dumbartonshire, Scotland—Gunner #1468406, 58th Light Anti-Aircraft Regiment, Royal Artillery

MASON, G: 66F, Malvina Place, Muirton, Perthshire—Driver, # 76993, Royal Army Service Corps

MAYS, JE: 25, Gladstone Street, Glasgow, Scotland—Royal Engineers

McCANN, M: 7, Elton Road, Bishopston, Bristol—Lance Sergeant, # 2322334, 2nd Divisional Signals, Royal Corps of Signals

McGUIGAN, E: 34, Garrock Street, Dalry, Ayrshire, Scotland—Private, # 2819002,

2nd Battalion, Seaforth Highlanders

MILLICAN, J: 13, Therlmere Avenue, Cockermouth—Private, # 3600422, 5th Battalion, Border Regiment

MILLER, George: 18, Monkland View Crescent, Old Monkland, Scotland—Private, # 2821264, 2nd Battalion, Seaforth Highlanders

MILNE, Benjamin: 101, West North Street, Aberdeen, Scotland—Corporal, # 2869156, No 1 Company, The Royal Corps of Signals

NICHOLS, F: 8, Heathcliffe Road, Tyseley, Birmingham—Lance Corporal, Royal Army Service Corps of Auxiliary Military Pioneer Corps

NICHOLSON, F: 6, Yard, 123, Highgate, Kendal—Private, # 3596145, 4th Battalion, Border Regiment

NORRIS, E: 34, Harriet Road, Kilmarnock, Ayrshire, Scotland—Royal Engineers

NORRIS, FC: 46, Redburn Road, Paignton, South Devon—Sapper, # 1911575, 670 Artizan Works Company, Royal Engineers

PASCALL, W: 1, Beaufoy Road, Dover, Kent—Sergeant, # 628124, 4th Battalion, Buffs (East Kent Regiment)

PEET, H: 62, The Headlands, Keswick—Private, # 3598094, 4th Battalion, Border Regiment

PENRICE, Tom: 19, Brough Street, Aspatria, Cumberland—Lance Corporal, # 3596017, 5th Battalion, Border Regiment

PERKINS, WC: 93, Muir-Kirk Road, Catford, London—Corporal, # 6925004, 4th Battalion, Royal Northumberland Fusiliers

PERRY, LE: 83, Stanstead Road, Forest Hill, London—Private, # 6018798, 7th Battalion, Queen's Own (Royal West Kent Regiment)

PHILLIPS, Frank: 113, Girton Avenue, Kingsbury, London—Private, # 5674414,

1st Battalion, Oxfordshire and Buckinghamshire Light Infantry

POW, L: 286, Thimble Mill Lane, Nechells, Birmingham—Driver, # 128390, Royal Army Service Corps

REGAN, Denis: 75, Bulk Road, Lancaster—Royal Army Service Corps

RELF, FL: 145, Northwood Road, Thornton Heath, Surrey—Fusilier, # 6466351, 14th Ordnance Battalion, Royal Fusiliers.

ROBERTSON, F: 38, Willow Avenue, Gloucester—Lance Corporal, # 5180056, 2nd Battalion, Gloucestershire Regiment

SAUNDERS, E: 53, Hardres Street, Ramsgate, Kent—Private, # 6288197, 5th Battalion, Buffs (East Kent Regiment)

SCOBIE, G: East Busby Farm, Methven, Perthshire, Scotland—Driver, # T84854525, 525 Ammunition Company, Royal Army Service Corps

SEAGER, Ian R: The Royal House, Dalston, Carlisle, Cumberland—Rifleman, # 6846324, 2nd Kings Royal Rifle Corps.

SETTLE, E: 66, Old Road, Heaton Norris, Stockport, Cheshire—Private, # 4139285, 1/8th Battalion, Middlesex Regiment

STAFFORD, FE: 3, Regents Road/Welford Road, Leicestershire—Private, # 4859258, 1/5th Battalion, Leicestershire Regiment

STARKEY, FG: 4, Boyland Road, Bromley, Kent—Sergeant, # 63450, 7th Battalion, Queen's Own (Royal West Kent Regiment)

SULLIVAN, J (Dan): 182, Bancroft Road, Mill End, London—Sergeant, # 6910684, Rifle Brigade

SUMMERHILL, Ernest: 34, Bamborough Terrace, North Shields, Northumberland—Driver, # 1868668, 58th Chemical Warfare Company, Royal Engineers

TAYLOR, G: 59, York Street, Oldham, Lancashire—Royal Army Service Corps

THOMAS, A: 44, Stoke Road, Ellesmere Port, Wirral, Cheshire—Private, # 4125885, 4th Battalion, Cheshire Regiment

TIMBERLAKE, E: 11, Dunny Lane, Chipperfield, Kings Langley, Hertfordshire—Sapper, # 1902836, Royal Engineers

TOLE, George: Chalet Cottage, Courtenay Road, Hoylake, Cheshire—Driver, # T 121876 Royal Army Service Corps

WATTS, W: 40, Quarry Road, Weoley Castle, Selly Oak, Birmingham—Private, # 5112817, 8th Battalion, Royal Warwickshire Regiment

WELTON, W: 54, Sandy Lane, Worksop, Nottinghamshire—Private, # 4976916, 8th Battalion, Sherwood Foresters.

WHITE, John: 11, Kiln Fields, Haslemere, Surrey—Private, # 6090394, 2/5th Battalion, Queen's (Royal West Surrey Regiment)

WILLIAMS, P: 75, Wood Lane, Shepherd's Bush, London—1st Battalion, The Welsh Guards

WILSON, C: 12, Grovebank Road, Trent-Vale, Stoke-on-Trent, Staffordshire—Private, 2nd Searchlight Regiment, Royal Artillery

WILSON, C: Benview, Blairnroar, Comrie, Perthshire—51st Highland Division, Royal Army Service Corps

WINUP, Arthur: 23, Belmont Road, Luton, Bedfordshire.

WRIGHT, W: Gerrard Road, Kings Cross, London—Private, # 13005924, Auxiliary Military Pioneer Corps

Other Soldiers named in Harry Jackson's Diary

ADAIR: Signaller

ASHBRIDGE, A: Private, # 3602241, 1st Battalion, Border Regiment

BAIN: Lance Corporal, Medical Orderly, Royal Army Medical Corps

BOWDEN

BUSH, JE: Private, # 127966, Royal Army Service Corps

CLEMENTS, H: Private, # 1077118, 1st Battalion, Border Regiment

DAVIDSON, GI: Captain, # 97960, Royal Army Medical Corps, Aberdeen

DUFFEY, Joseph Patrick: Block 6/Flat 48 Erskineville Housing Estate, Sydney, Australia—Private, # NX18121, 2/13 Australian Infantry Battalion

FRASER, M: Sergeant

GILL: Corporal

HANKEY, GT: Lieutenant Colonel, # 38907, Royal Army Medical Corps

JOHNSTON: Lieutenant

KAY: Captain, Medical Officer, Royal Army Medical Corps

KINGSBURY, K J: Lance Corporal, #7356316, Medical Orderly, Royal Army Medical Corps

KNOWLES, GSA: Captain, # 104022, Royal Army Medical Corps

LANSDELL, NR: Captain, # 87659, Royal Army Medical Corps

McBRIDE: Corporal
MELLOR, AW: Captain, # 107324, Royal Army Medical Corps
MULHOLLAND: Sergeant Major
ORR, Edward: Private, # 3597427, Border Regiment
PEARSON
POTTS: Royal Engineers, Stoke
PRESTON, Lewis Lionel: Private, # 5183303, 2nd Battalion, Gloucestershire Regiment
REES: New Zealand
REIGERFELD: Lieutenant
RITCHIE, Jack
SMITH: Company Sergeant Major
TEASDALE, G: Private, # 3601262, 4th Battalion, Border Regiment
WESTON: Sergeant
WYNN: Royal Engineers, Stoke

LEST WE FORGET.

AUTHOR'S NOTE

Harry Jackson was my grandfather. All his grandchildren called him Grandda Jackson. My mother Joan is his and Mabel's youngest daughter.

As a child, I'd adored my grandda. I can still see his face in my mind's eye: his twinkling eyes, ruddy complexion, laughing mouth, his red hair transfused with grey like a mix of exotic spices. I can smell his earthy, hops-laden breath filling my young nostrils. I can recall sitting on his lap stroking his vast pendulous earlobes, their velvety feel between my thumb and forefinger a constant soother for me.

My grandfather was indeed an accomplished musician. He particularly loved playing the piano, a permanent fixture in any of his homes that my family visited. I have a fond memory of watching him lead a marching band in the streets of Whitehaven—the uniforms flamboyant, the drums loud and powerful, all men marching in time, my grandfather at the helm, twirling his mace around, his expression proud. I also saw him perform on a stone bandstand in Castle Park, Whitehaven. From the perspective of a little girl, these experiences become woven into a colourful tapestry of adult memories.

Harry Jackson had a wicked sense of humour. Shortly before my family headed off to Singapore in 1963 (one of my father's overseas postings with the Royal Air Force), I surreptitiously whispered to Grandda, 'Who is your favourite grandchild?', giving him only a choice between myself and my older brother. He chuckled in his unique way, and then raised a gnarled, nicotine-stained finger at me, wagging it back and forth before shaking his head: 'I'll not say, Jacqueline.'

I pleaded with him to tell me. After all, I was going away, a long way away, to an unknown tropical country on the other side of the world. So, with this in mind, surely I could leave civilisation behind as *someone's* favourite? I turned a crestfallen face to my grandda and my ruse worked. He chuckled in resignation, pulling me close to him, nestling me into his rattling chest as he whispered, 'You are, my pet, but you didn't hear that from me.'

I didn't understand. How could you not hear something from the person who said it? I asked him that question, and he roared with laughter.

That was the last time I ever saw my grandda Jackson. He passed away a year later in 1964 at the age of 65.

Mona Jackson, Harry Jackson's eldest living daughter, brought his World War II diary and photographs to Australia in the early 2000s, where my family had emigrated from England years prior. She left them in my mother's keeping.

My grandfather started writing his diary in January 1941, and some of the dates, sequences of events, times and places prior to this time (and even after) are a bit of a jumble, understandably so given his horrific situation, so I have had to rearrange and add to some entries. Grandda's spelling of cities and villages was not great and also many borders and names of places have now changed. As a result of my persistent research I believe I have recorded his journey and timelines fairly accurately. Some events he only alluded to, obviously due to the danger he would have faced had his diary been discovered by the enemy, and I have expanded upon them. I have also taken the creative licence of adding emotional tones to certain diary entries. Men in those days simply didn't express their emotions, and certainly not in war diaries. In relation to Harry Jackson's life prior to and following the war, I have relied upon family oral and written history and research. Every effort has been made to seek permission to use material provided by others in my grandfather's diary.

ACKNOWLEDGEMENTS

This book has been a collaboration of love and there are many people I would like to thank for helping in that collaboration.

Of course, my first acknowledgement goes to my grandfather, Henry Barnes Jackson, 1898–1964, without whose war diary this story would not have existed.

My mother, Joan Barnett, and aunt, Mona Jackson, Harry Snr's last remaining offspring, for giving me permission to publish their father's diary and photographs and giving freely of their memories.

My cousins: Harry Jackson Jr for graciously allowing me to write of his secretive birth, adoption and childhood and providing me with information pertaining to our grandfather and grandmother. Patricia Coyle (nee Byrne) (the late Betty Byrne (nee Jackson) and the late Bill Byrne's daughter) for providing me with documentation pertaining to family, and for reading the manuscript prior to publishing, despite how confronting it was for her to do so. Family historian Jean McDowell (nee Cranston) (the late Bert and Marjorie Cranston's daughter). Jackie Baldock (nee Sumner) (the late John and Mary Sumner's daughter) for providing information, photos and documentation on the Cranston clan.

My brother, Gary Smitham, and my son, Liam McCallum, for help with photos.

My husband, Doug Byrne, for his enduring patience, encouragement and relentless reading of redraft after redraft of *The Music Maker*. He is a man of whom I know my grandfather would heartily approve.

Kenneth G Ross, Australian playwright, for his endless constructive comments and suggestions.

Angela Farmer, artwork.

Bev Harrison, proofreading.

Heather Williams, Tara Moran and all the Pen and Sword design, editorial, production and marketing team.

Rosemary Peers and Lynk Manuscript Assessment Service, editing.